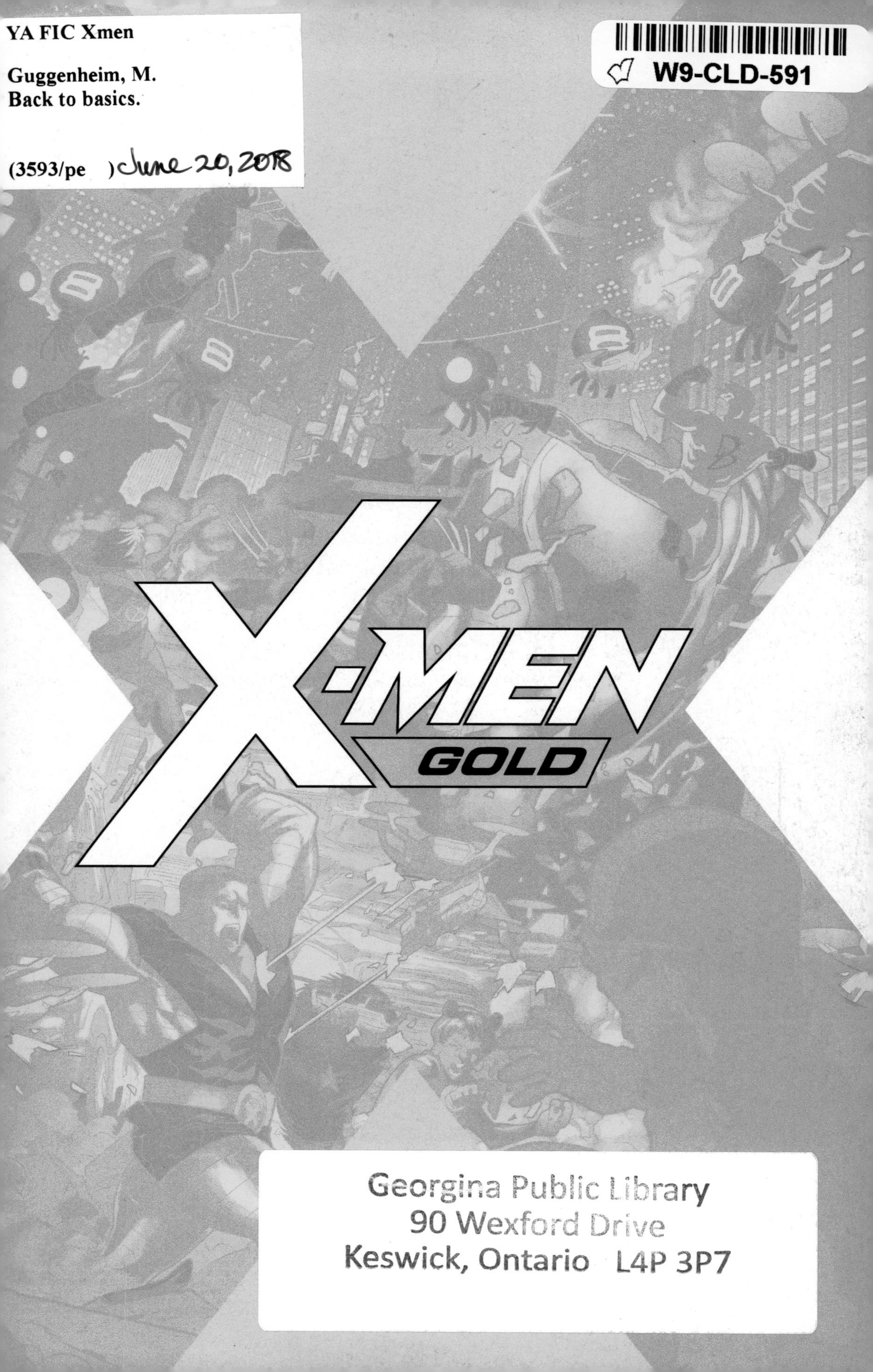
X-MEN
GOLD

GENETICALLY GIFTED WITH UNCANNY ABILITIES, MUTANTS ARE BELIEVED TO BE THE NEXT STAGE OF HUMAN EVOLUTION. WHILE THE WORLD HATES AND FEARS THEM, KITTY PRYDE HAS REFORMED THE TEAM OF MUTANT HEROES KNOWN AS THE X-MEN TO USE THEIR POWERS FOR GOOD AND SPREAD A POSITIVE IMAGE OF MUTANTKIND.

Collection Editor/**JENNIFER GRÜNWALD** · Assistant Editor/**CAITLIN O'CONNELL**
Associate Managing Editor/**KATERI WOODY** · Editor, Special Projects/**MARK D. BEAZLEY**
VP Production & Special Projects/**JEFF YOUNGQUIST** · SVP Print, Sales & Marketing/**DAVID GABRIEL**
Book Designer/**JAY BOWEN**

Editor in Chief/**AXEL ALONSO** · Chief Creative Officer/**JOE QUESADA**
President/**DAN BUCKLEY** · Executive Producer/**ALAN FINE**

X-MEN GOLD VOL. 1: BACK TO THE BASICS. Contains material originally published in magazine form as X-MEN GOLD #1-6. First printing 2017. ISBN# 978-1-302-90730-3. Published by MARVEL WORLDWIDE, INC., a subsidiary of MARVEL ENTERTAINMENT, LLC. OFFICE OF PUBLICATION: 135 West 50th Street, New York, NY 10020. Copyright © 2017 MARVEL No similarity between any of the names, characters, persons, and/or institutions in this magazine with those of any living or dead person or institution is intended, and any such similarity which may exist is purely coincidental. **Printed in the U.S.A.** DAN BUCKLEY, President, Marvel Entertainment; JOE QUESADA, Chief Creative Officer; TOM BREVOORT, SVP of Publishing; DAVID BOGART, SVP of Business Affairs & Operations, Publishing & Partnership; C.B. CEBULSKI, VP of Brand Management & Development, Asia; DAVID GABRIEL, SVP of Sales & Marketing, Publishing; JEFF YOUNGQUIST, VP of Production & Special Projects; DAN CARR, Executive Director of Publishing Technology; ALEX MORALES, Director of Publishing Operations; SUSAN CRESPI, Production Manager; STAN LEE, Chairman Emeritus. For information regarding advertising in Marvel Comics or on Marvel.com, please contact Vit DeBellis, Integrated Sales Manager, at vdebellis@marvel.com. For Marvel subscription inquiries, please call 888-511-5480. **Manufactured between 6/30/2017 and 7/31/2017 by QUAD/GRAPHICS WASECA, WASECA, MN, USA.**

10 9 8 7 6 5 4 3 2 1

X-MEN GOLD

BACK TO THE BASICS

Writer/**MARC GUGGENHEIM**

ISSUES #1-3
Penciler/**ARDIAN SYAF**
Inkers/**JAY LEISTEN** with **CRAIG YEUNG** (#3)
Colorist/**FRANK MARTIN**
with **ANDREW CROSSLEY** (#6)

ISSUES #4-6
Penciler/**R.B. SILVA**
Inker/**ADRIANO DI BENEDETTO**
Color Artist/**FRANK MARTIN**
with **ANDREW CROSSLEY** (#6)

Letterer/**VC's CORY PETIT**

Cover Artists/**ARDIAN SYAF & JAY LEISTEN**
with **LAURA MARTIN** (#1) & **FRANK MARTIN** (#2-6)

Assistant Editor/**CHRIS ROBINSON**
Editor/**DANIEL KETCHUM**
X-Men Group Editor/**MARK PANICCIA**

X-MEN CREATED BY **STAN LEE** & **JACK KIRBY**

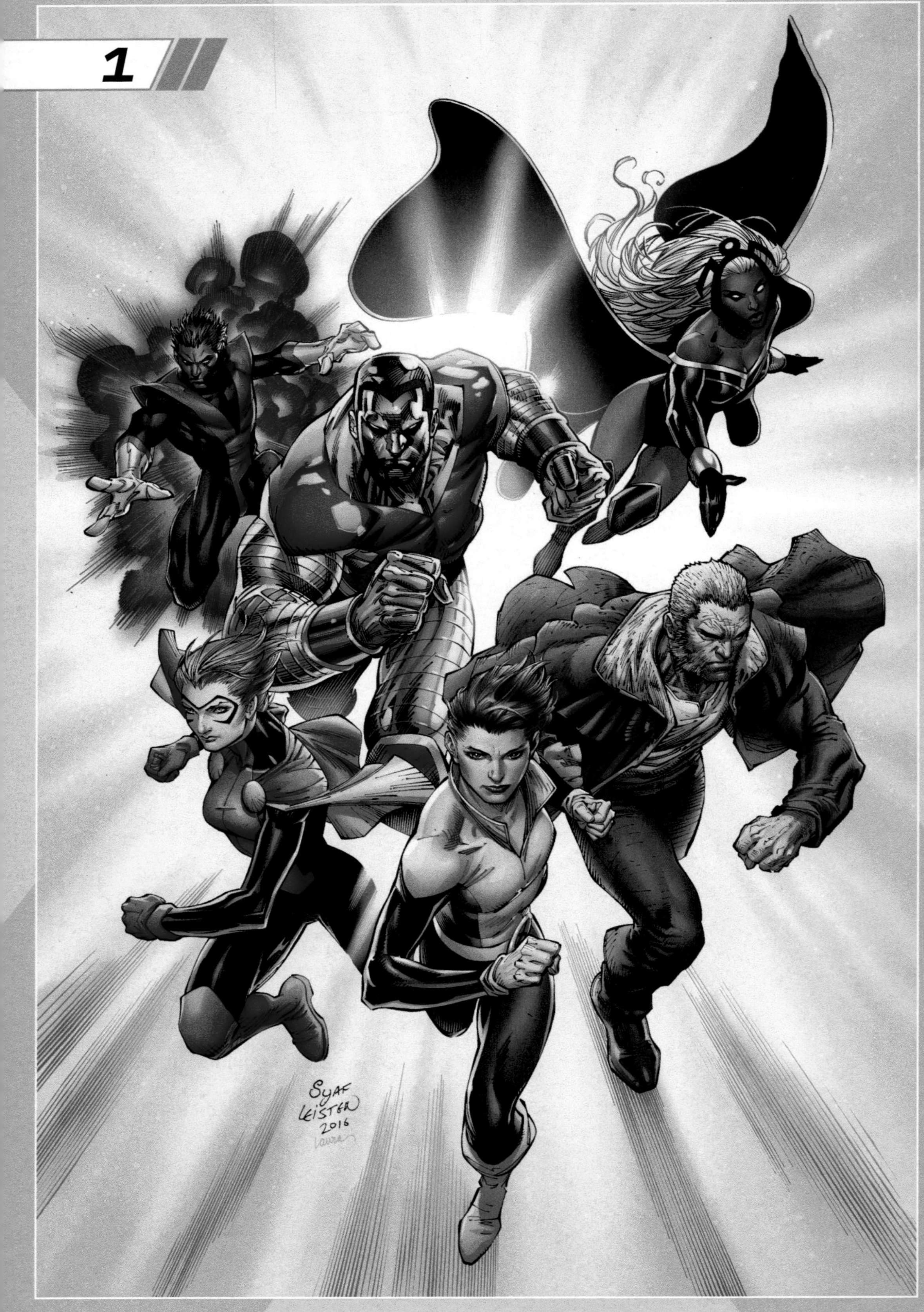
1
SYAF
LEISTER
2016

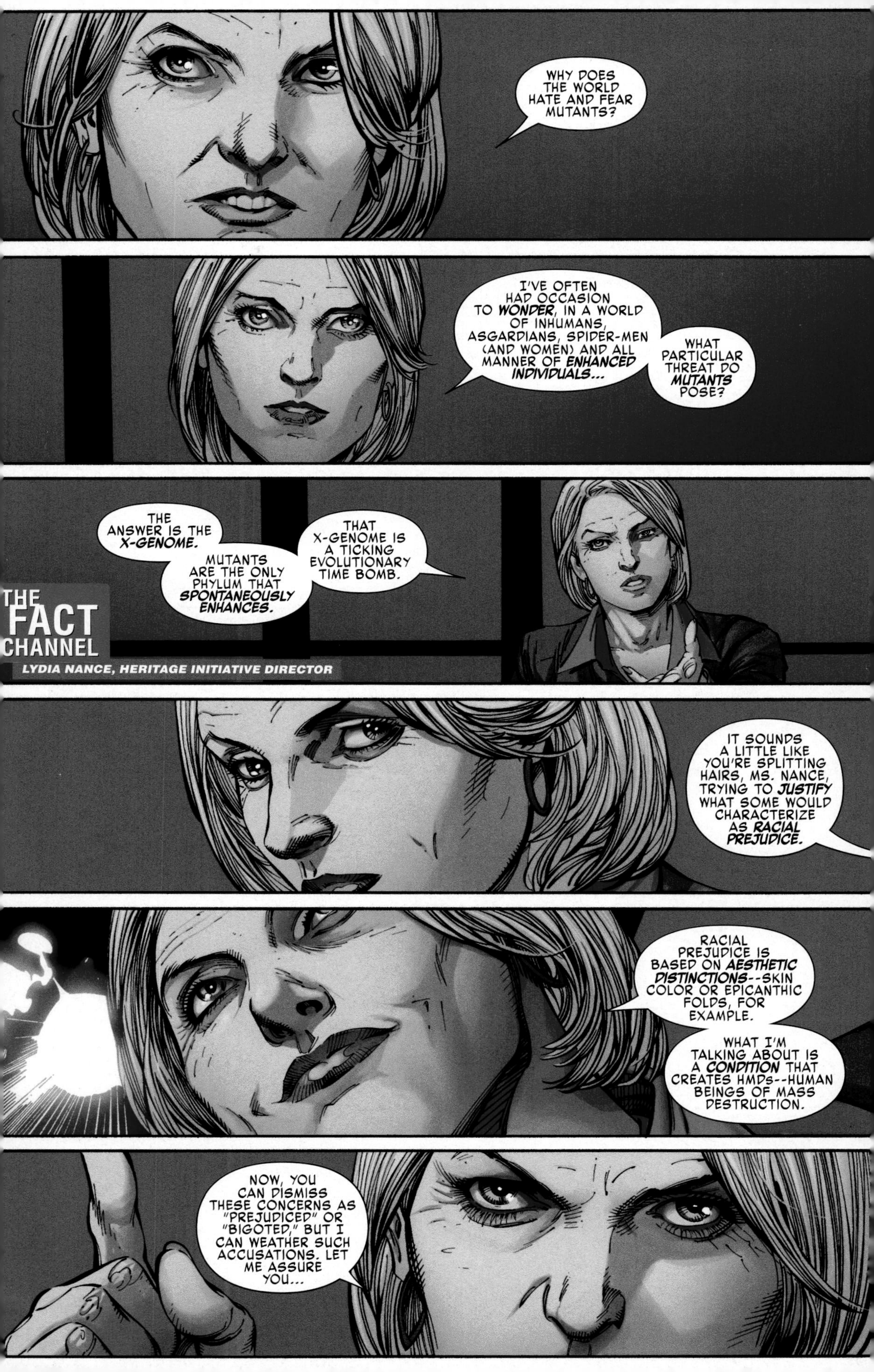
WHY DOES THE WORLD HATE AND FEAR MUTANTS?
I'VE OFTEN HAD OCCASION TO WONDER, IN A WORLD OF INHUMANS, ASGARDIANS, SPIDER-MEN (AND WOMEN) AND ALL MANNER OF ENHANCED INDIVIDUALS...
WHAT PARTICULAR THREAT DO MUTANTS POSE?
THE ANSWER IS THE X-GENOME.
MUTANTS ARE THE ONLY PHYLUM THAT SPONTANEOUSLY ENHANCES.
THAT X-GENOME IS A TICKING EVOLUTIONARY TIME BOMB.
THE FACT CHANNEL
LYDIA NANCE, HERITAGE INITIATIVE DIRECTOR
IT SOUNDS A LITTLE LIKE YOU'RE SPLITTING HAIRS, MS. NANCE, TRYING TO JUSTIFY WHAT SOME WOULD CHARACTERIZE AS RACIAL PREJUDICE.
RACIAL PREJUDICE IS BASED ON AESTHETIC DISTINCTIONS--SKIN COLOR OR EPICANTHIC FOLDS, FOR EXAMPLE.
WHAT I'M TALKING ABOUT IS A CONDITION THAT CREATES HMDs--HUMAN BEINGS OF MASS DESTRUCTION.
NOW, YOU CAN DISMISS THESE CONCERNS AS "PREJUDICED" OR "BIGOTED," BUT I CAN WEATHER SUCH ACCUSATIONS. LET ME ASSURE YOU...

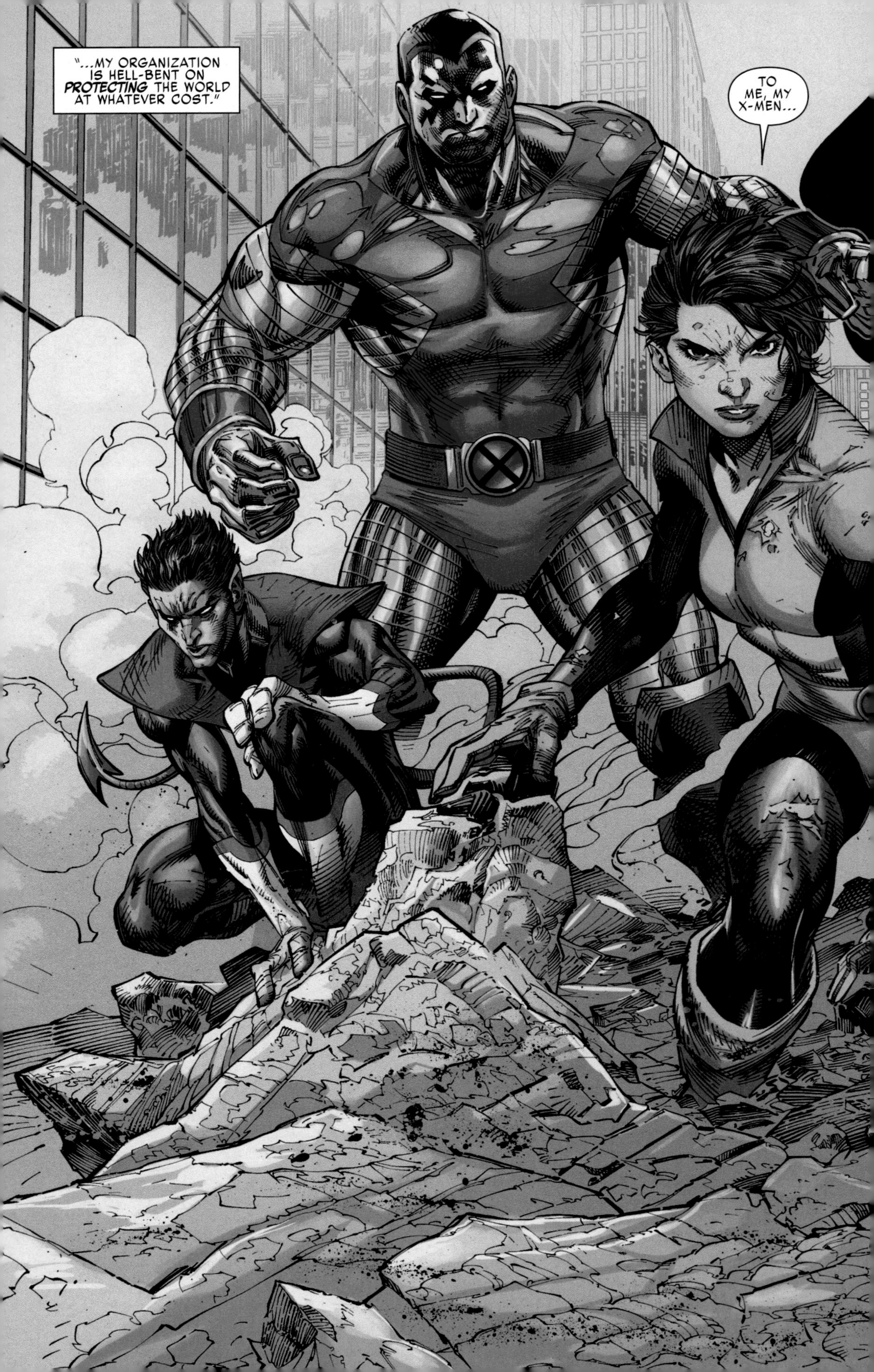
"...MY ORGANIZATION IS HELL-BENT ON PROTECTING THE WORLD AT WHATEVER COST."
TO ME, MY X-MEN...

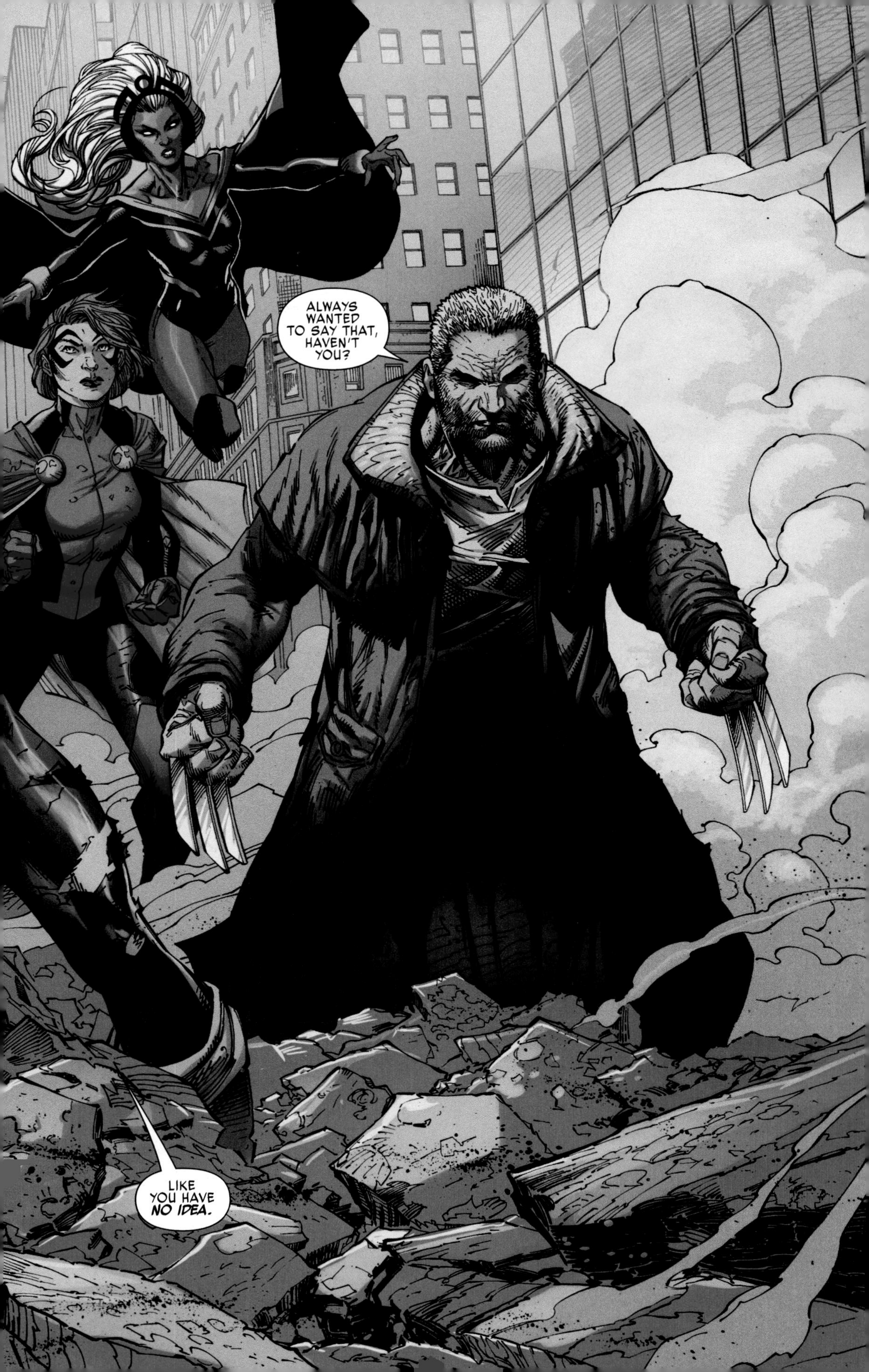
ALWAYS WANTED TO SAY THAT, HAVEN'T YOU?
LIKE YOU HAVE *NO IDEA.*

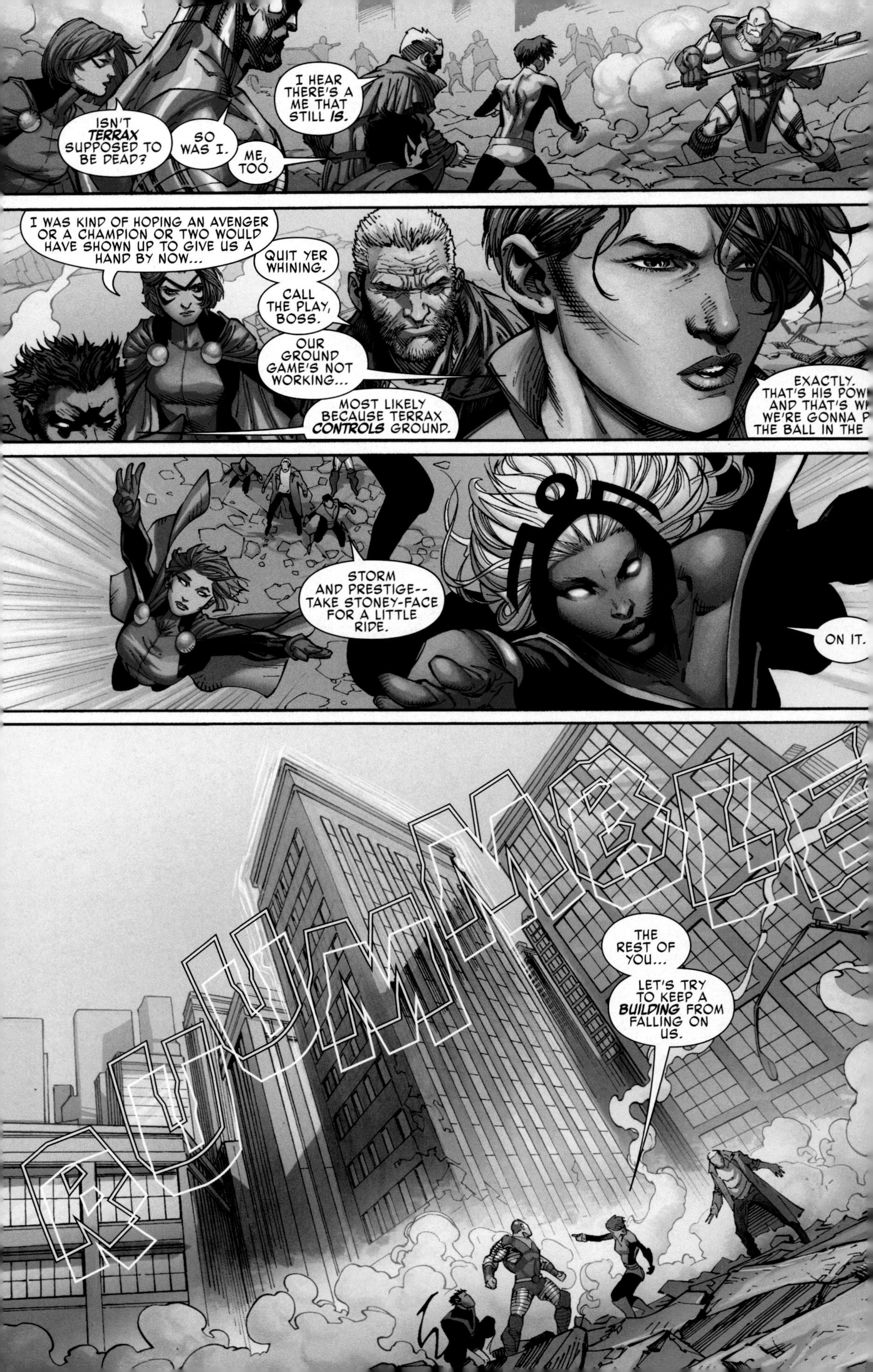
ISN'T TERRAX SUPPOSED TO BE DEAD?
SO WAS I.
ME, TOO.
I HEAR THERE'S A ME THAT STILL IS.
I WAS KIND OF HOPING AN AVENGER OR A CHAMPION OR TWO WOULD HAVE SHOWN UP TO GIVE US A HAND BY NOW...
QUIT YER WHINING.
CALL THE PLAY, BOSS.
OUR GROUND GAME'S NOT WORKING...
MOST LIKELY BECAUSE TERRAX CONTROLS GROUND.
STORM AND PRESTIGE-- TAKE STONEY-FACE FOR A LITTLE RIDE.
ON IT.
RUUMMBLE
THE REST OF YOU...
LET'S TRY TO KEEP A BUILDING FROM FALLING ON US.

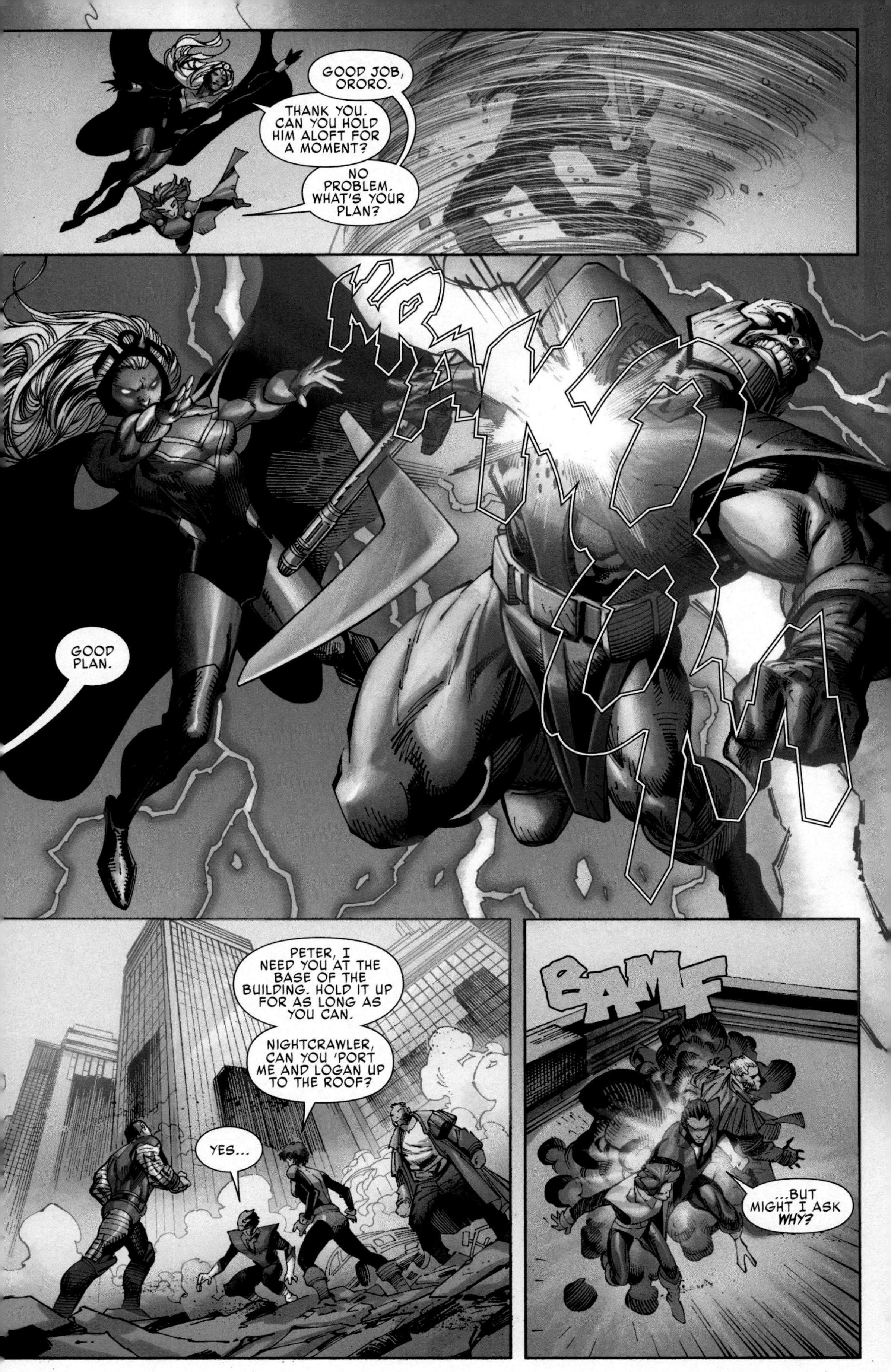
GOOD JOB, ORORO.
THANK YOU. CAN YOU HOLD HIM ALOFT FOR A MOMENT?
NO PROBLEM. WHAT'S YOUR PLAN?
KRAKOOOM
GOOD PLAN.
PETER, I NEED YOU AT THE BASE OF THE BUILDING. HOLD IT UP FOR AS LONG AS YOU CAN.
NIGHTCRAWLER, CAN YOU 'PORT ME AND LOGAN UP TO THE ROOF?
YES...
BAMF
...BUT MIGHT I ASK WHY?

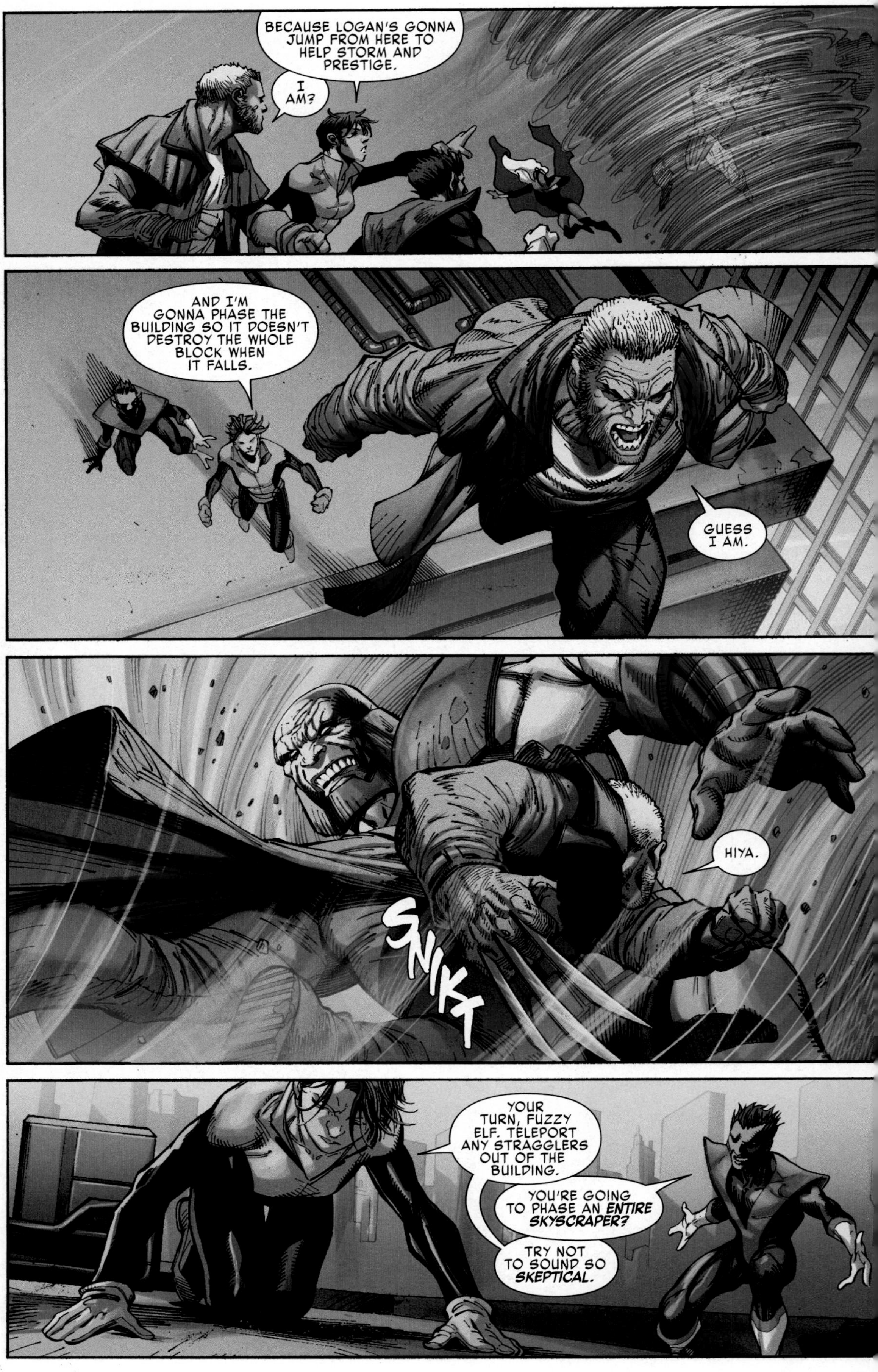
BECAUSE LOGAN'S GONNA JUMP FROM HERE TO HELP STORM AND PRESTIGE.
I AM?
AND I'M GONNA PHASE THE BUILDING SO IT DOESN'T DESTROY THE WHOLE BLOCK WHEN IT FALLS.
GUESS I AM.
HIYA.
SNIKT
YOUR TURN, FUZZY ELF. TELEPORT ANY STRAGGLERS OUT OF THE BUILDING.
YOU'RE GOING TO PHASE AN *ENTIRE SKYSCRAPER?*
TRY NOT TO SOUND SO *SKEPTICAL.*

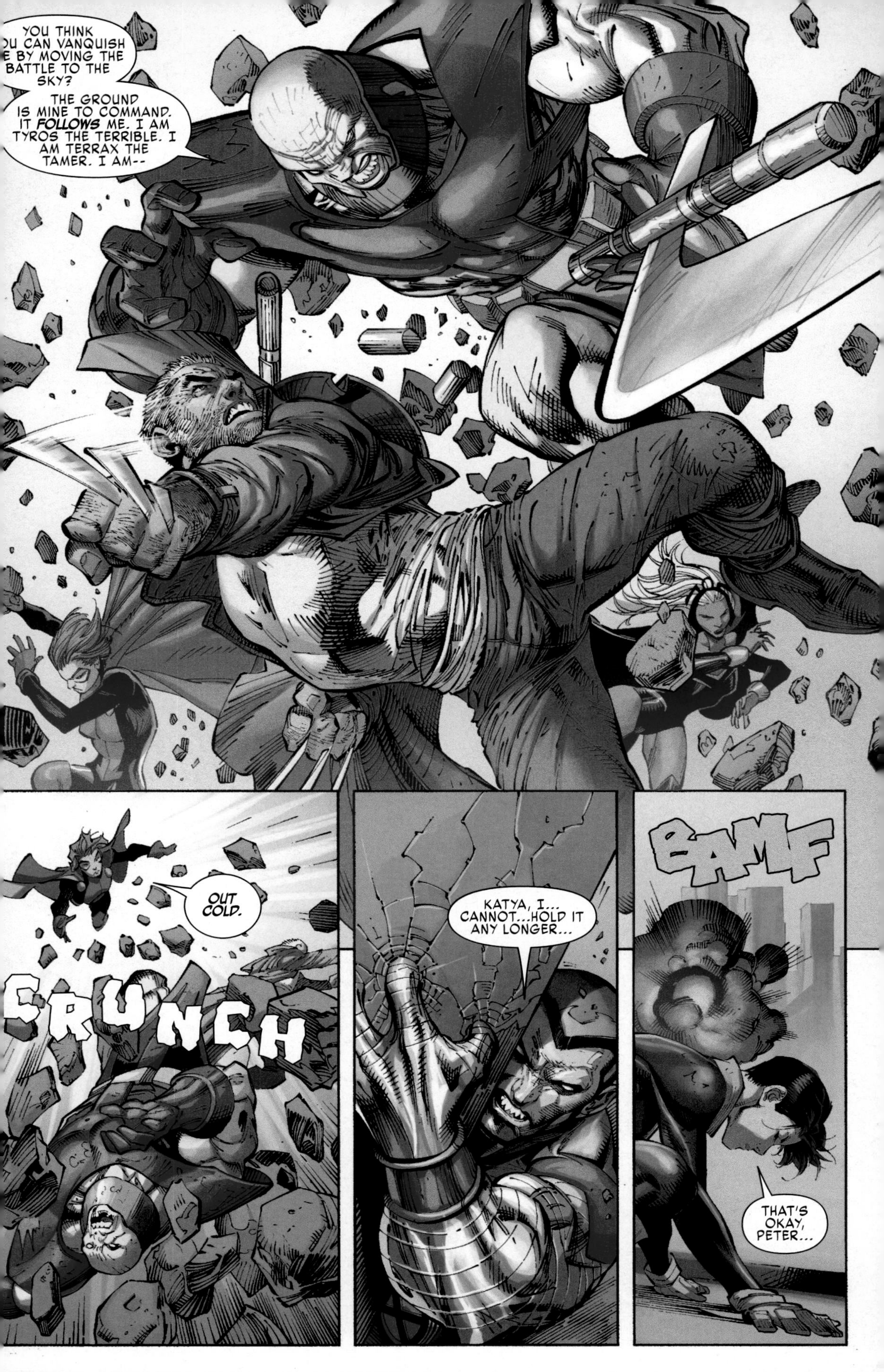
YOU THINK OU CAN VANQUISH E BY MOVING THE BATTLE TO THE SKY?
THE GROUND IS MINE TO COMMAND. IT FOLLOWS ME. I AM TYROS THE TERRIBLE. I AM TERRAX THE TAMER. I AM--
OUT COLD.
CRUNCH
KATYA, I... CANNOT...HOLD IT ANY LONGER...
BAMF
THAT'S OKAY, PETER...

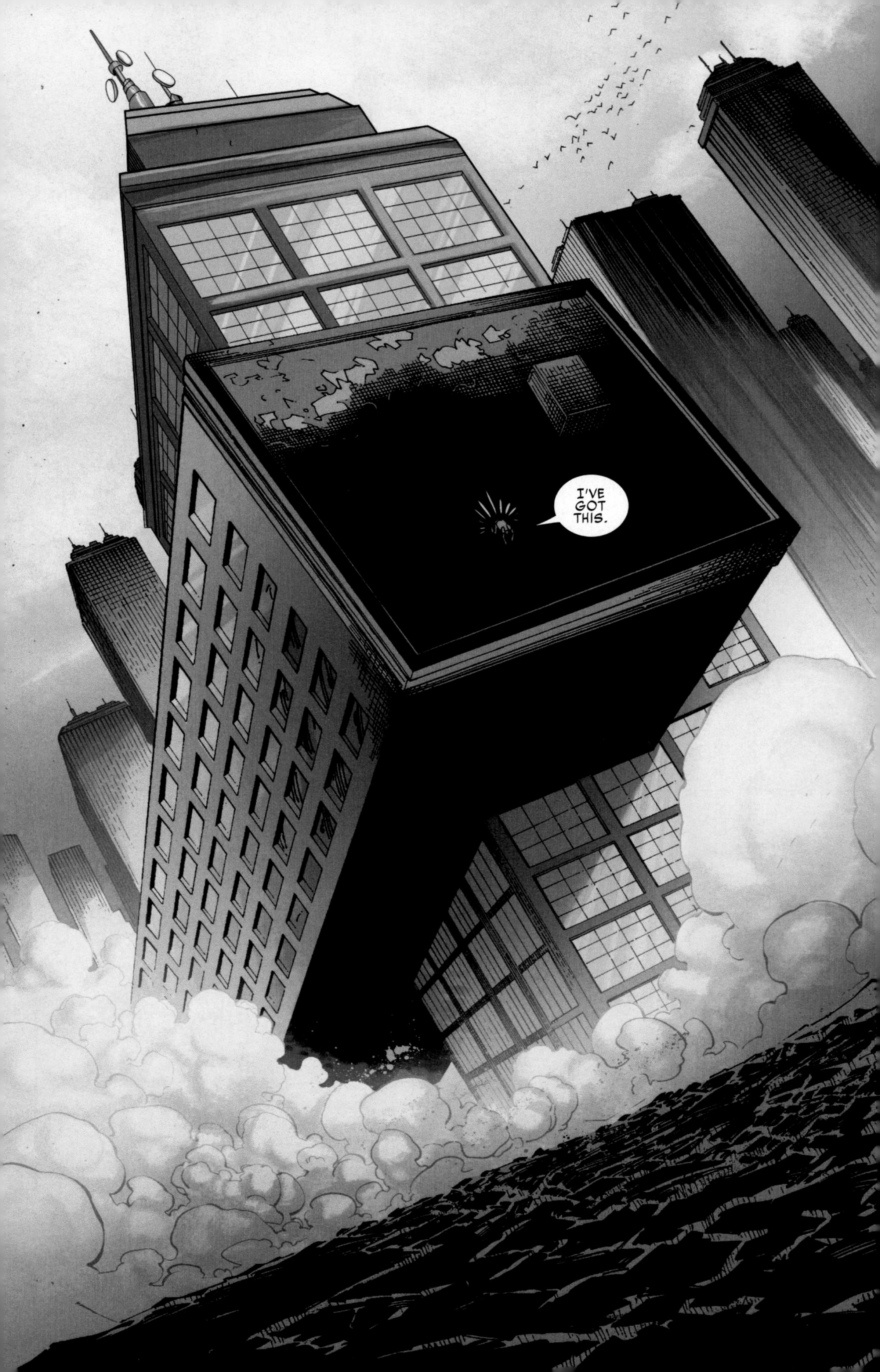
I'VE GOT THIS.

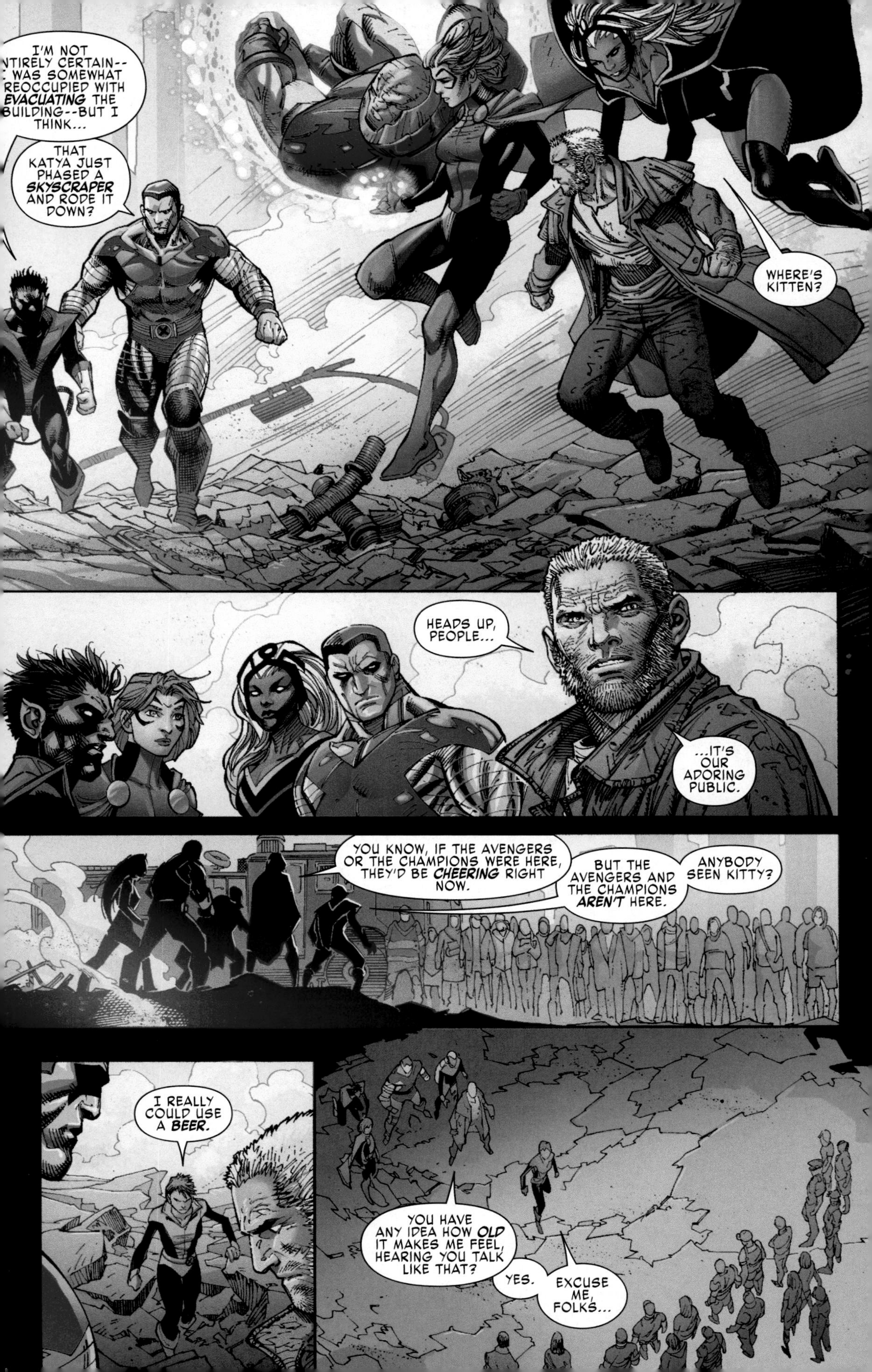
I'M NOT ...NTIRELY CERTAIN-- ...I WAS SOMEWHAT ...REOCCUPIED WITH EVACUATING THE ...BUILDING--BUT I THINK...
THAT KATYA JUST PHASED A SKYSCRAPER AND RODE IT DOWN?
WHERE'S KITTEN?
HEADS UP, PEOPLE...
...IT'S OUR ADORING PUBLIC.
YOU KNOW, IF THE AVENGERS OR THE CHAMPIONS WERE HERE, THEY'D BE CHEERING RIGHT NOW.
BUT THE AVENGERS AND THE CHAMPIONS AREN'T HERE.
ANYBODY SEEN KITTY?
I REALLY COULD USE A BEER.
YOU HAVE ANY IDEA HOW OLD IT MAKES ME FEEL, HEARING YOU TALK LIKE THAT?
YES.
EXCUSE ME, FOLKS...

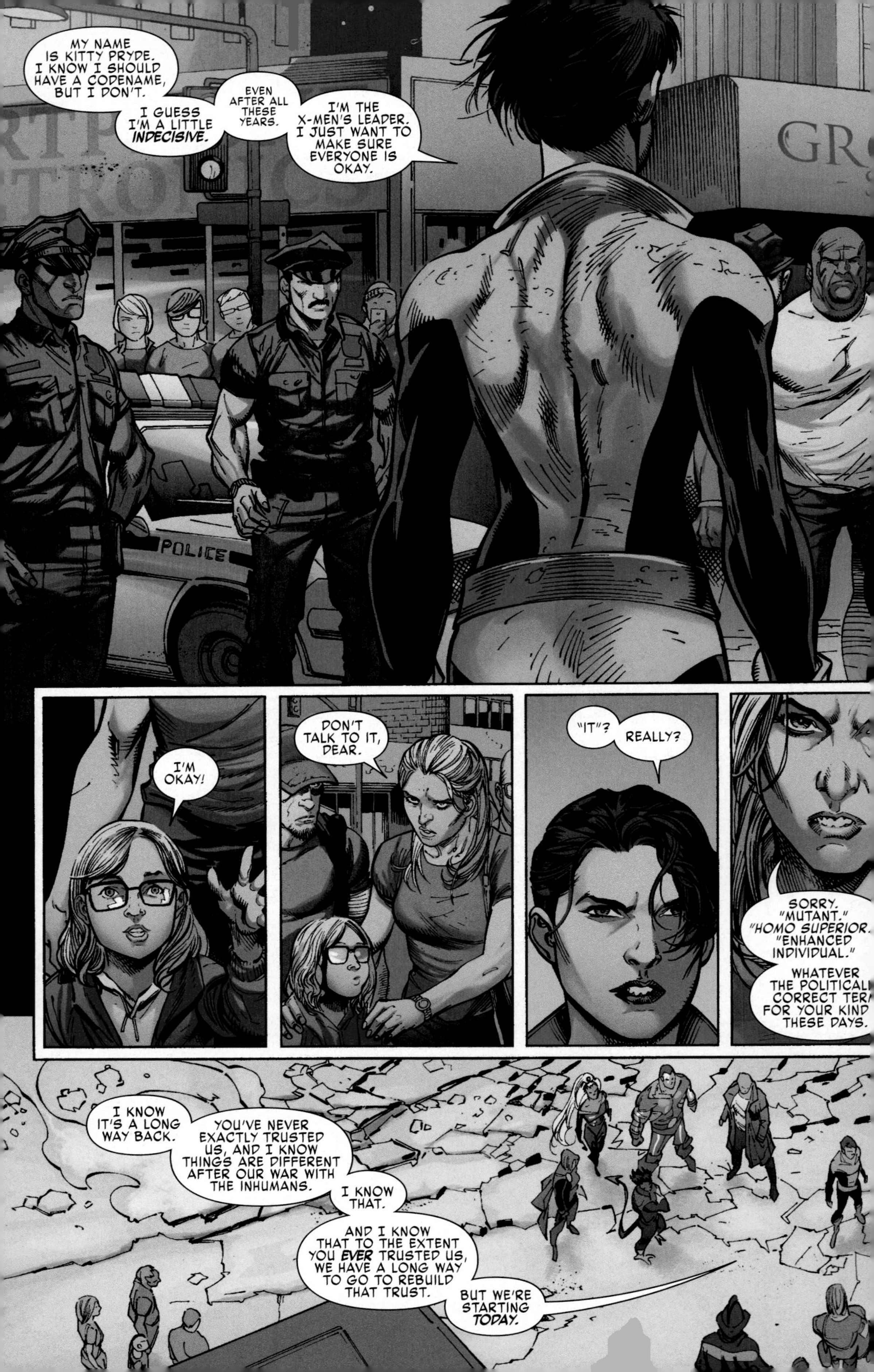
MY NAME IS KITTY PRYDE. I KNOW I SHOULD HAVE A CODENAME, BUT I DON'T.
I GUESS I'M A LITTLE *INDECISIVE.*
EVEN AFTER ALL THESE YEARS.
I'M THE X-MEN'S LEADER. I JUST WANT TO MAKE SURE EVERYONE IS OKAY.
POLICE
I'M OKAY!
DON'T TALK TO IT, DEAR.
"IT"?
REALLY?
SORRY. "MUTANT." "*HOMO SUPERIOR.*" "ENHANCED INDIVIDUAL."
WHATEVER THE POLITICALL CORRECT TER FOR YOUR KIND THESE DAYS.
I KNOW IT'S A LONG WAY BACK.
YOU'VE NEVER EXACTLY TRUSTED US, AND I KNOW THINGS ARE DIFFERENT AFTER OUR WAR WITH THE INHUMANS.
I KNOW THAT.
AND I KNOW THAT TO THE EXTENT YOU *EVER* TRUSTED US, WE HAVE A LONG WAY TO GO TO REBUILD THAT TRUST.
BUT WE'RE STARTING *TODAY.*

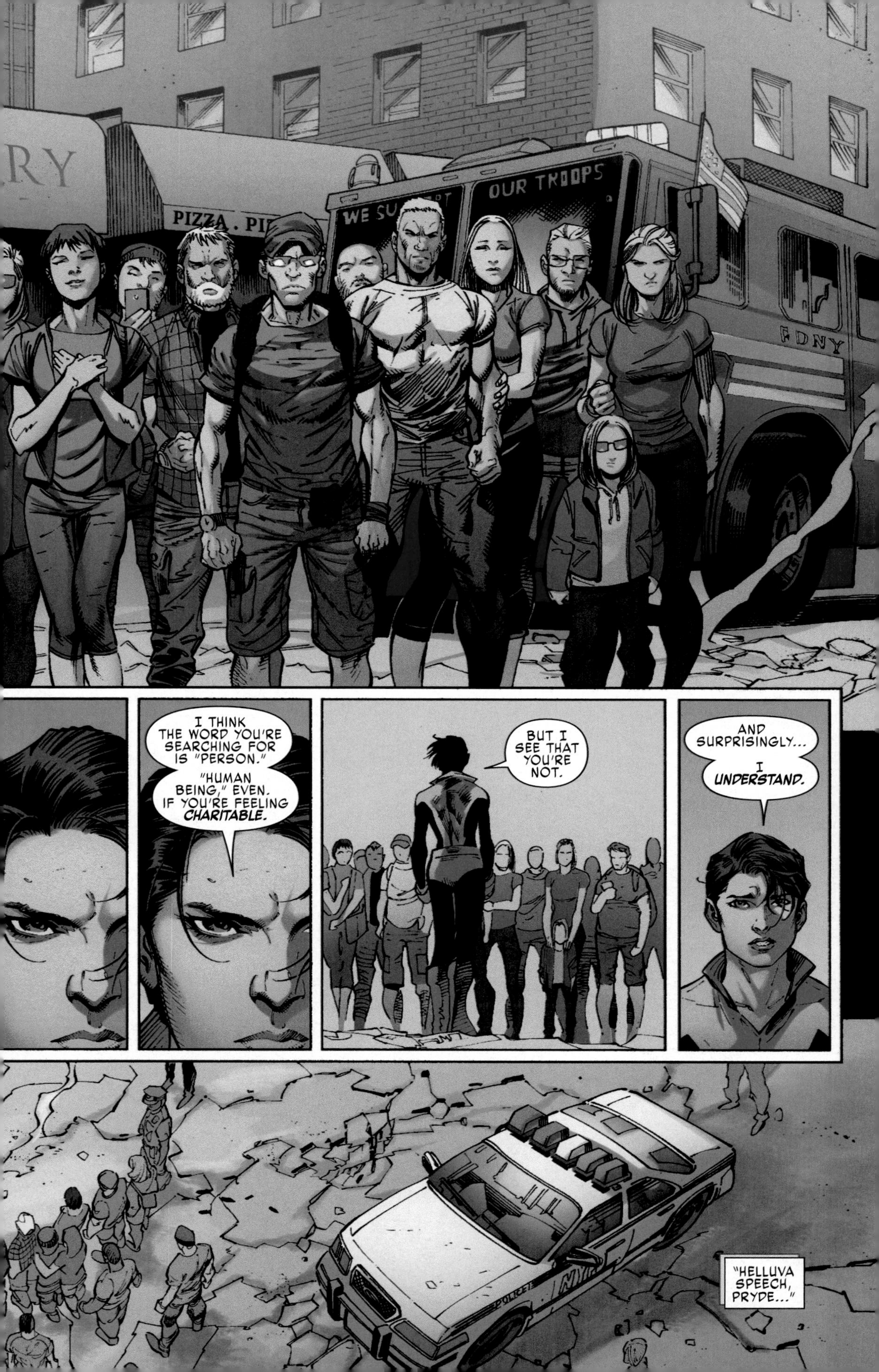
RY
PIZZA . PI
WE SU RT
OUR TROOPS
FDNY
I THINK THE WORD YOU'RE SEARCHING FOR IS "PERSON."
"HUMAN BEING," EVEN. IF YOU'RE FEELING CHARITABLE.
BUT I SEE THAT YOU'RE NOT.
AND SURPRISINGLY...
I UNDERSTAND.
"HELLUVA SPEECH, PRYDE..."

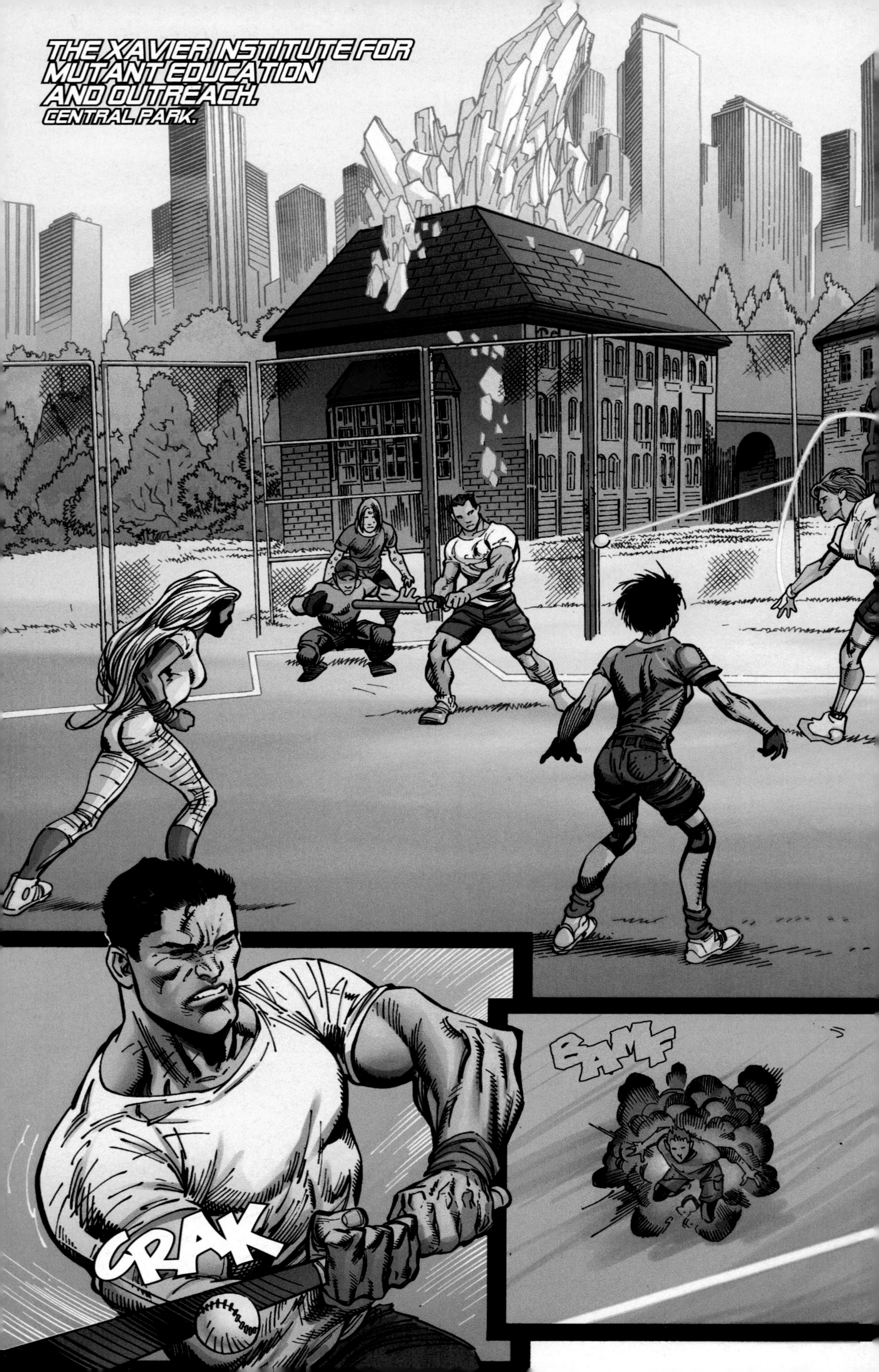
THE XAVIER INSTITUTE FOR MUTANT EDUCATION AND OUTREACH.
CENTRAL PARK.
CRAK
BAMF

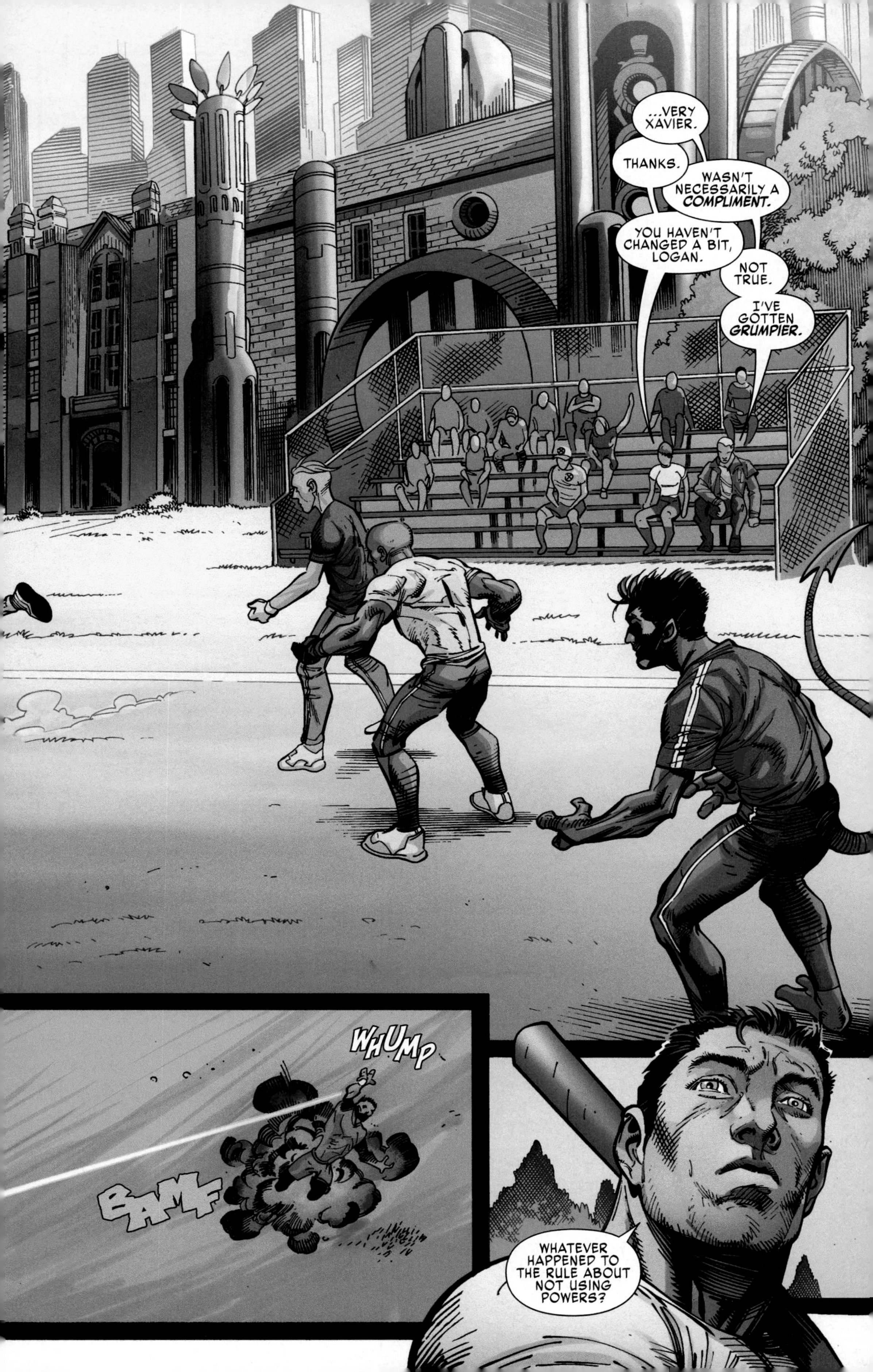
...VERY XAVIER.
THANKS.
WASN'T NECESSARILY A COMPLIMENT.
YOU HAVEN'T CHANGED A BIT, LOGAN.
NOT TRUE.
I'VE GOTTEN GRUMPIER.
WHUMP
BAMF
WHATEVER HAPPENED TO THE RULE ABOUT NOT USING POWERS?

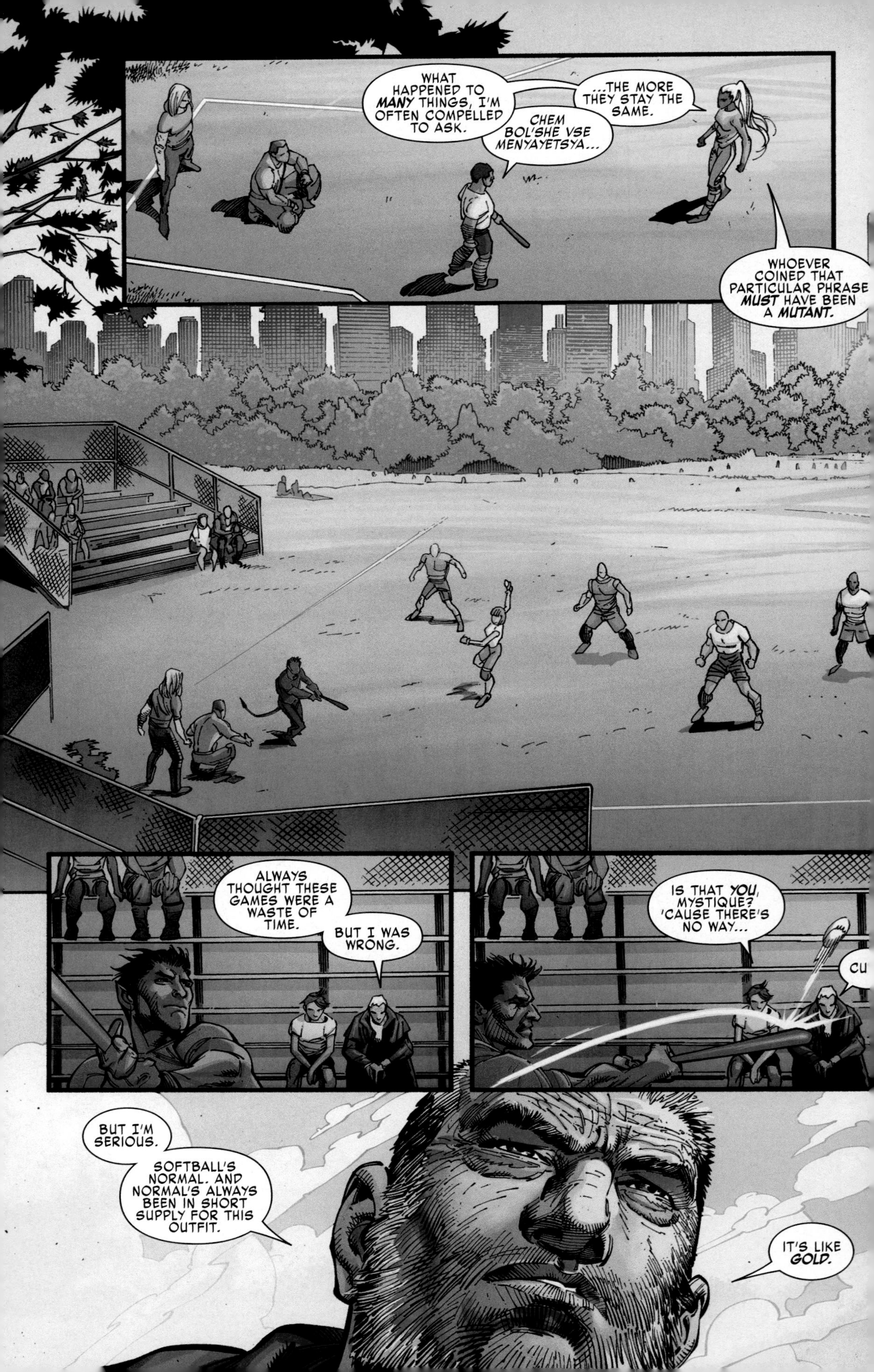
WHAT HAPPENED TO MANY THINGS, I'M OFTEN COMPELLED TO ASK.
CHEM BOL'SHE VSE MENYAYETSYA...
...THE MORE THEY STAY THE SAME.
WHOEVER COINED THAT PARTICULAR PHRASE MUST HAVE BEEN A MUTANT.
ALWAYS THOUGHT THESE GAMES WERE A WASTE OF TIME.
BUT I WAS WRONG.
IS THAT YOU, MYSTIQUE? 'CAUSE THERE'S NO WAY...
CU
BUT I'M SERIOUS.
SOFTBALL'S NORMAL. AND NORMAL'S ALWAYS BEEN IN SHORT SUPPLY FOR THIS OUTFIT.
IT'S LIKE GOLD.

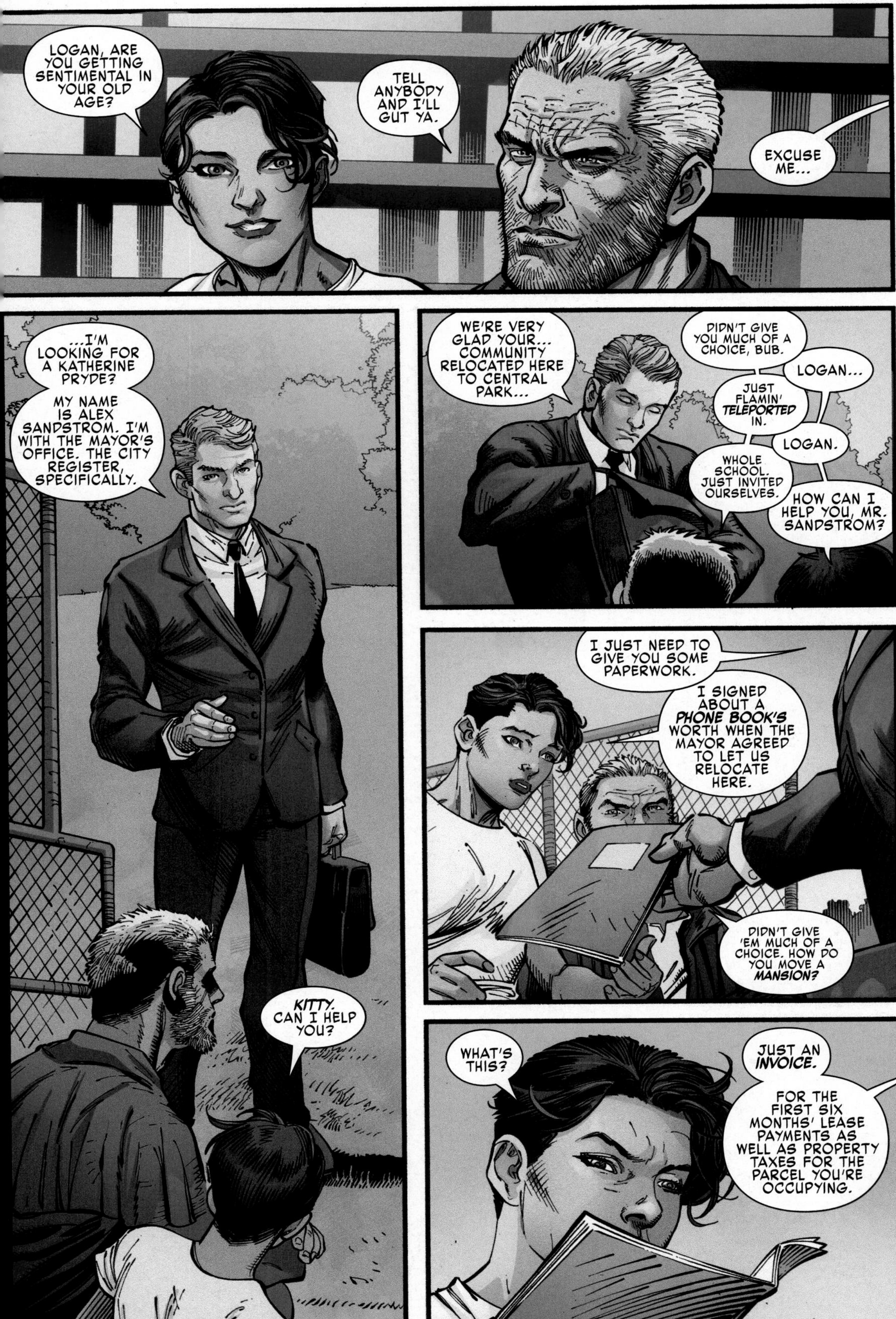
LOGAN, ARE YOU GETTING SENTIMENTAL IN YOUR OLD AGE?
TELL ANYBODY AND I'LL GUT YA.
EXCUSE ME...
...I'M LOOKING FOR A KATHERINE PRYDE?
MY NAME IS ALEX SANDSTROM. I'M WITH THE MAYOR'S OFFICE. THE CITY REGISTER, SPECIFICALLY.
KITTY. CAN I HELP YOU?
WE'RE VERY GLAD YOUR... COMMUNITY RELOCATED HERE TO CENTRAL PARK...
DIDN'T GIVE YOU MUCH OF A CHOICE, BUB.
JUST FLAMIN' TELEPORTED IN.
WHOLE SCHOOL. JUST INVITED OURSELVES.
LOGAN...
LOGAN.
HOW CAN I HELP YOU, MR. SANDSTROM?
I JUST NEED TO GIVE YOU SOME PAPERWORK.
I SIGNED ABOUT A PHONE BOOK'S WORTH WHEN THE MAYOR AGREED TO LET US RELOCATE HERE.
DIDN'T GIVE 'EM MUCH OF A CHOICE. HOW DO YOU MOVE A MANSION?
WHAT'S THIS?
JUST AN INVOICE.
FOR THE FIRST SIX MONTHS' LEASE PAYMENTS AS WELL AS PROPERTY TAXES FOR THE PARCEL YOU'RE OCCUPYING.

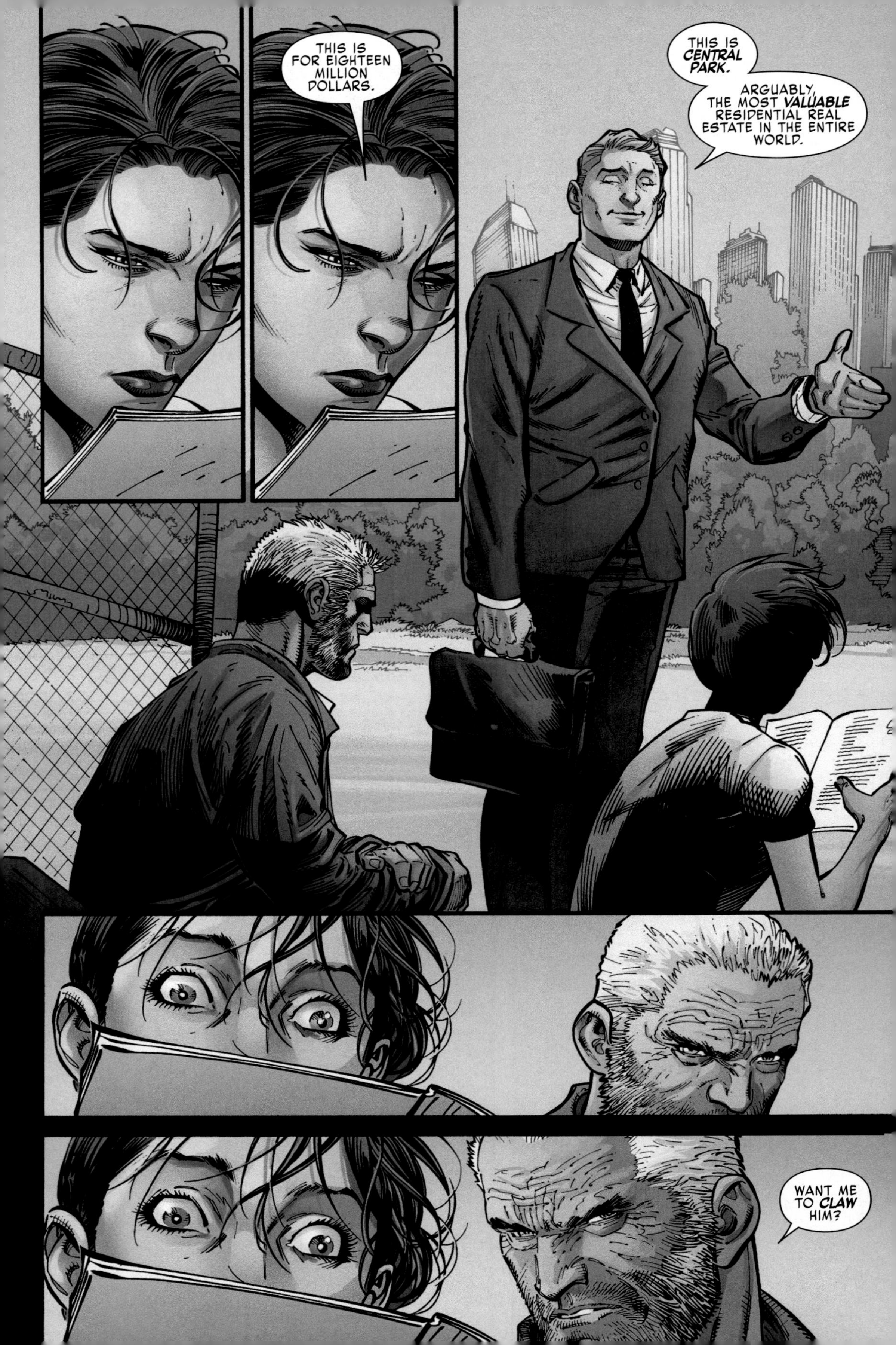
THIS IS FOR EIGHTEEN MILLION DOLLARS.
THIS IS CENTRAL PARK.
ARGUABLY, THE MOST VALUABLE RESIDENTIAL REAL ESTATE IN THE ENTIRE WORLD.
WANT ME TO CLAW HIM?

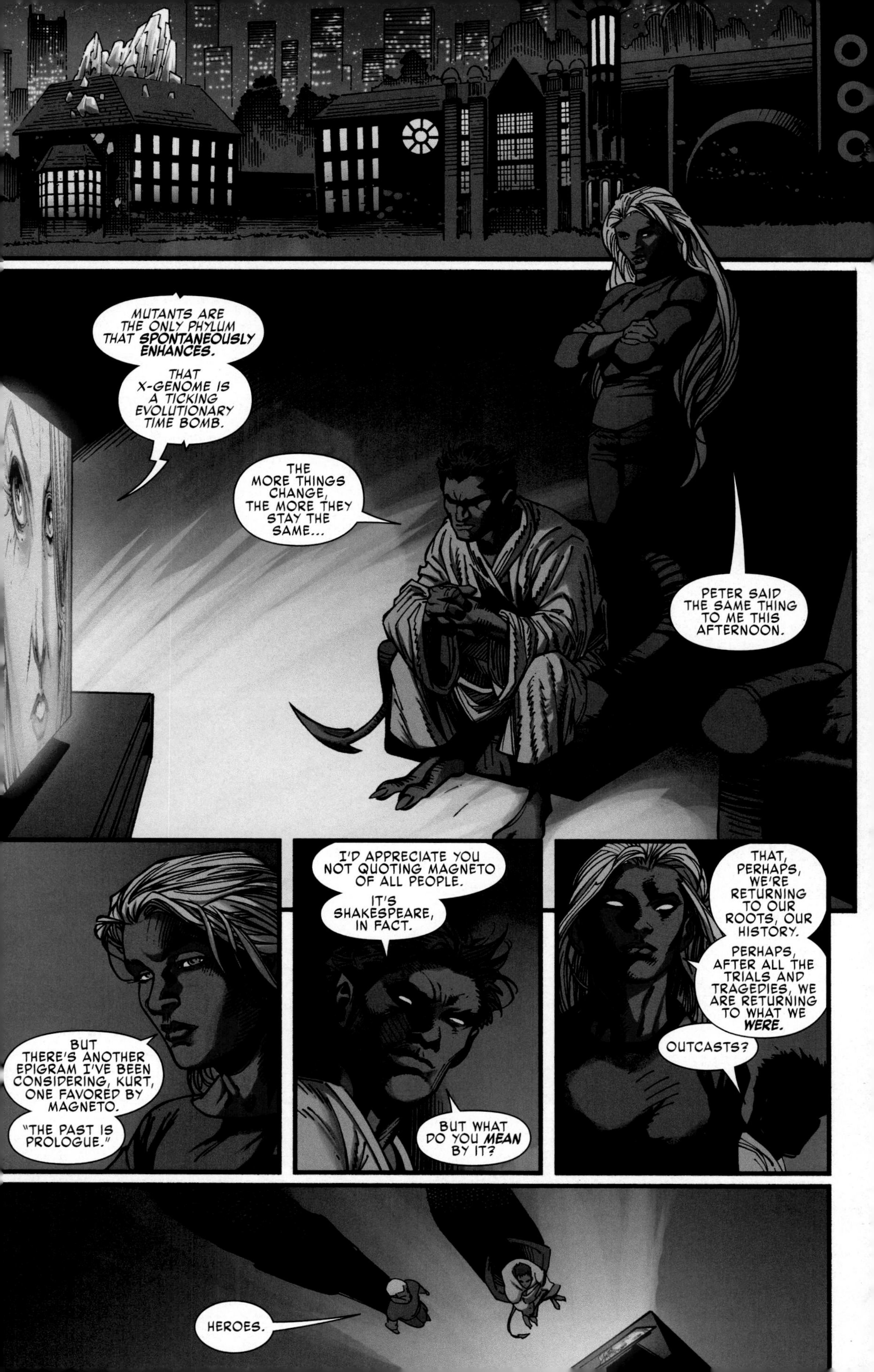
MUTANTS ARE THE ONLY PHYLUM THAT SPONTANEOUSLY ENHANCES.
THAT X-GENOME IS A TICKING EVOLUTIONARY TIME BOMB.
THE MORE THINGS CHANGE, THE MORE THEY STAY THE SAME...
PETER SAID THE SAME THING TO ME THIS AFTERNOON.
BUT THERE'S ANOTHER EPIGRAM I'VE BEEN CONSIDERING, KURT, ONE FAVORED BY MAGNETO.
"THE PAST IS PROLOGUE."
I'D APPRECIATE YOU NOT QUOTING MAGNETO OF ALL PEOPLE.
IT'S SHAKESPEARE, IN FACT.
BUT WHAT DO YOU MEAN BY IT?
THAT, PERHAPS, WE'RE RETURNING TO OUR ROOTS, OUR HISTORY.
PERHAPS, AFTER ALL THE TRIALS AND TRAGEDIES, WE ARE RETURNING TO WHAT WE WERE.
OUTCASTS?
HEROES.

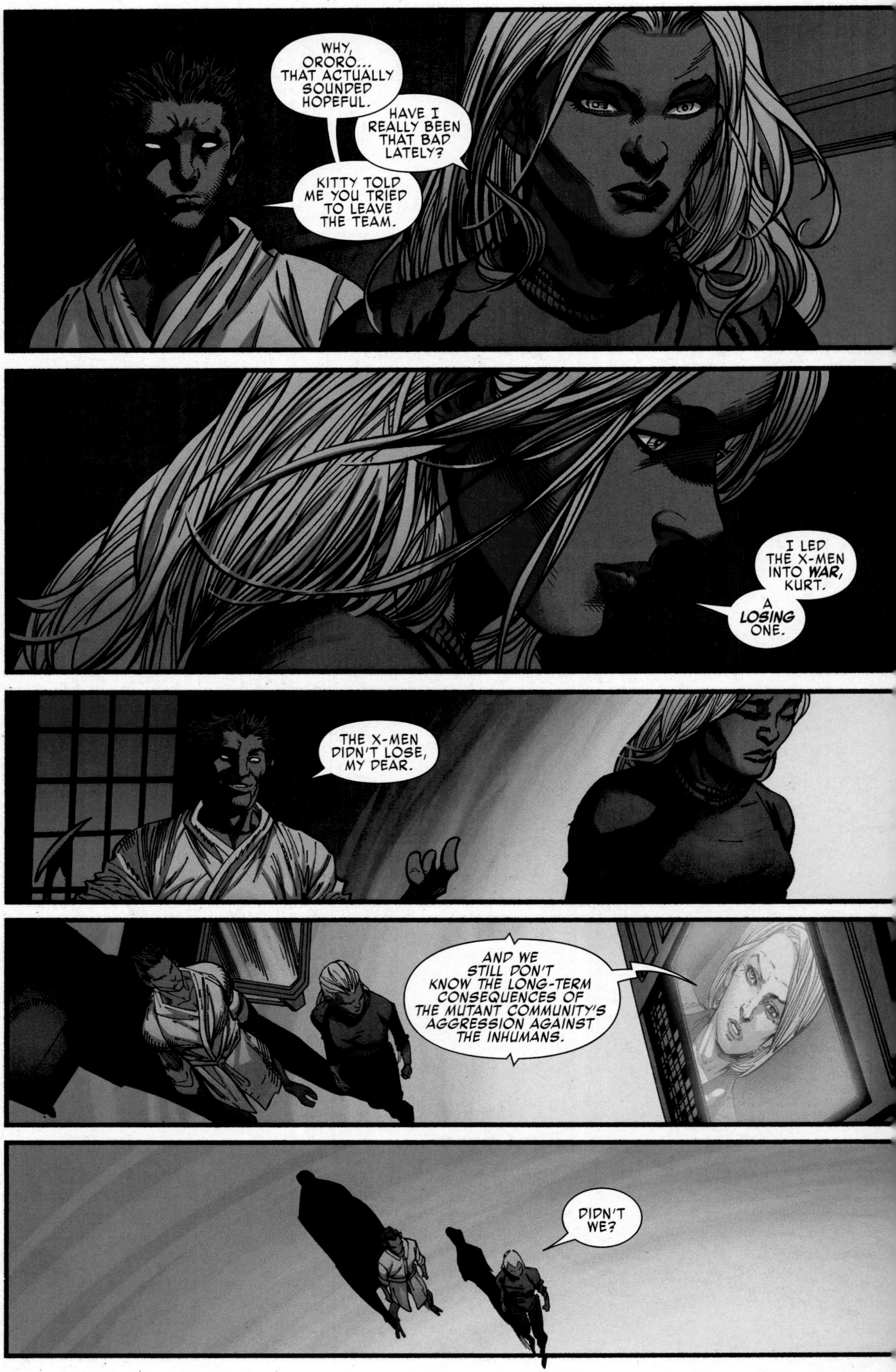
WHY, ORORO... THAT ACTUALLY SOUNDED HOPEFUL.
HAVE I REALLY BEEN THAT BAD LATELY?
KITTY TOLD ME YOU TRIED TO LEAVE THE TEAM.
I LED THE X-MEN INTO *WAR,* KURT.
A *LOSING* ONE.
THE X-MEN DIDN'T LOSE, MY DEAR.
AND WE STILL DON'T KNOW THE LONG-TERM CONSEQUENCES OF THE MUTANT COMMUNITY'S AGGRESSION AGAINST THE INHUMANS.
DIDN'T WE?

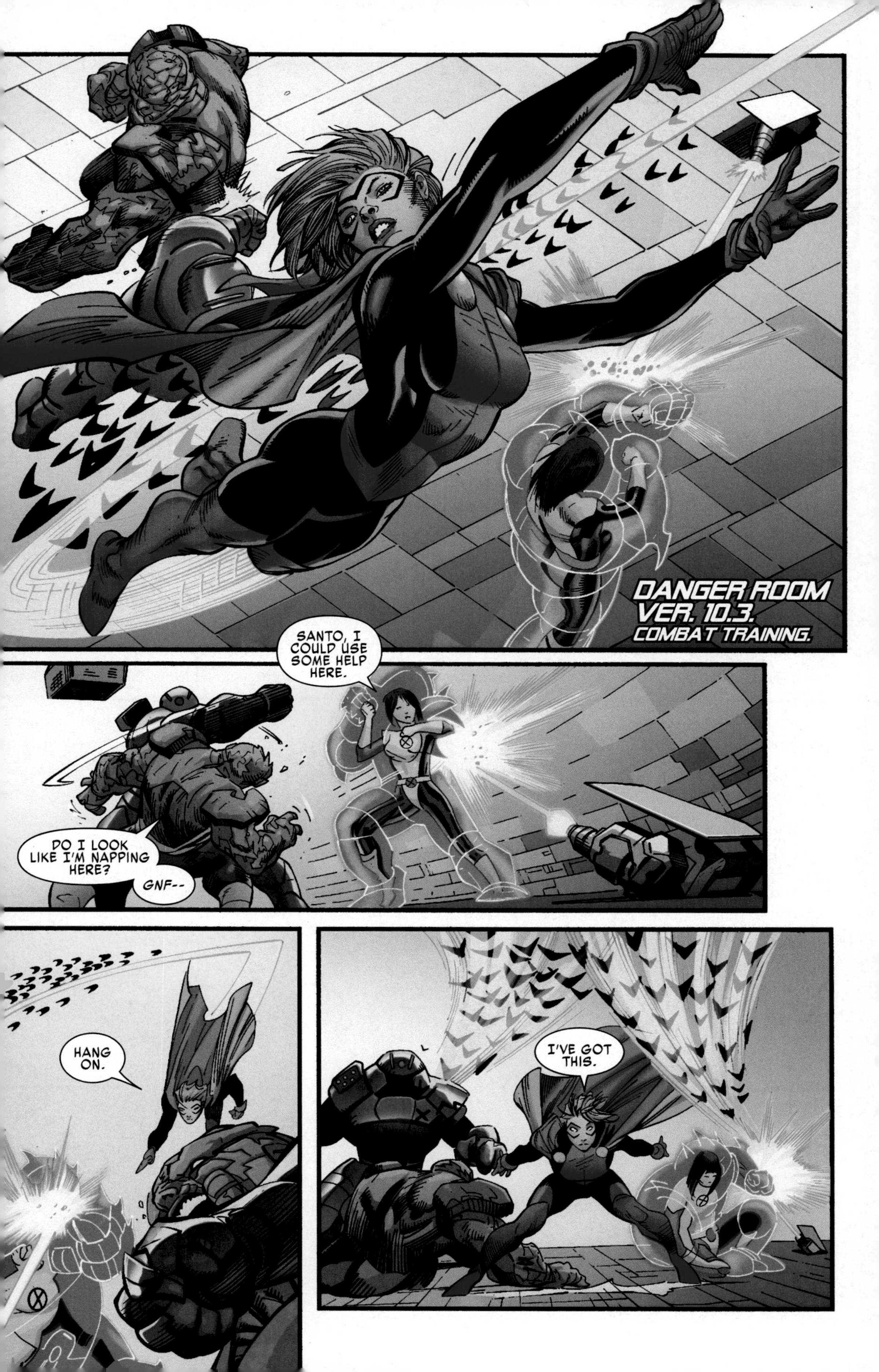

DANGER ROOM VER. 10.3.
COMBAT TRAINING.
SANTO, I COULD USE SOME HELP HERE.
DO I LOOK LIKE I'M NAPPING HERE?
GNF--
HANG ON.
I'VE GOT THIS.

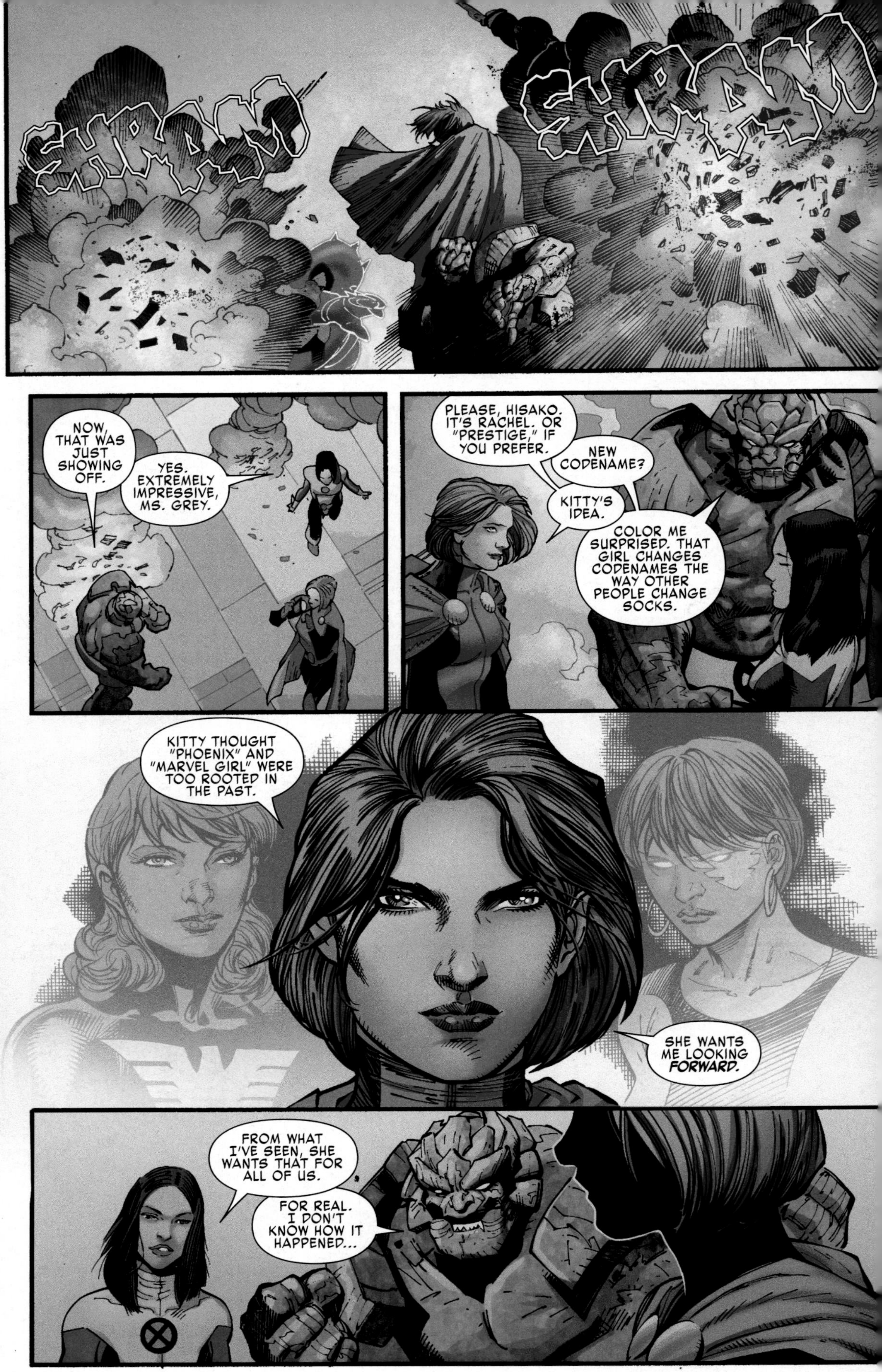
SHRAAM
SHRAAM
NOW, THAT WAS JUST SHOWING OFF.
YES. EXTREMELY IMPRESSIVE, MS. GREY.
PLEASE, HISAKO. IT'S RACHEL. OR "PRESTIGE," IF YOU PREFER.
NEW CODENAME?
KITTY'S IDEA.
COLOR ME SURPRISED. THAT GIRL CHANGES CODENAMES THE WAY OTHER PEOPLE CHANGE SOCKS.
KITTY THOUGHT "PHOENIX" AND "MARVEL GIRL" WERE TOO ROOTED IN THE PAST.
SHE WANTS ME LOOKING *FORWARD.*
FROM WHAT I'VE SEEN, SHE WANTS THAT FOR ALL OF US.
FOR REAL. I DON'T KNOW HOW IT HAPPENED...

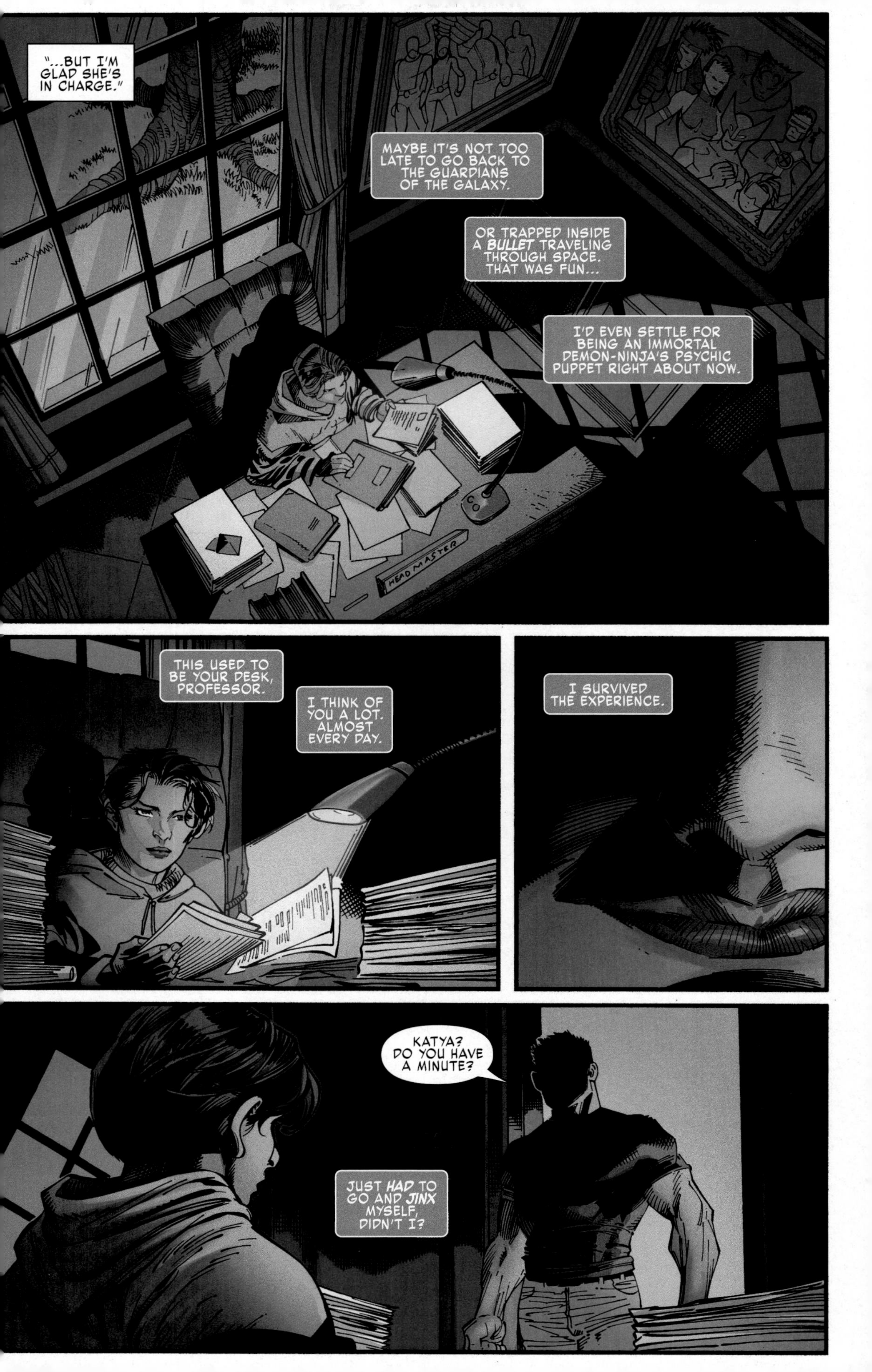

"...BUT I'M GLAD SHE'S IN CHARGE."
MAYBE IT'S NOT TOO LATE TO GO BACK TO THE GUARDIANS OF THE GALAXY.
OR TRAPPED INSIDE A BULLET TRAVELING THROUGH SPACE. THAT WAS FUN...
I'D EVEN SETTLE FOR BEING AN IMMORTAL DEMON-NINJA'S PSYCHIC PUPPET RIGHT ABOUT NOW.
HEAD MASTER
THIS USED TO BE YOUR DESK, PROFESSOR.
I THINK OF YOU A LOT. ALMOST EVERY DAY.
I SURVIVED THE EXPERIENCE.
KATYA? DO YOU HAVE A MINUTE?
JUST HAD TO GO AND JINX MYSELF, DIDN'T I?

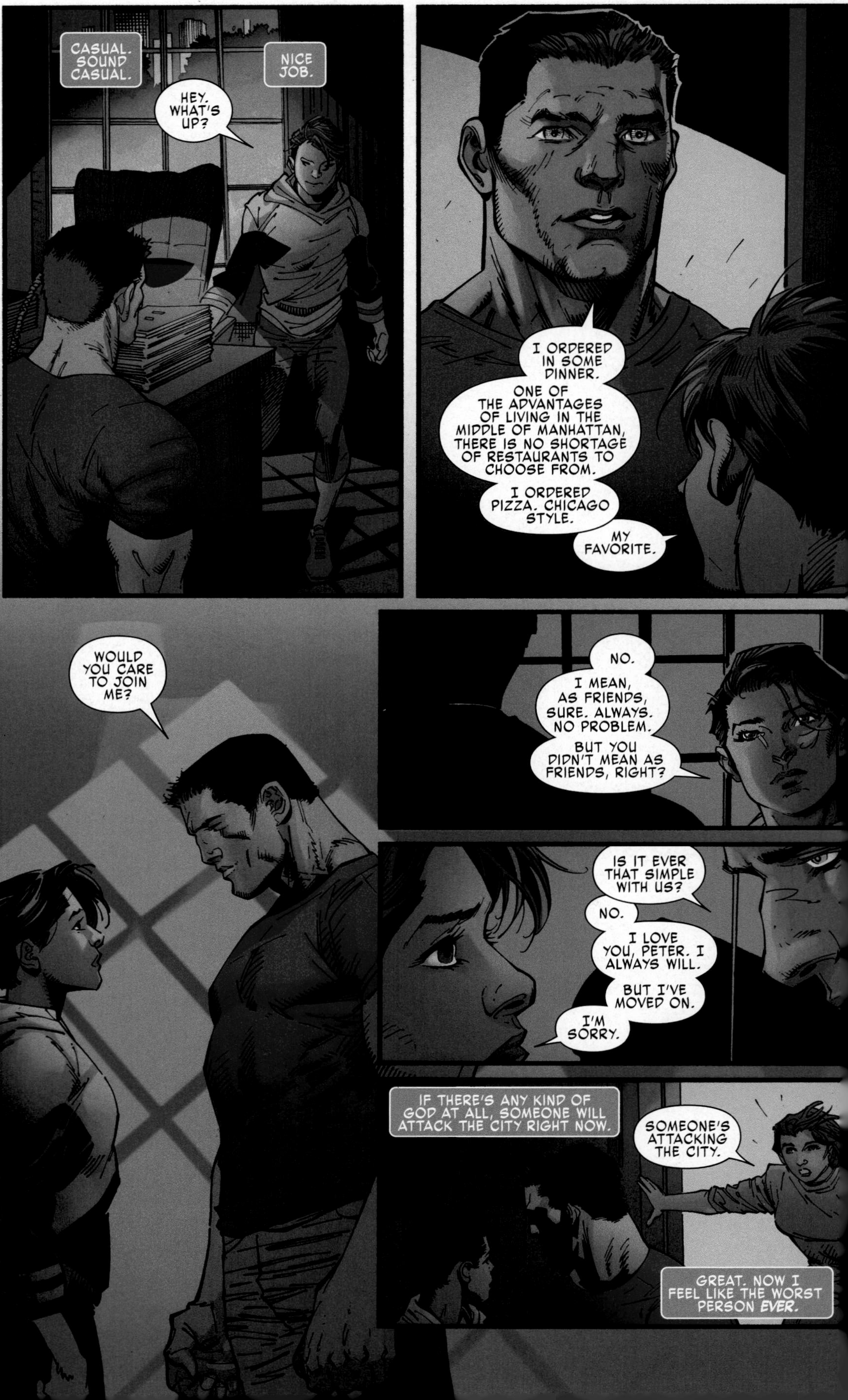

CASUAL. SOUND CASUAL.
HEY. WHAT'S UP?
NICE JOB.
I ORDERED IN SOME DINNER.
ONE OF THE ADVANTAGES OF LIVING IN THE MIDDLE OF MANHATTAN, THERE IS NO SHORTAGE OF RESTAURANTS TO CHOOSE FROM.
I ORDERED PIZZA. CHICAGO STYLE.
MY FAVORITE.
WOULD YOU CARE TO JOIN ME?
NO.
I MEAN, AS FRIENDS, SURE. ALWAYS. NO PROBLEM.
BUT YOU DIDN'T MEAN AS FRIENDS, RIGHT?
IS IT EVER THAT SIMPLE WITH US?
NO.
I LOVE YOU, PETER. I ALWAYS WILL.
BUT I'VE MOVED ON.
I'M SORRY.
IF THERE'S ANY KIND OF GOD AT ALL, SOMEONE WILL ATTACK THE CITY RIGHT NOW.
SOMEONE'S ATTACKING THE CITY.
GREAT. NOW I FEEL LIKE THE WORST PERSON *EVER.*

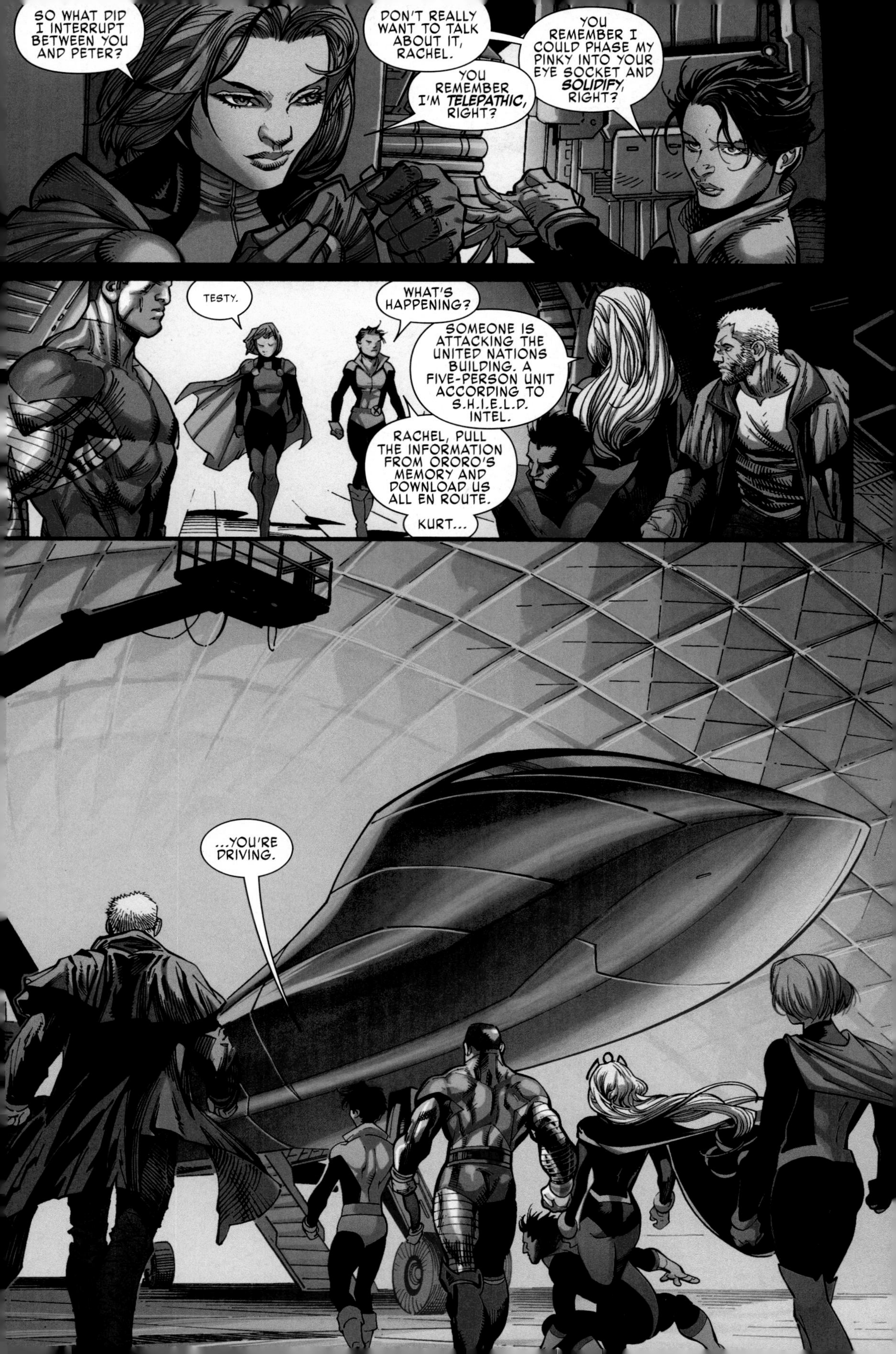
SO WHAT DID I INTERRUPT BETWEEN YOU AND PETER?
DON'T REALLY WANT TO TALK ABOUT IT, RACHEL.
YOU REMEMBER I'M TELEPATHIC, RIGHT?
YOU REMEMBER I COULD PHASE MY PINKY INTO YOUR EYE SOCKET AND SOLIDIFY, RIGHT?
TESTY.
WHAT'S HAPPENING?
SOMEONE IS ATTACKING THE UNITED NATIONS BUILDING. A FIVE-PERSON UNIT ACCORDING TO S.H.I.E.L.D. INTEL.
RACHEL, PULL THE INFORMATION FROM ORORO'S MEMORY AND DOWNLOAD US ALL EN ROUTE.
KURT...
...YOU'RE DRIVING.

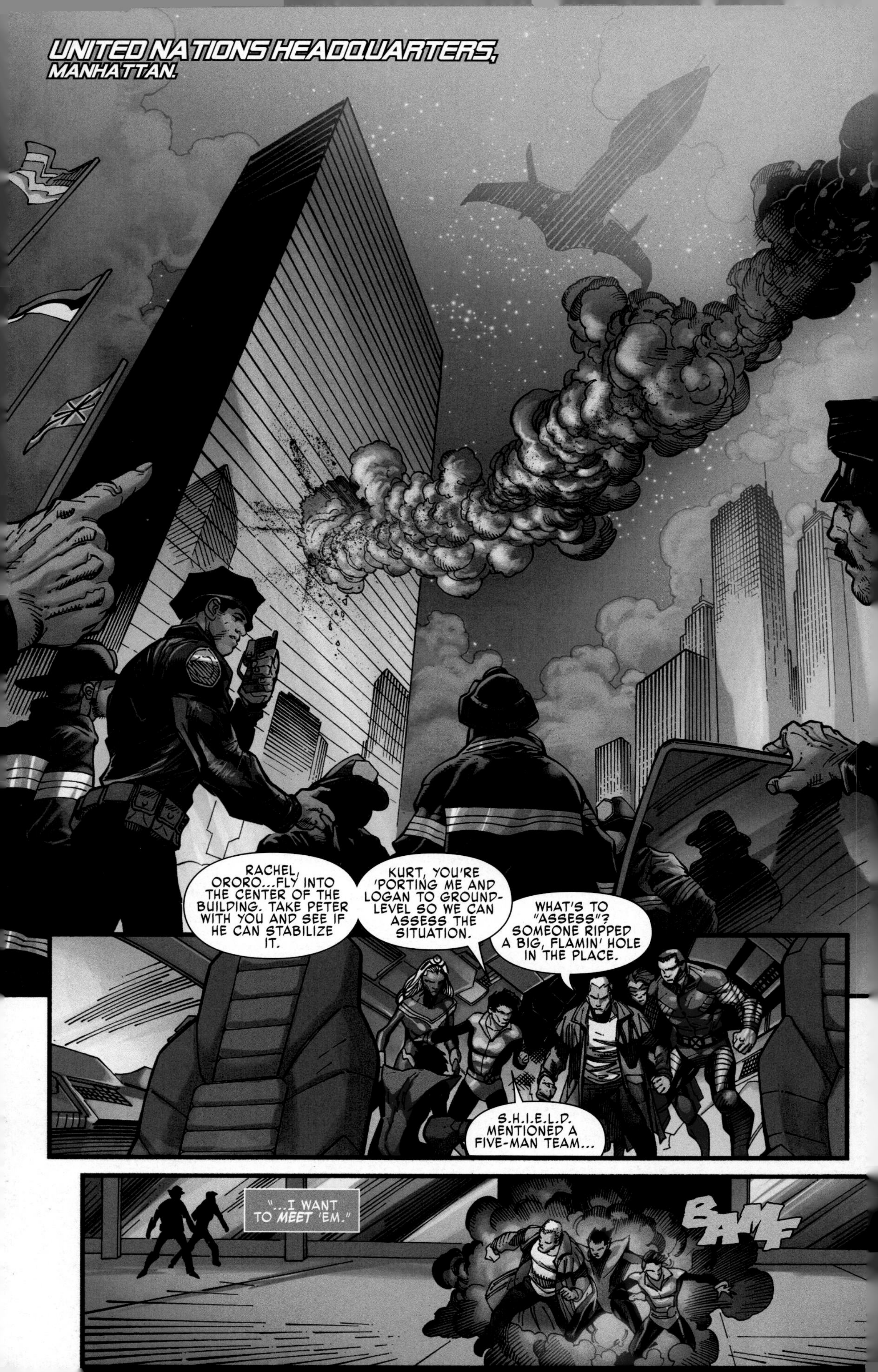
UNITED NATIONS HEADQUARTERS, MANHATTAN.
RACHEL, ORORO...FLY INTO THE CENTER OF THE BUILDING. TAKE PETER WITH YOU AND SEE IF HE CAN STABILIZE IT.
KURT, YOU'RE 'PORTING ME AND LOGAN TO GROUND-LEVEL SO WE CAN ASSESS THE SITUATION.
WHAT'S TO "ASSESS"? SOMEONE RIPPED A BIG, FLAMIN' HOLE IN THE PLACE.
S.H.I.E.L.D. MENTIONED A FIVE-MAN TEAM...
"...I WANT TO MEET 'EM."
BAMF

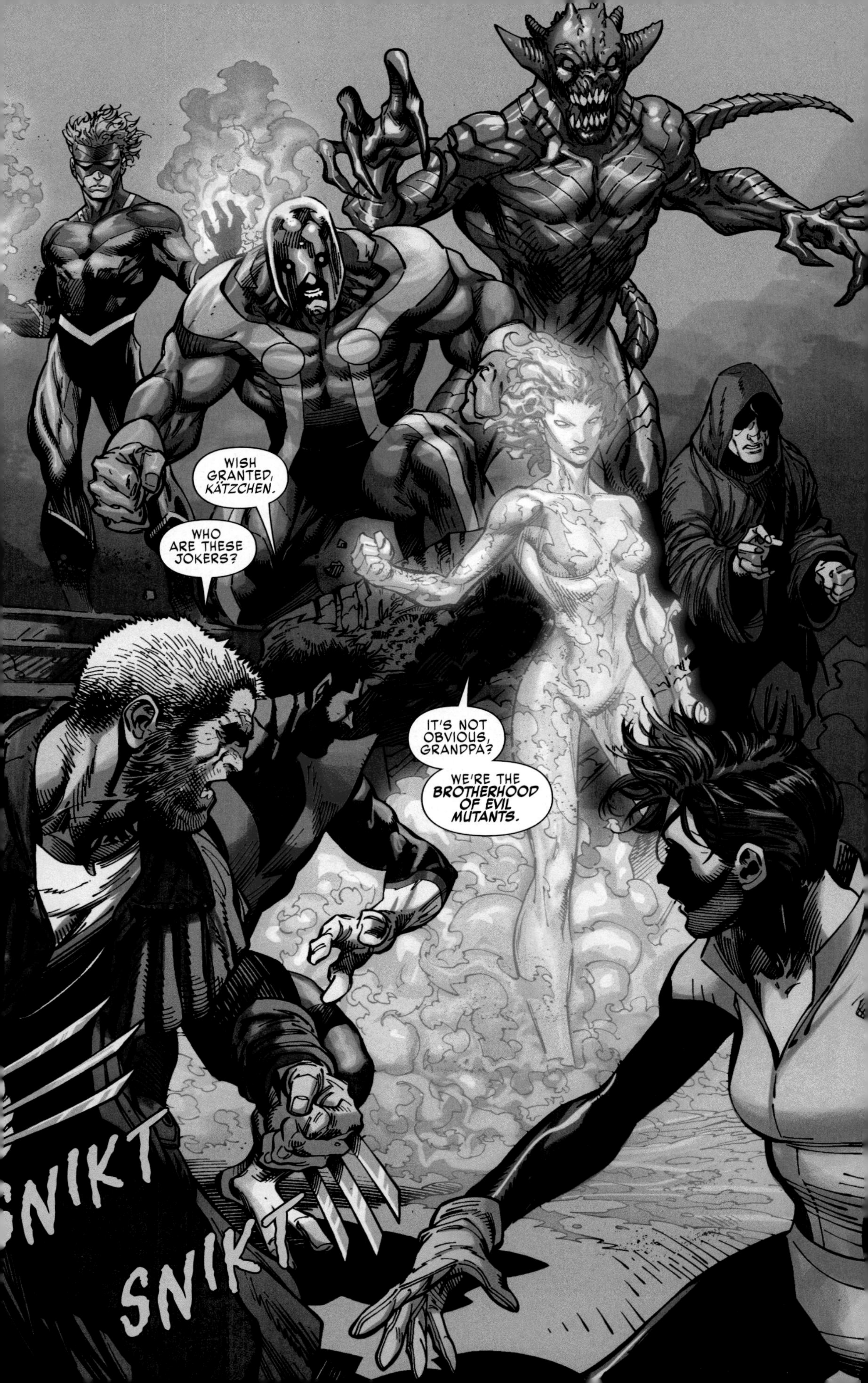
WISH GRANTED, KÄTZCHEN.
WHO ARE THESE JOKERS?
IT'S NOT OBVIOUS, GRANDPA?
WE'RE THE BROTHERHOOD OF EVIL MUTANTS.
SNIKT
SNIKT

2

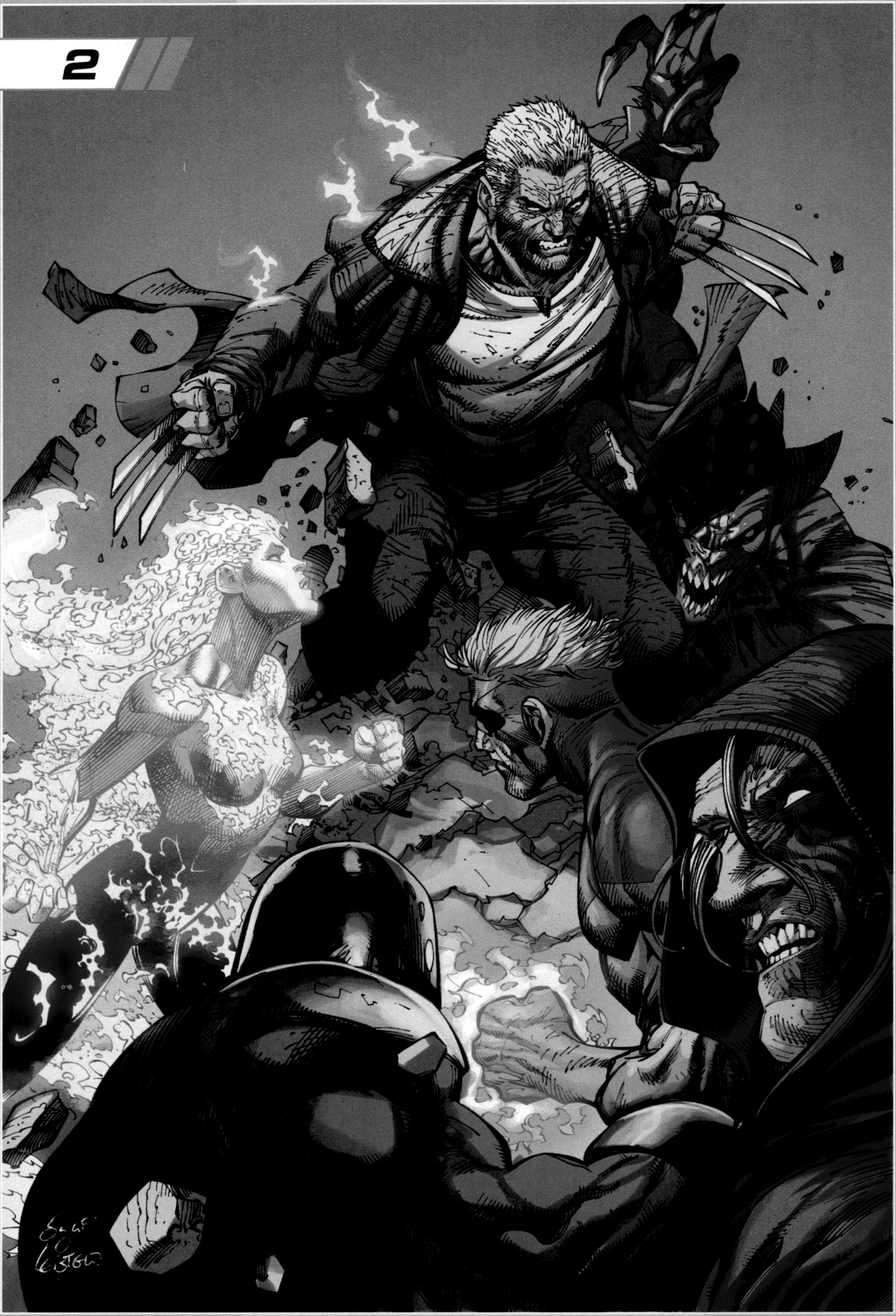

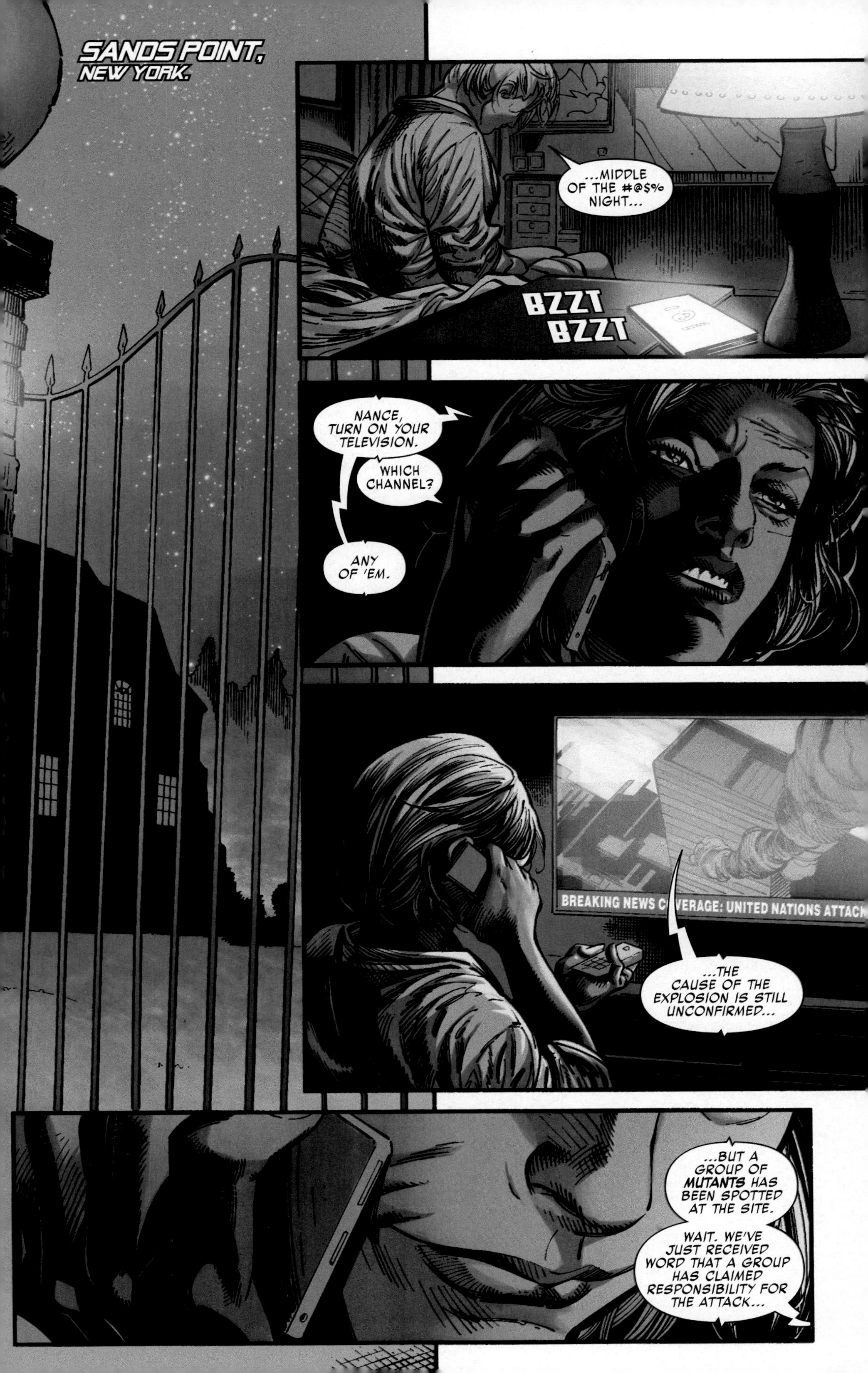
SANDS POINT, NEW YORK.
...MIDDLE OF THE #@$% NIGHT...
BZZT BZZT
NANCE, TURN ON YOUR TELEVISION.
WHICH CHANNEL?
ANY OF 'EM.
BREAKING NEWS COVERAGE: UNITED NATIONS ATTACK
...THE CAUSE OF THE EXPLOSION IS STILL UNCONFIRMED...
...BUT A GROUP OF MUTANTS HAS BEEN SPOTTED AT THE SITE.
WAIT. WE'VE JUST RECEIVED WORD THAT A GROUP HAS CLAIMED RESPONSIBILITY FOR THE ATTACK...

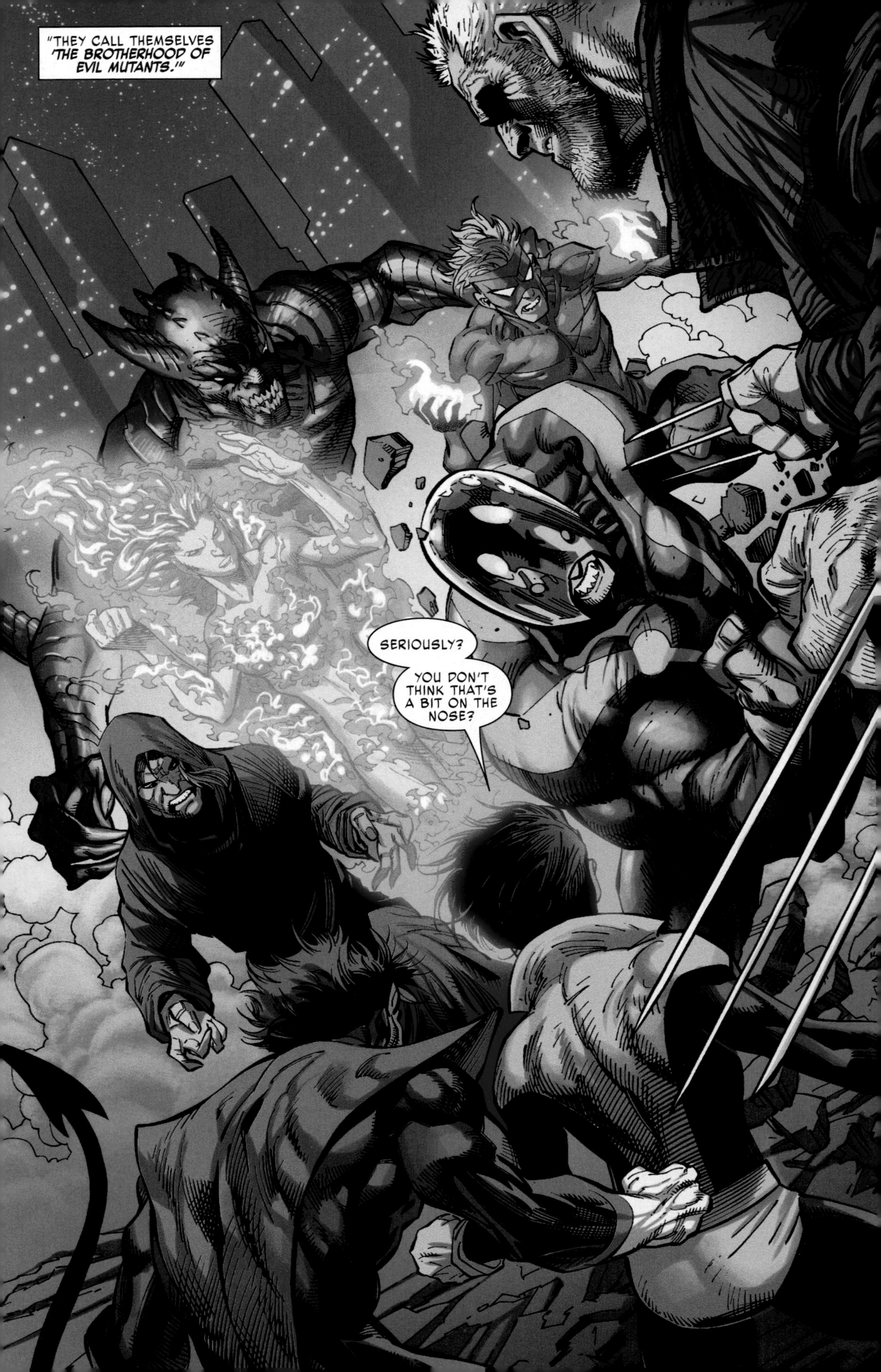
"THEY CALL THEMSELVES *'THE BROTHERHOOD OF EVIL MUTANTS.'"*
SERIOUSLY?
YOU DON'T THINK THAT'S A BIT ON THE NOSE?

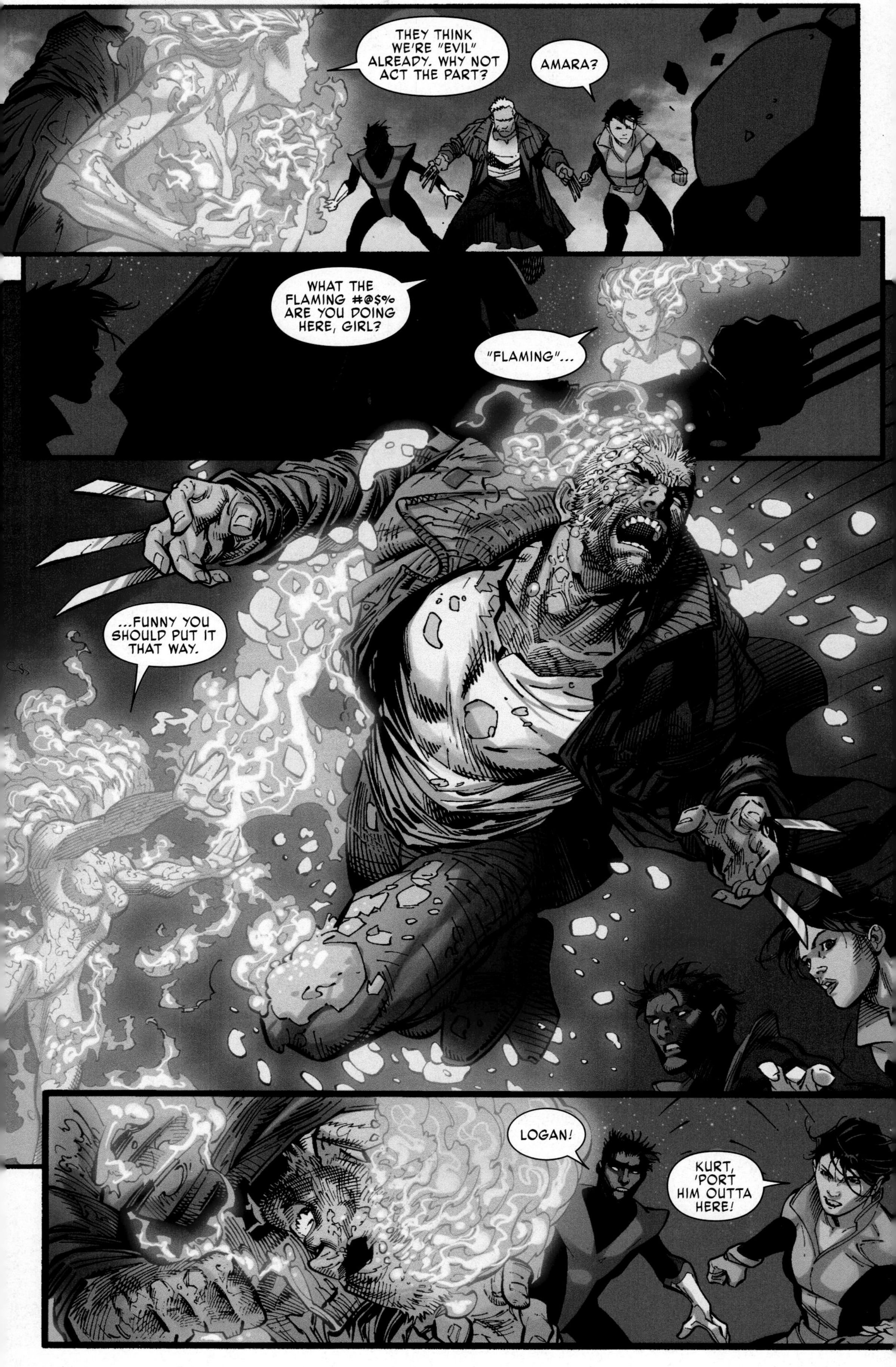
THEY THINK WE'RE "EVIL" ALREADY. WHY NOT ACT THE PART?
AMARA?
WHAT THE FLAMING #@$% ARE YOU DOING HERE, GIRL?
"FLAMING"...
...FUNNY YOU SHOULD PUT IT THAT WAY.
LOGAN!
KURT, 'PORT HIM OUTTA HERE!

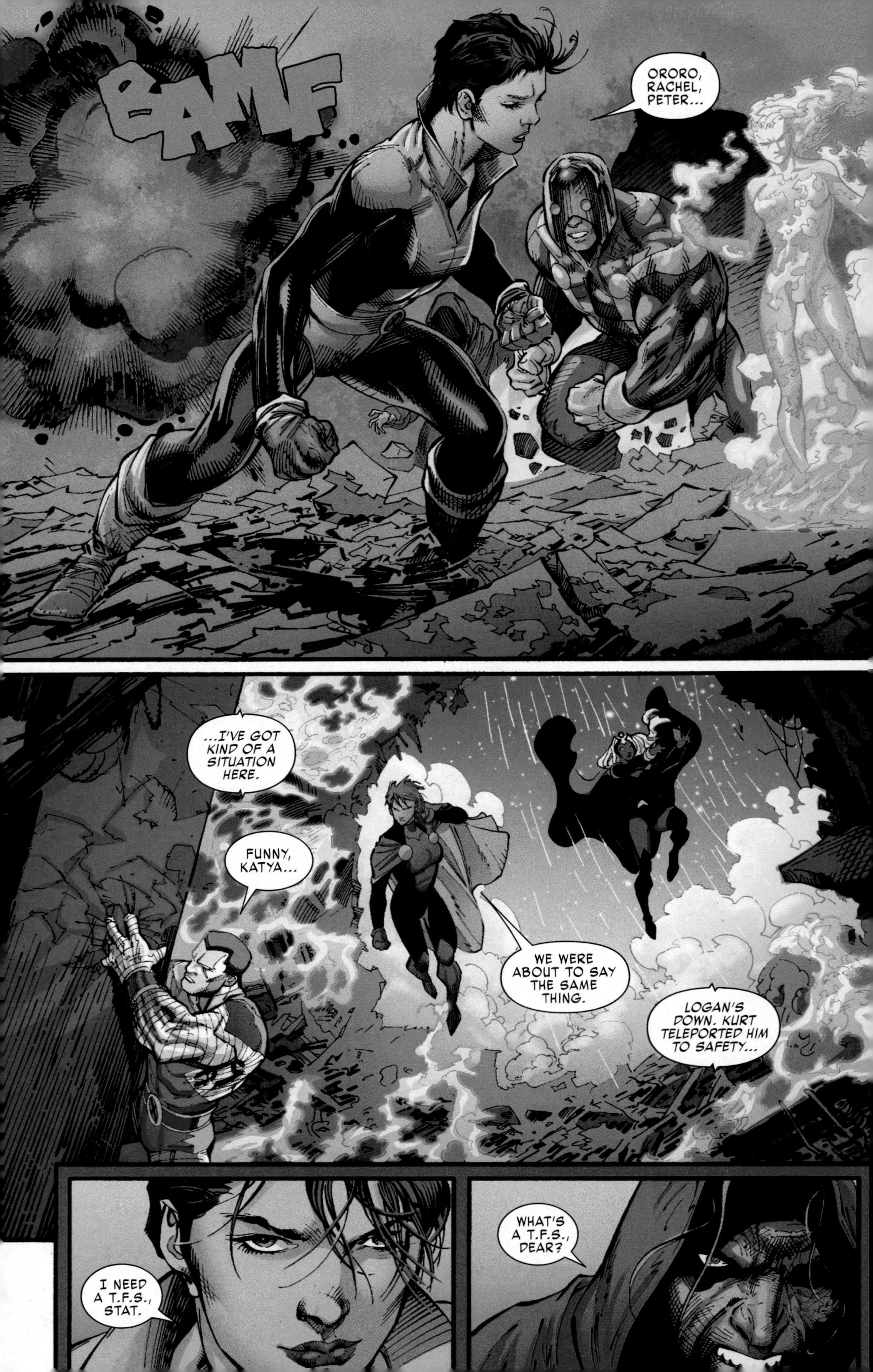
BAMF
ORORO, RACHEL, PETER...
...I'VE GOT KIND OF A SITUATION HERE.
FUNNY, KATYA...
WE WERE ABOUT TO SAY THE SAME THING.
LOGAN'S DOWN. KURT TELEPORTED HIM TO SAFETY...
I NEED A T.F.S., STAT.
WHAT'S A T.F.S., DEAR?

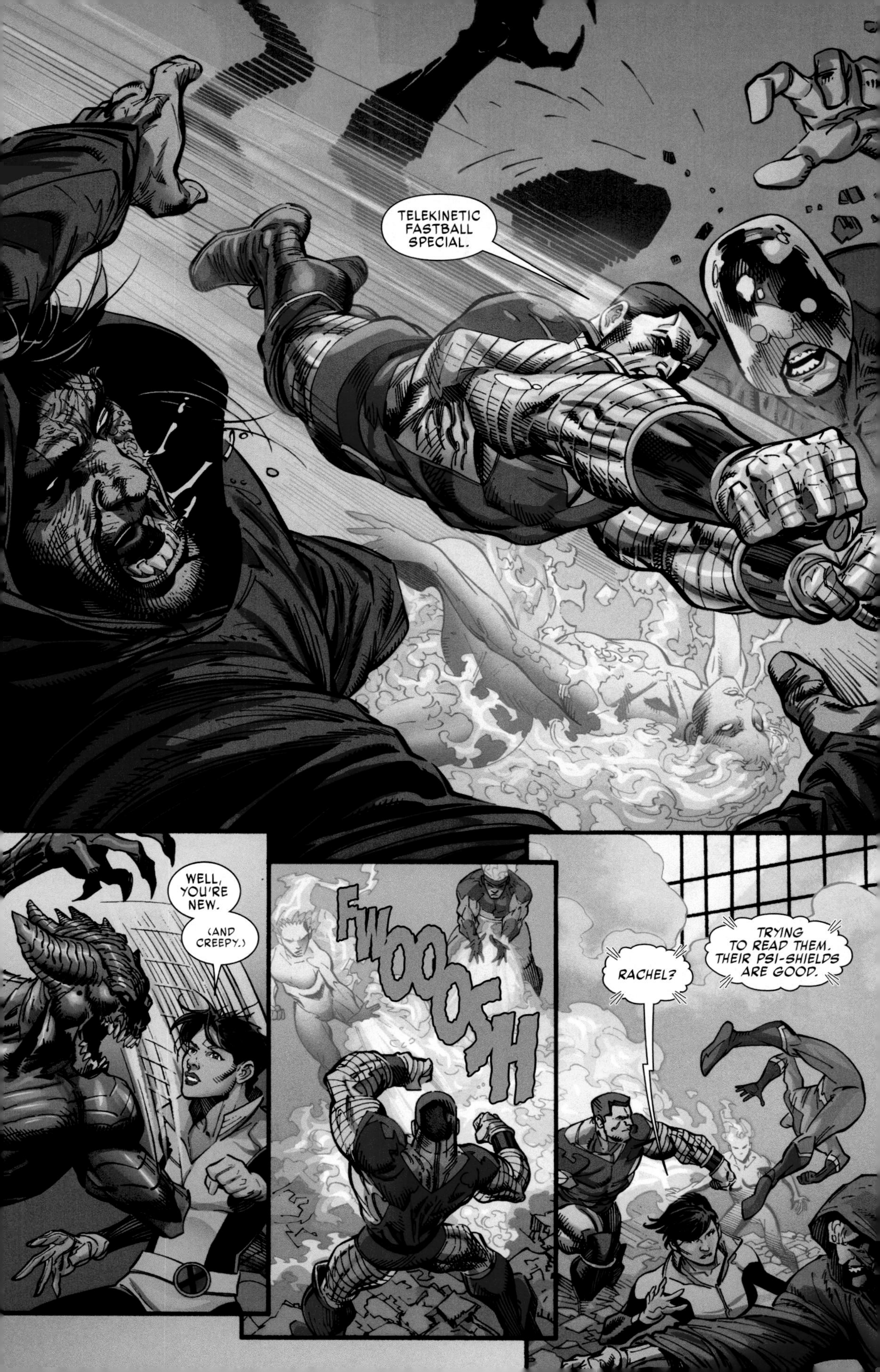
TELEKINETIC FASTBALL SPECIAL.
WELL, YOU'RE NEW.
(AND CREEPY.)
FWOOOOSH
RACHEL?
TRYING TO READ THEM. THEIR PSI-SHIELDS ARE GOOD.

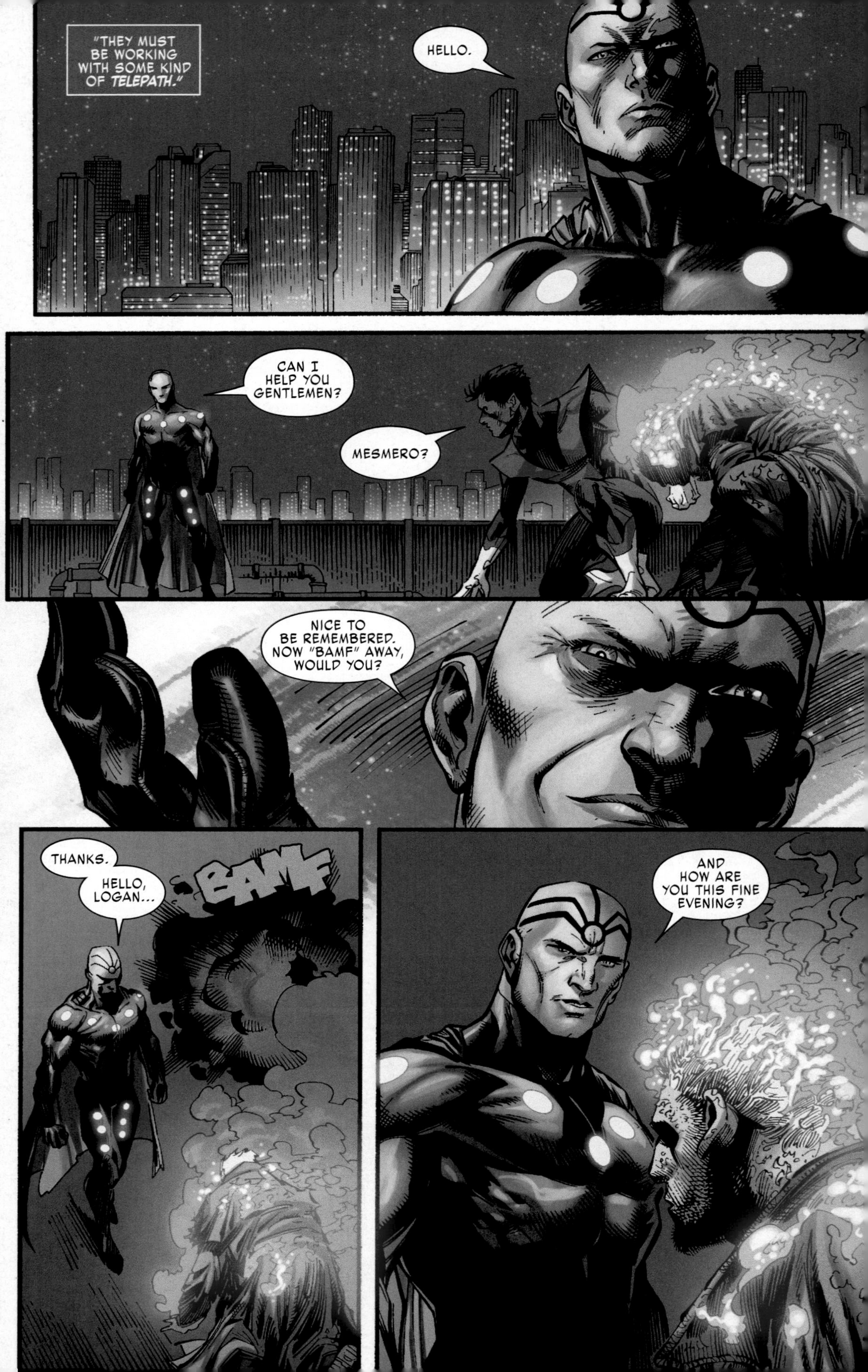
"THEY MUST BE WORKING WITH SOME KIND OF TELEPATH."
HELLO.
CAN I HELP YOU GENTLEMEN?
MESMERO?
NICE TO BE REMEMBERED. NOW "BAMF" AWAY, WOULD YOU?
THANKS.
BAMF
HELLO, LOGAN...
AND HOW ARE YOU THIS FINE EVENING?

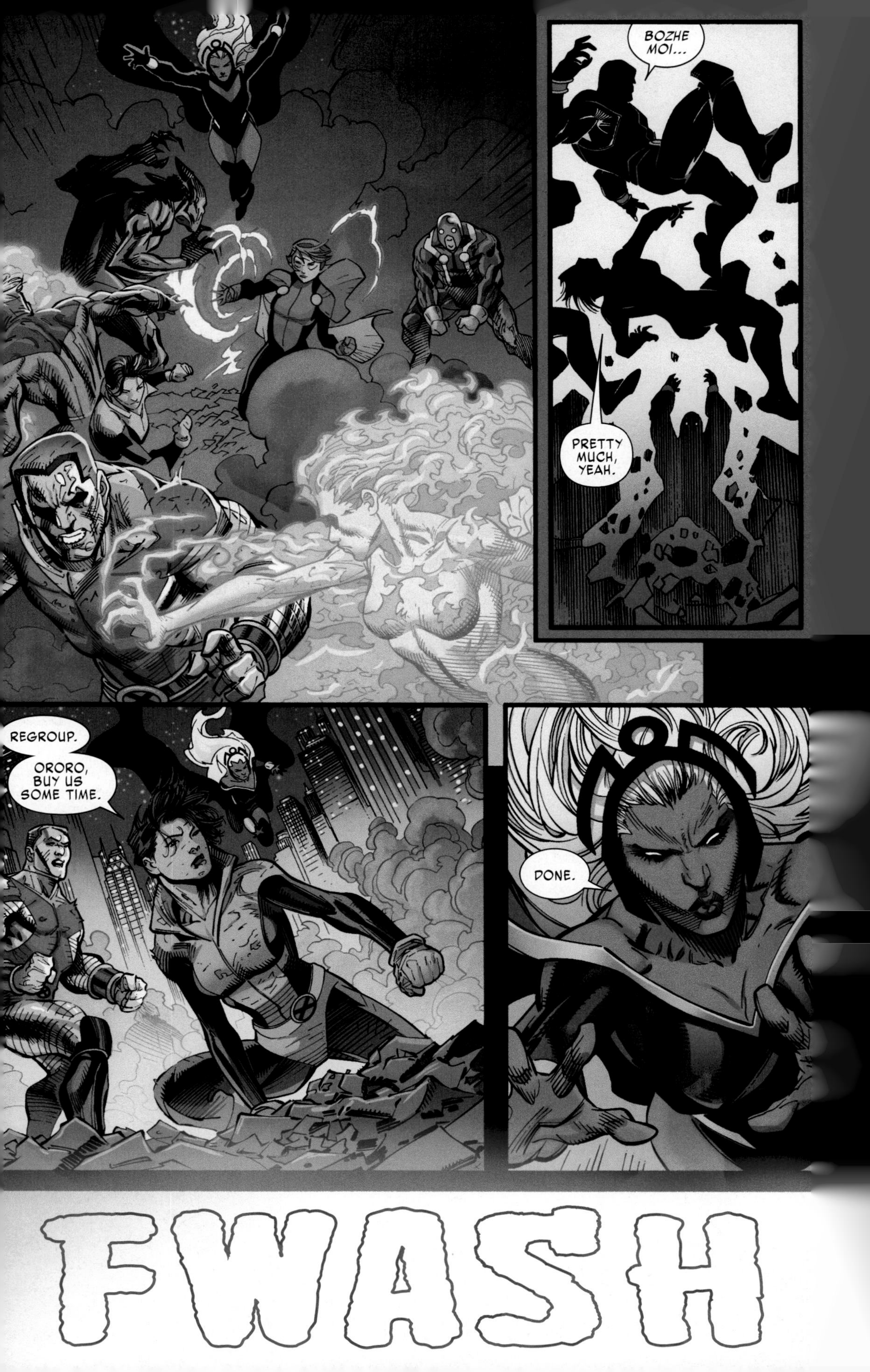
BOZHE MOI...
PRETTY MUCH, YEAH.
REGROUP.
ORORO, BUY US SOME TIME.
DONE.
FWASH

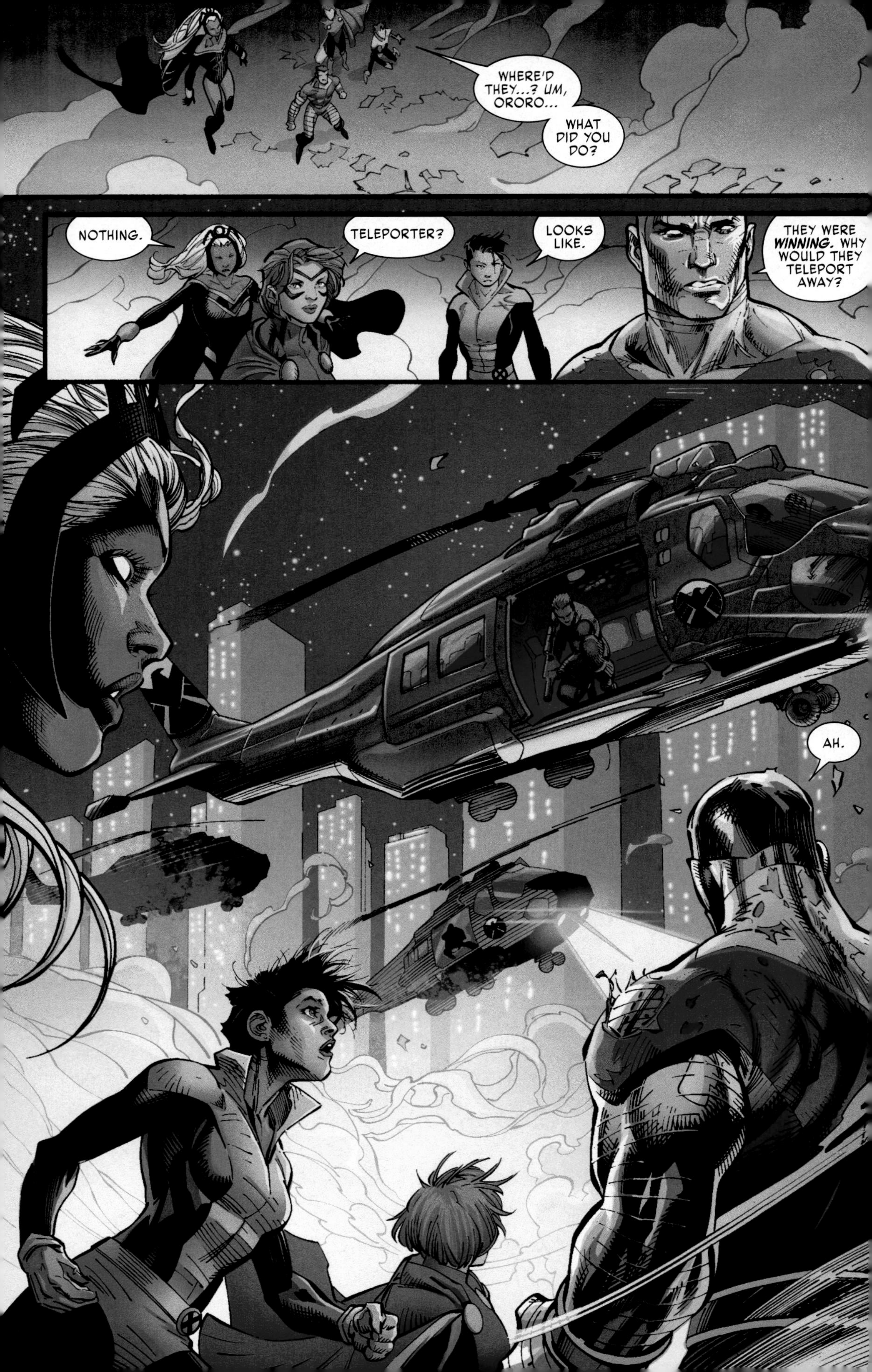

WHERE'D THEY...? UM, ORORO...
WHAT DID YOU DO?
NOTHING.
TELEPORTER?
LOOKS LIKE.
THEY WERE WINNING. WHY WOULD THEY TELEPORT AWAY?
AH.

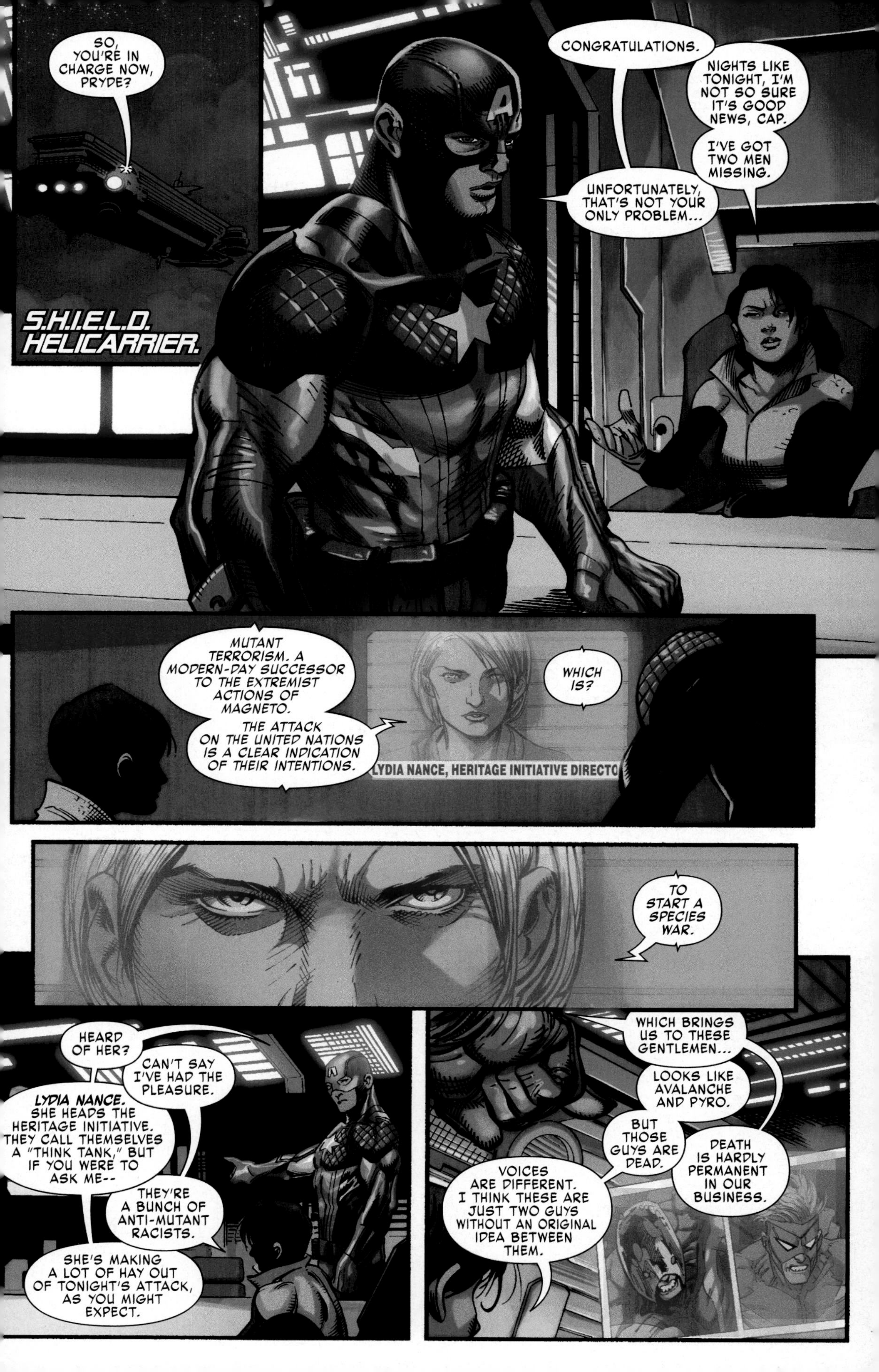
S.H.I.E.L.D. HELICARRIER.
SO, YOU'RE IN CHARGE NOW, PRYDE?
CONGRATULATIONS.
NIGHTS LIKE TONIGHT, I'M NOT SO SURE IT'S GOOD NEWS, CAP.
I'VE GOT TWO MEN MISSING.
UNFORTUNATELY, THAT'S NOT YOUR ONLY PROBLEM...
MUTANT TERRORISM. A MODERN-DAY SUCCESSOR TO THE EXTREMIST ACTIONS OF MAGNETO.
THE ATTACK ON THE UNITED NATIONS IS A CLEAR INDICATION OF THEIR INTENTIONS.
LYDIA NANCE, HERITAGE INITIATIVE DIRECTO
WHICH IS?
TO START A SPECIES WAR.
HEARD OF HER?
CAN'T SAY I'VE HAD THE PLEASURE.
LYDIA NANCE. SHE HEADS THE HERITAGE INITIATIVE. THEY CALL THEMSELVES A "THINK TANK," BUT IF YOU WERE TO ASK ME--
THEY'RE A BUNCH OF ANTI-MUTANT RACISTS.
SHE'S MAKING A LOT OF HAY OUT OF TONIGHT'S ATTACK, AS YOU MIGHT EXPECT.
WHICH BRINGS US TO THESE GENTLEMEN...
LOOKS LIKE AVALANCHE AND PYRO.
BUT THOSE GUYS ARE DEAD.
DEATH IS HARDLY PERMANENT IN OUR BUSINESS.
VOICES ARE DIFFERENT. I THINK THESE ARE JUST TWO GUYS WITHOUT AN ORIGINAL IDEA BETWEEN THEM.

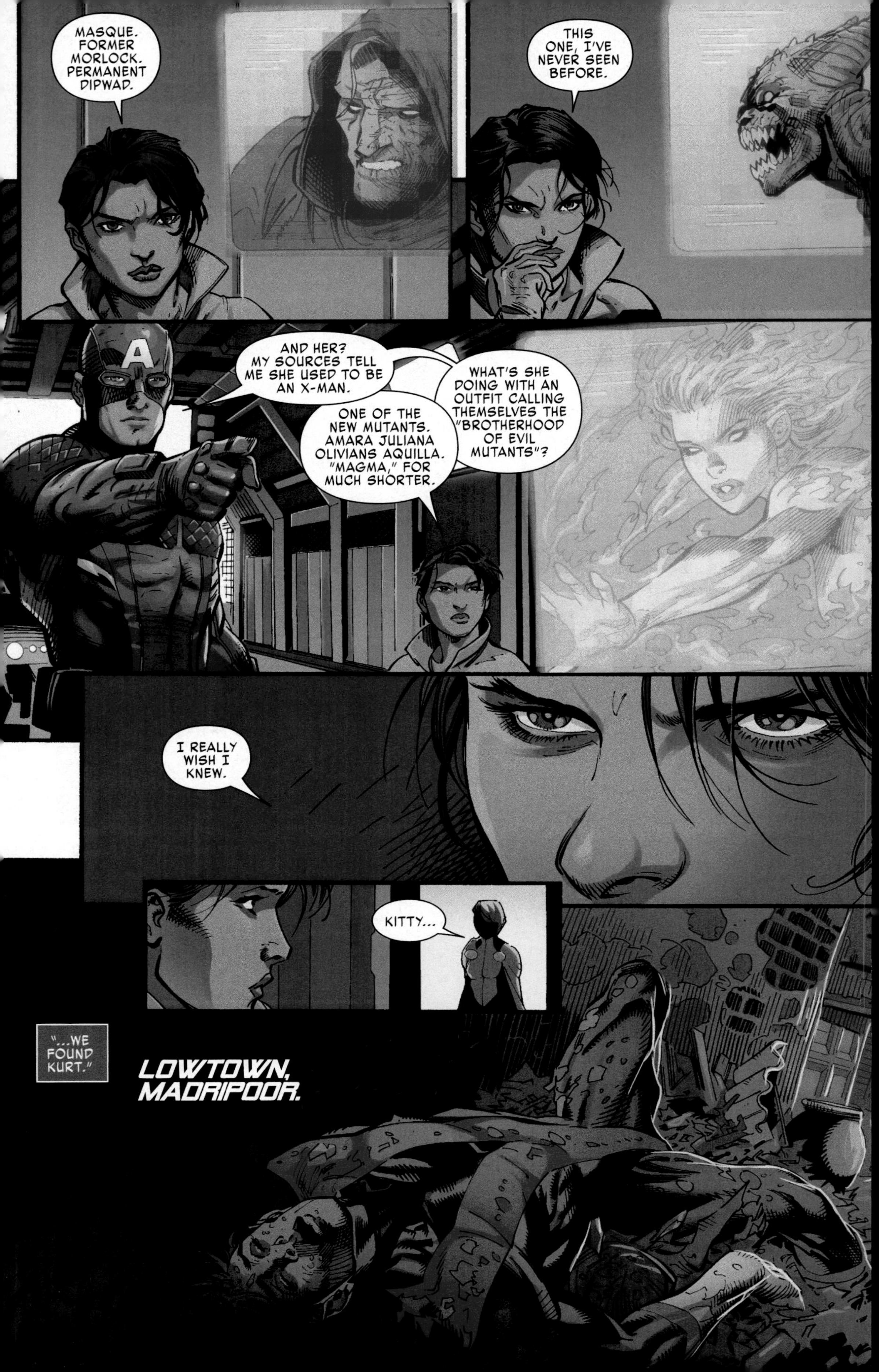
MASQUE. FORMER MORLOCK. PERMANENT DIPWAD.
THIS ONE, I'VE NEVER SEEN BEFORE.
AND HER? MY SOURCES TELL ME SHE USED TO BE AN X-MAN.
ONE OF THE NEW MUTANTS. AMARA JULIANA OLIVIANS AQUILLA. "MAGMA," FOR MUCH SHORTER.
WHAT'S SHE DOING WITH AN OUTFIT CALLING THEMSELVES THE "BROTHERHOOD OF EVIL MUTANTS"?
I REALLY WISH I KNEW.
KITTY...
"...WE FOUND KURT."
LOWTOWN, MADRIPOOR.

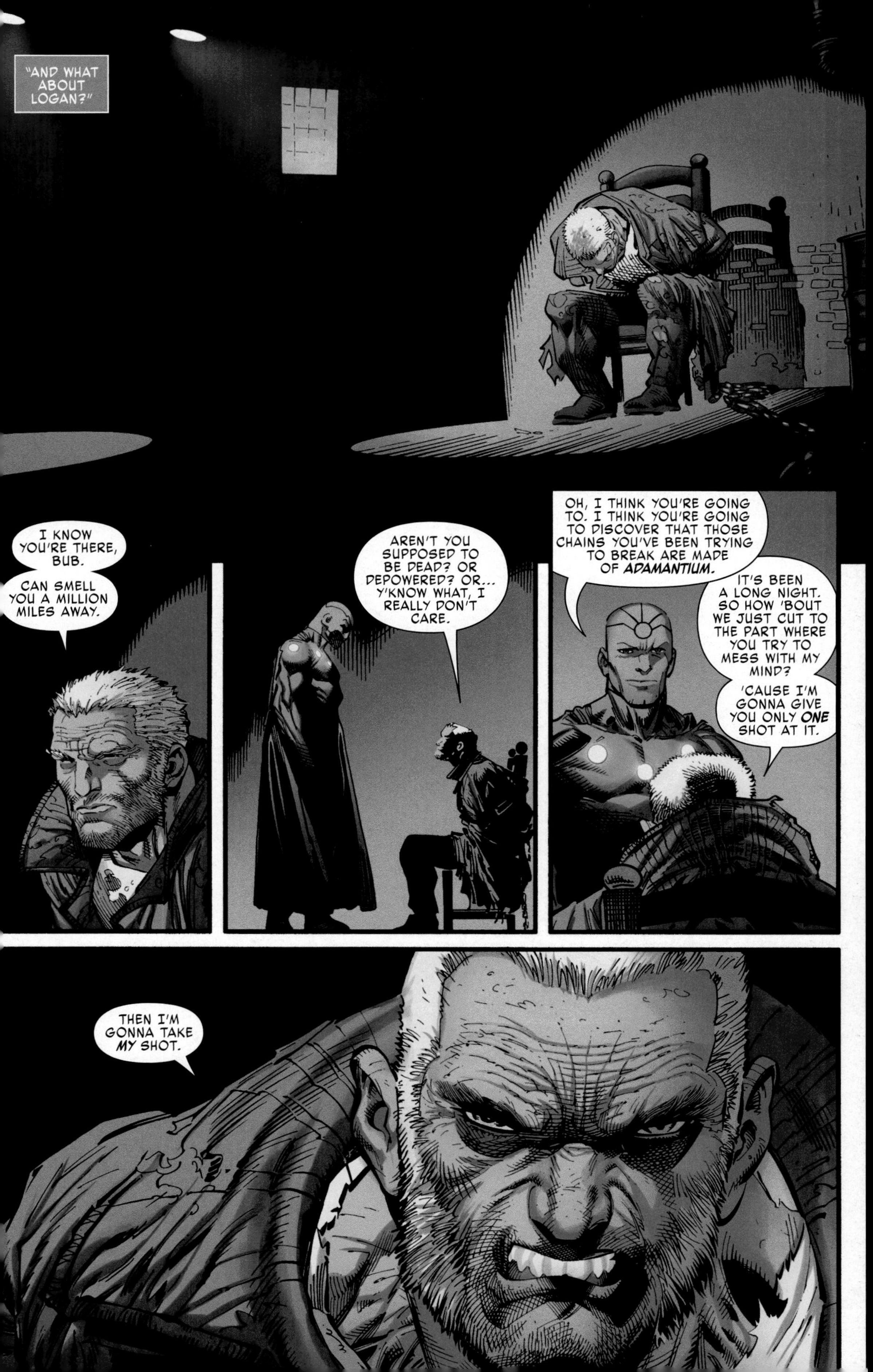
"AND WHAT ABOUT LOGAN?"
I KNOW YOU'RE THERE, BUB.
CAN SMELL YOU A MILLION MILES AWAY.
AREN'T YOU SUPPOSED TO BE DEAD? OR DEPOWERED? OR... Y'KNOW WHAT, I REALLY DON'T CARE.
OH, I THINK YOU'RE GOING TO. I THINK YOU'RE GOING TO DISCOVER THAT THOSE CHAINS YOU'VE BEEN TRYING TO BREAK ARE MADE OF ADAMANTIUM.
IT'S BEEN A LONG NIGHT. SO HOW 'BOUT WE JUST CUT TO THE PART WHERE YOU TRY TO MESS WITH MY MIND?
'CAUSE I'M GONNA GIVE YOU ONLY ONE SHOT AT IT.
THEN I'M GONNA TAKE MY SHOT.

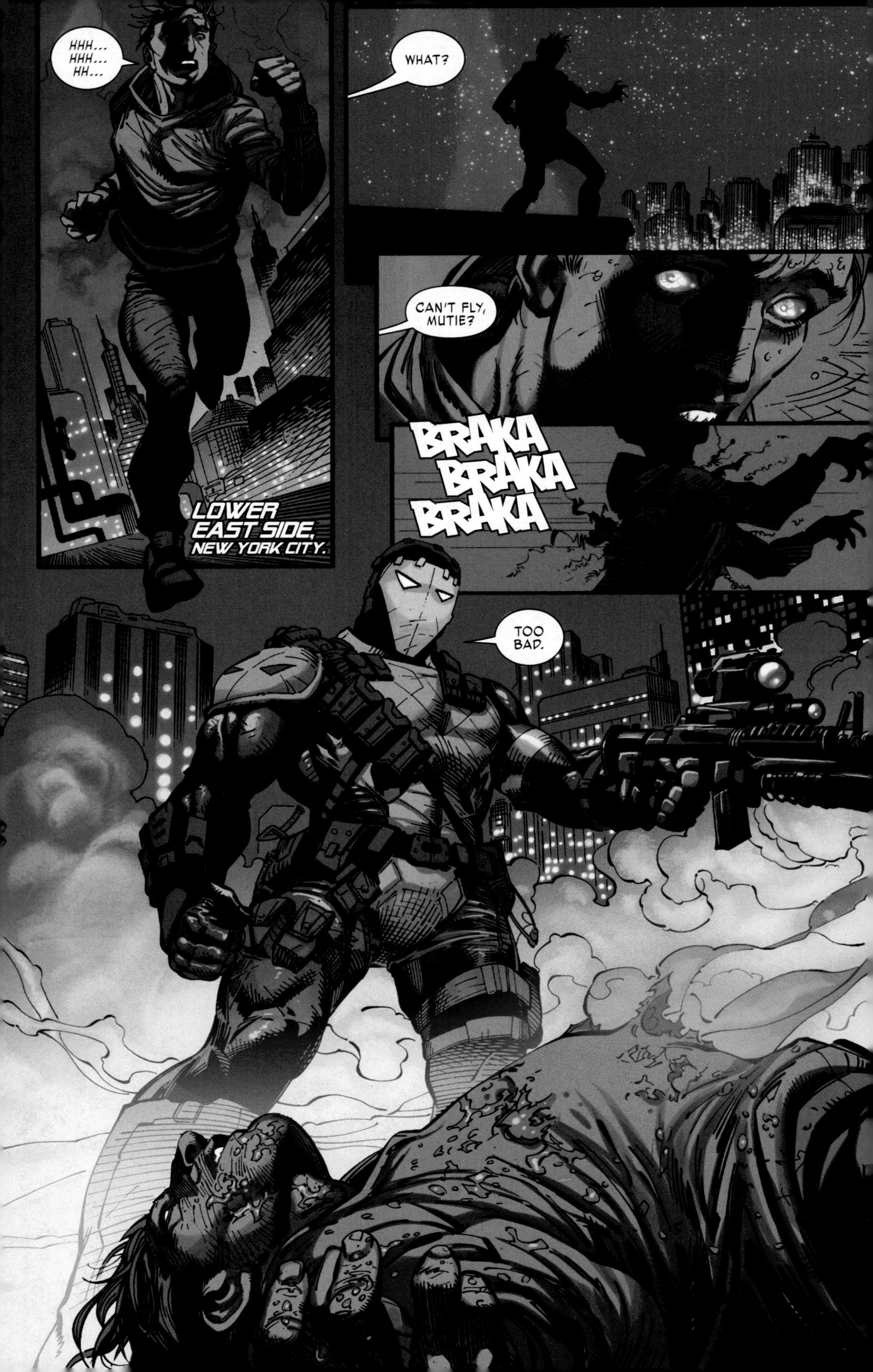
HHH... HHH... HH...
WHAT?
LOWER EAST SIDE, NEW YORK CITY.
CAN'T FLY, MUTIE?
BRAKA BRAKA BRAKA
TOO BAD.

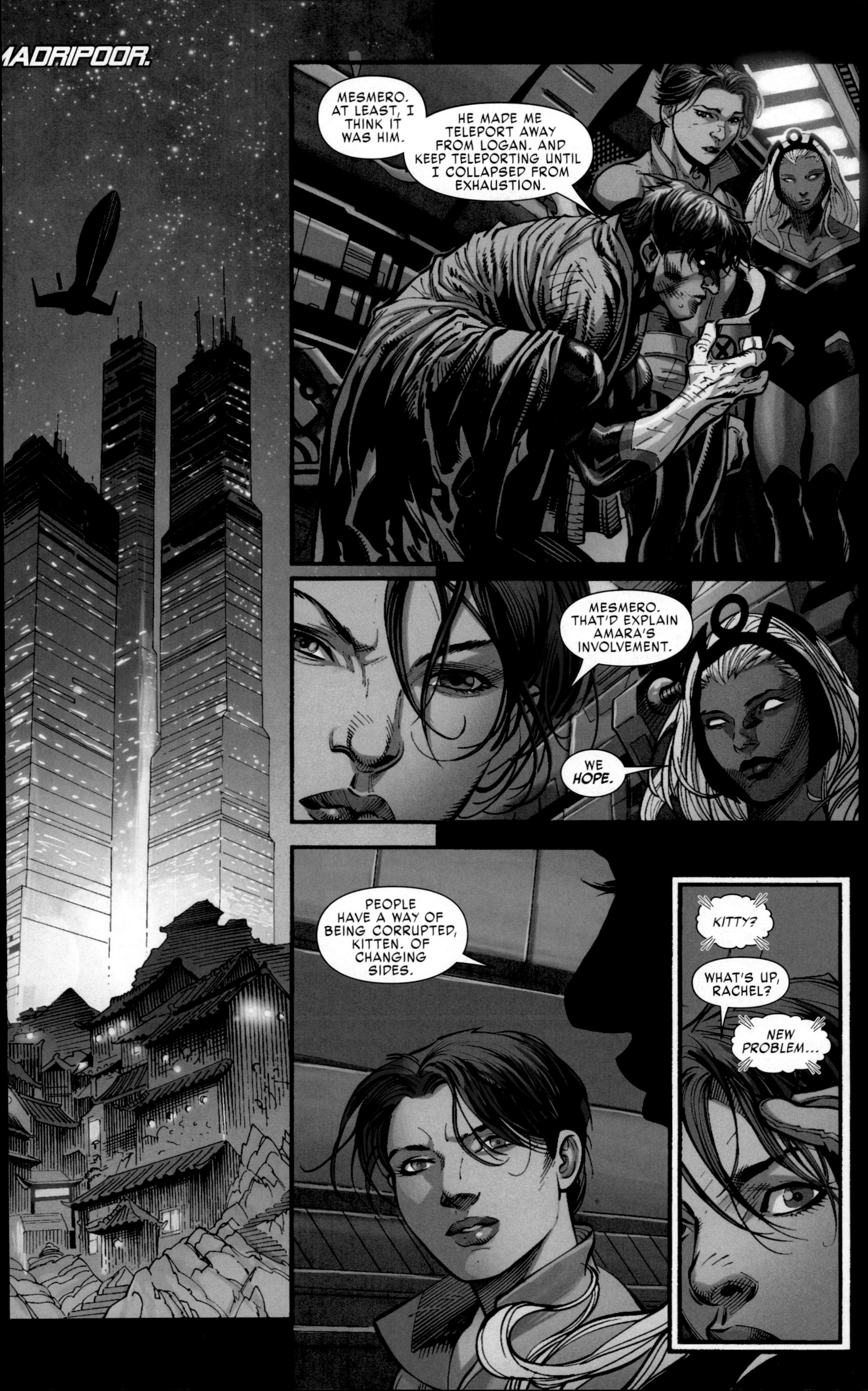
MADRIPOOR.
MESMERO. AT LEAST, I THINK IT WAS HIM.
HE MADE ME TELEPORT AWAY FROM LOGAN. AND KEEP TELEPORTING UNTIL I COLLAPSED FROM EXHAUSTION.
MESMERO. THAT'D EXPLAIN AMARA'S INVOLVEMENT.
WE HOPE.
PEOPLE HAVE A WAY OF BEING CORRUPTED, KITTEN. OF CHANGING SIDES.
KITTY?
WHAT'S UP, RACHEL?
NEW PROBLEM...

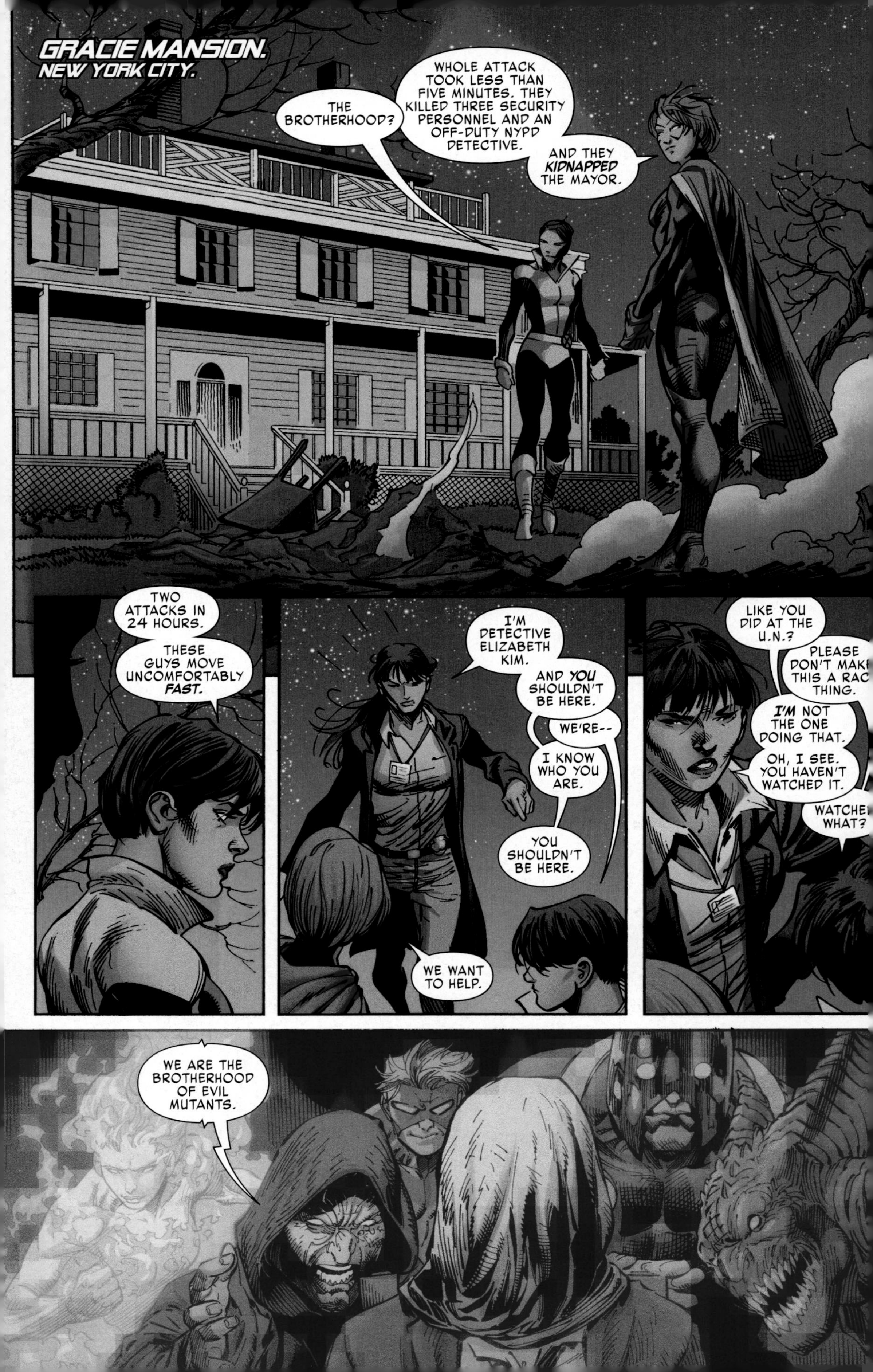
GRACIE MANSION. NEW YORK CITY.
THE BROTHERHOOD?
WHOLE ATTACK TOOK LESS THAN FIVE MINUTES. THEY KILLED THREE SECURITY PERSONNEL AND AN OFF-DUTY NYPD DETECTIVE.
AND THEY KIDNAPPED THE MAYOR.
TWO ATTACKS IN 24 HOURS.
THESE GUYS MOVE UNCOMFORTABLY FAST.
I'M DETECTIVE ELIZABETH KIM.
AND YOU SHOULDN'T BE HERE.
WE'RE--
I KNOW WHO YOU ARE.
YOU SHOULDN'T BE HERE.
WE WANT TO HELP.
LIKE YOU DID AT THE U.N.?
PLEASE DON'T MAK
THIS A RAC
THING.
I'M NOT THE ONE DOING THAT.
OH, I SEE. YOU HAVEN'T WATCHED IT.
WATCHE
WHAT?
WE ARE THE BROTHERHOOD OF EVIL MUTANTS.

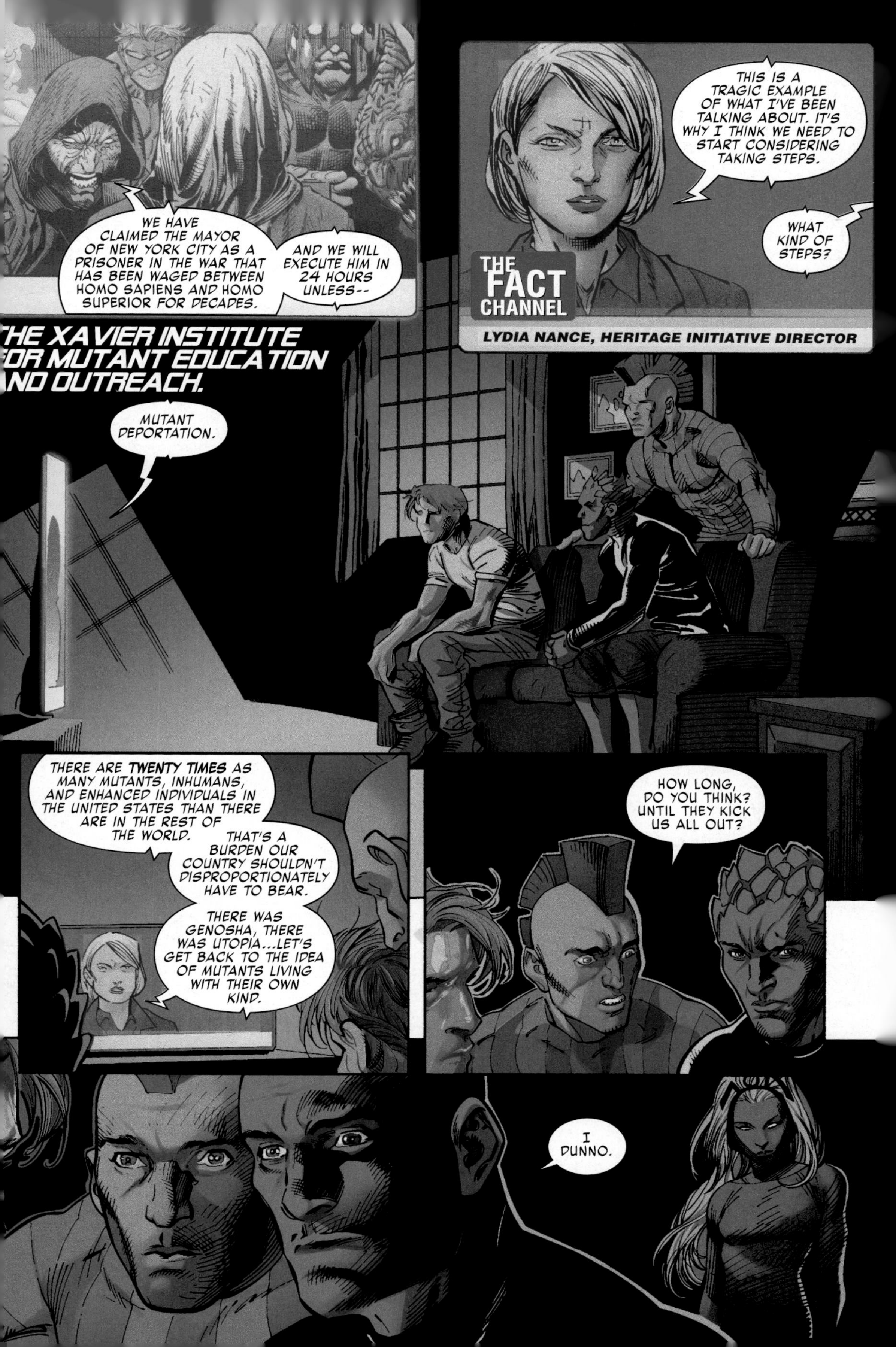
WE HAVE CLAIMED THE MAYOR OF NEW YORK CITY AS A PRISONER IN THE WAR THAT HAS BEEN WAGED BETWEEN HOMO SAPIENS AND HOMO SUPERIOR FOR DECADES.
AND WE WILL EXECUTE HIM IN 24 HOURS UNLESS--
THIS IS A TRAGIC EXAMPLE OF WHAT I'VE BEEN TALKING ABOUT. IT'S WHY I THINK WE NEED TO START CONSIDERING TAKING STEPS.
WHAT KIND OF STEPS?
THE FACT CHANNEL
LYDIA NANCE, HERITAGE INITIATIVE DIRECTOR
THE XAVIER INSTITUTE FOR MUTANT EDUCATION AND OUTREACH.
MUTANT DEPORTATION.
THERE ARE TWENTY TIMES AS MANY MUTANTS, INHUMANS, AND ENHANCED INDIVIDUALS IN THE UNITED STATES THAN THERE ARE IN THE REST OF THE WORLD.
THAT'S A BURDEN OUR COUNTRY SHOULDN'T DISPROPORTIONATELY HAVE TO BEAR.
THERE WAS GENOSHA, THERE WAS UTOPIA...LET'S GET BACK TO THE IDEA OF MUTANTS LIVING WITH THEIR OWN KIND.
HOW LONG, DO YOU THINK? UNTIL THEY KICK US ALL OUT?
I DUNNO.

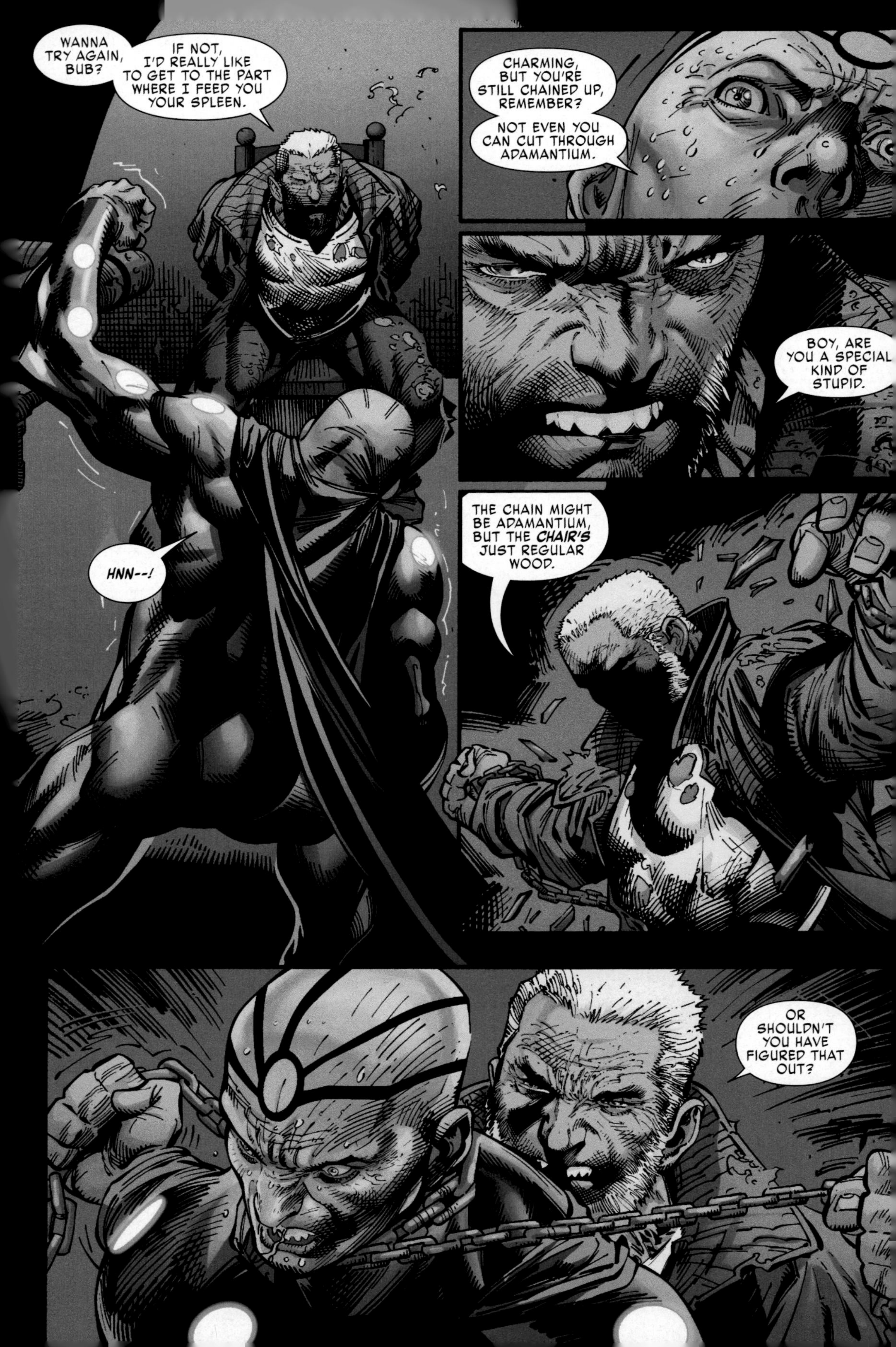
WANNA TRY AGAIN, BUB?
IF NOT, I'D REALLY LIKE TO GET TO THE PART WHERE I FEED YOU YOUR SPLEEN.
CHARMING, BUT YOU'RE STILL CHAINED UP, REMEMBER?
NOT EVEN YOU CAN CUT THROUGH ADAMANTIUM.
BOY, ARE YOU A SPECIAL KIND OF STUPID.
HNN--!
THE CHAIN MIGHT BE ADAMANTIUM, BUT THE CHAIR'S JUST REGULAR WOOD.
OR SHOULDN'T YOU HAVE FIGURED THAT OUT?

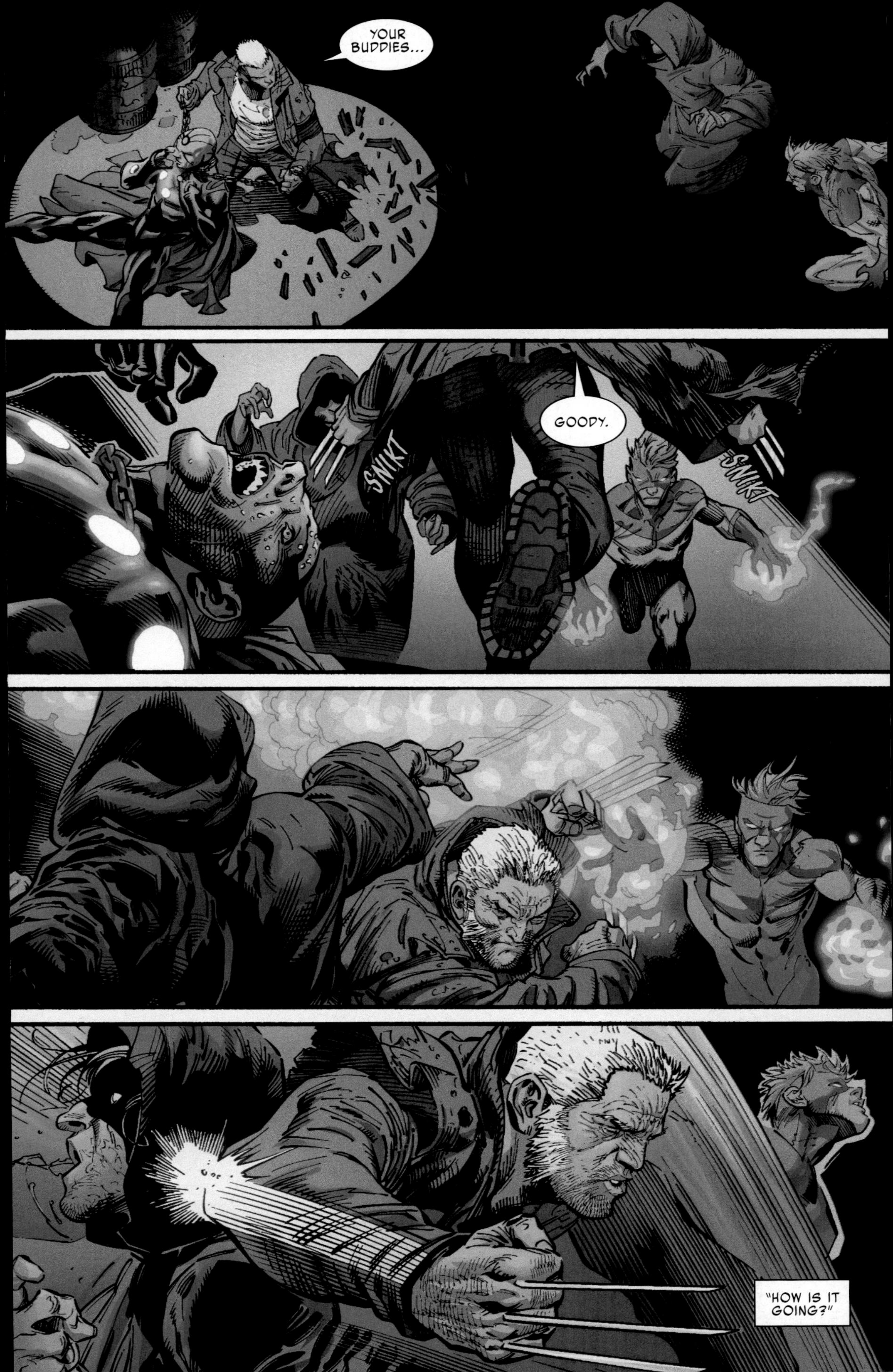
YOUR BUDDIES...
SNIKT
GOODY.
SNIKT
"HOW IS IT GOING?"

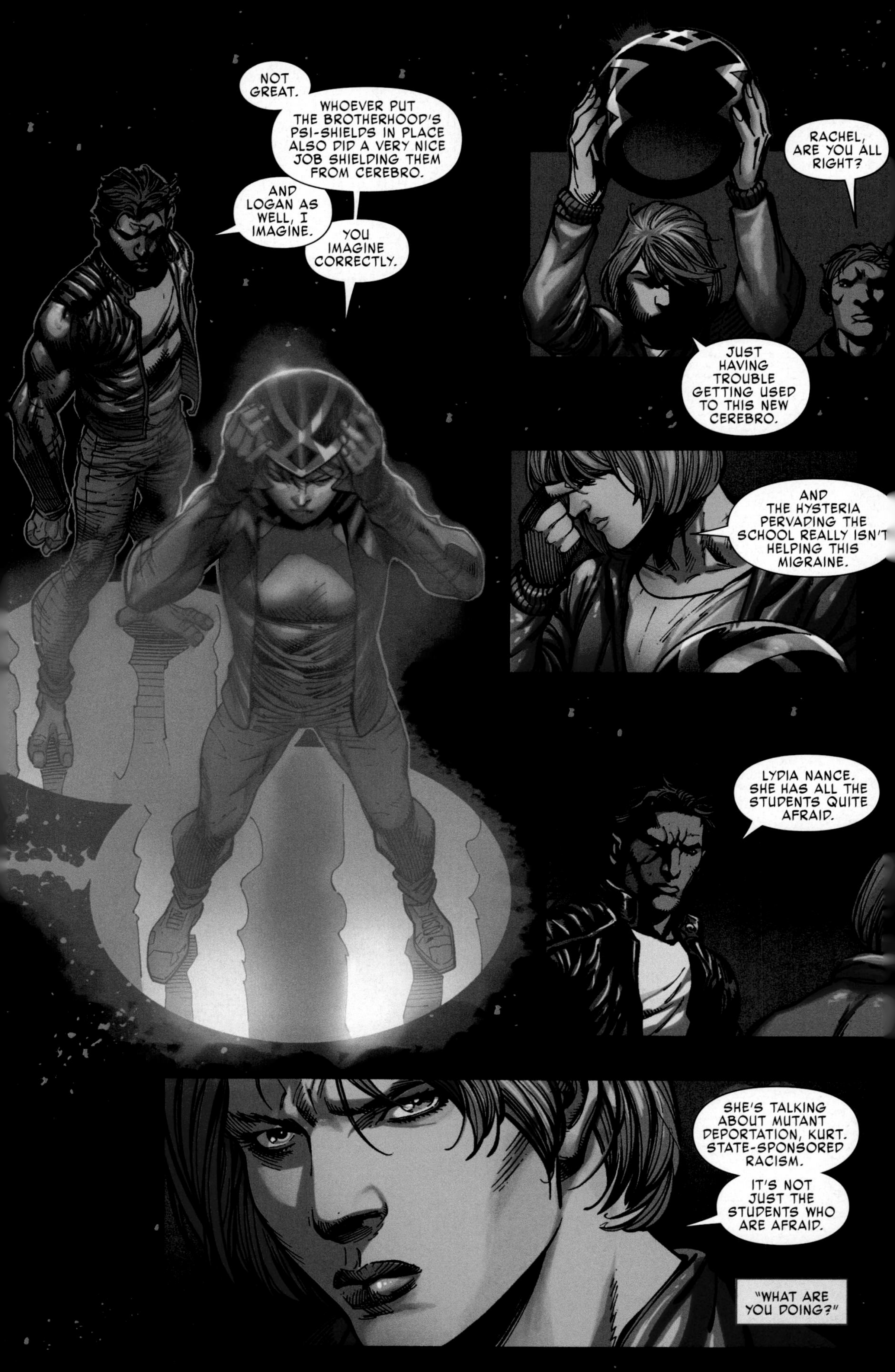
NOT GREAT.
WHOEVER PUT THE BROTHERHOOD'S PSI-SHIELDS IN PLACE ALSO DID A VERY NICE JOB SHIELDING THEM FROM CEREBRO.
AND LOGAN AS WELL, I IMAGINE.
YOU IMAGINE CORRECTLY.
RACHEL, ARE YOU ALL RIGHT?
JUST HAVING TROUBLE GETTING USED TO THIS NEW CEREBRO.
AND THE HYSTERIA PERVADING THE SCHOOL REALLY ISN'T HELPING THIS MIGRAINE.
LYDIA NANCE. SHE HAS ALL THE STUDENTS QUITE AFRAID.
SHE'S TALKING ABOUT MUTANT DEPORTATION, KURT. STATE-SPONSORED RACISM.
IT'S NOT JUST THE STUDENTS WHO ARE AFRAID.
"WHAT ARE YOU DOING?"

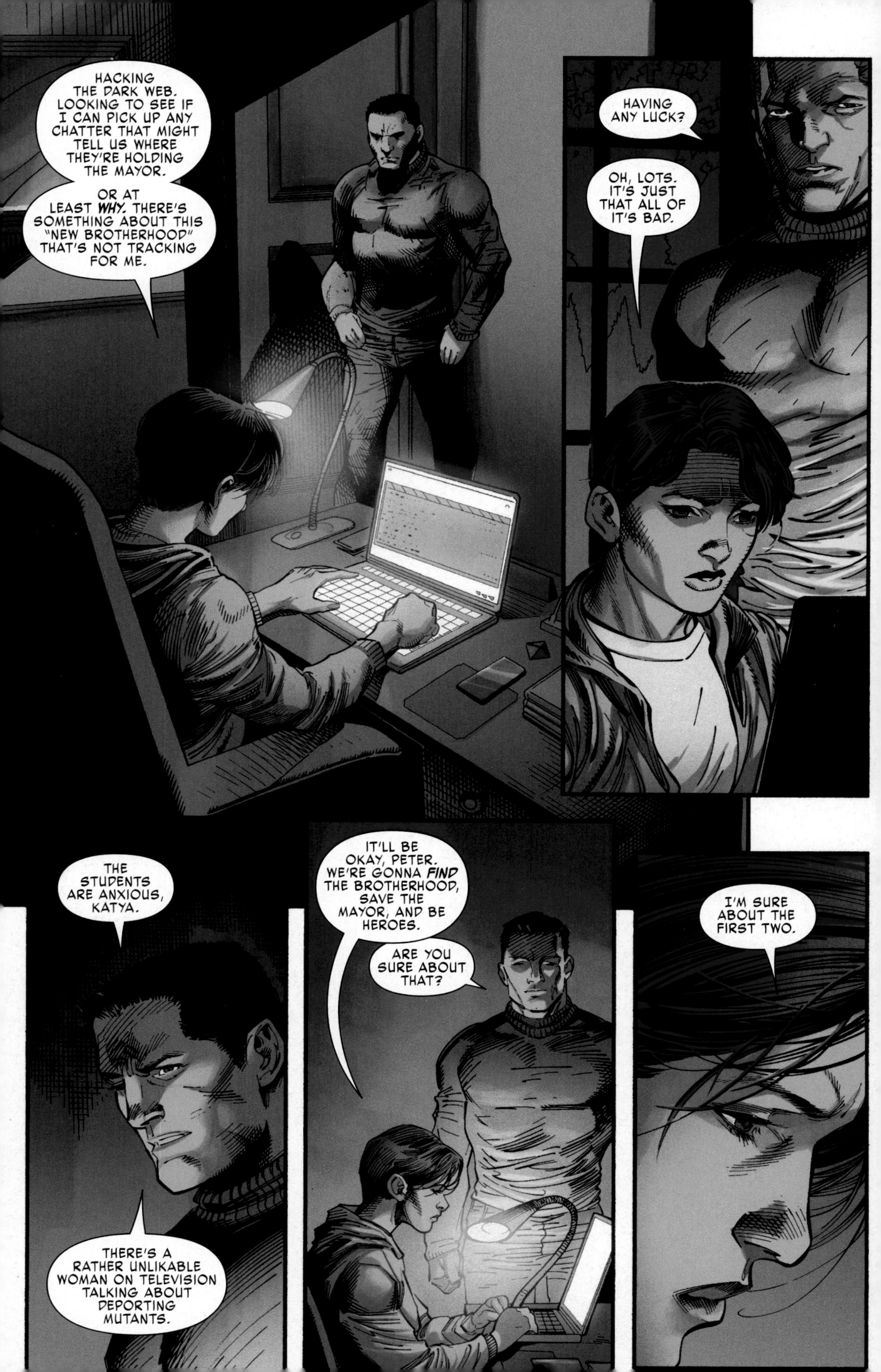
HACKING THE DARK WEB. LOOKING TO SEE IF I CAN PICK UP ANY CHATTER THAT MIGHT TELL US WHERE THEY'RE HOLDING THE MAYOR.
OR AT LEAST *WHY.* THERE'S SOMETHING ABOUT THIS "NEW BROTHERHOOD" THAT'S NOT TRACKING FOR ME.
HAVING ANY LUCK?
OH, LOTS. IT'S JUST THAT ALL OF IT'S BAD.
THE STUDENTS ARE ANXIOUS, KATYA.
THERE'S A RATHER UNLIKABLE WOMAN ON TELEVISION TALKING ABOUT DEPORTING MUTANTS.
IT'LL BE OKAY, PETER. WE'RE GONNA *FIND* THE BROTHERHOOD, SAVE THE MAYOR, AND BE HEROES.
ARE YOU SURE ABOUT THAT?
I'M SURE ABOUT THE FIRST TWO.

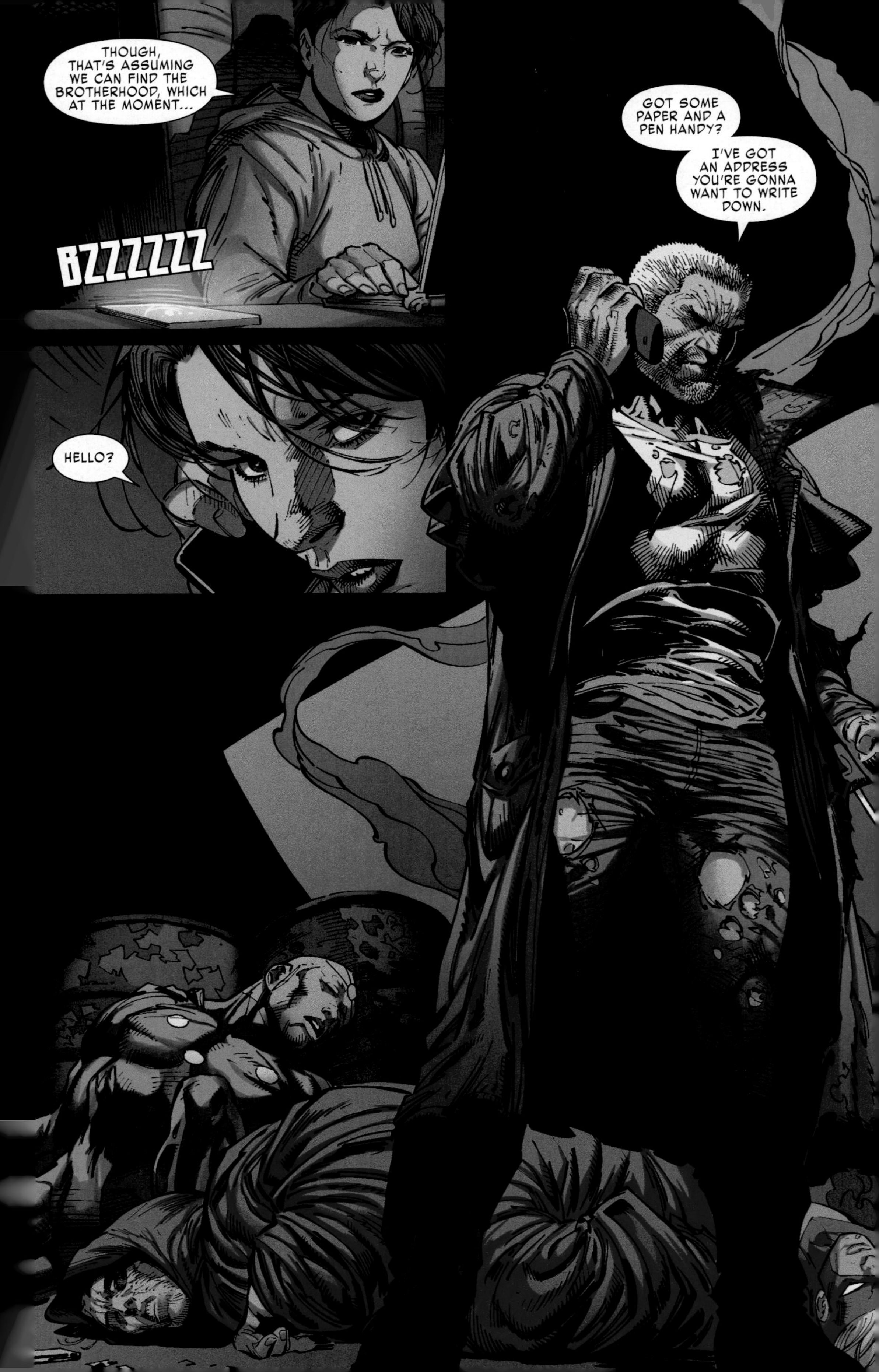
THOUGH, THAT'S ASSUMING WE CAN FIND THE BROTHERHOOD, WHICH AT THE MOMENT...
BZZZZZZ
HELLO?
GOT SOME PAPER AND A PEN HANDY?
I'VE GOT AN ADDRESS YOU'RE GONNA WANT TO WRITE DOWN.

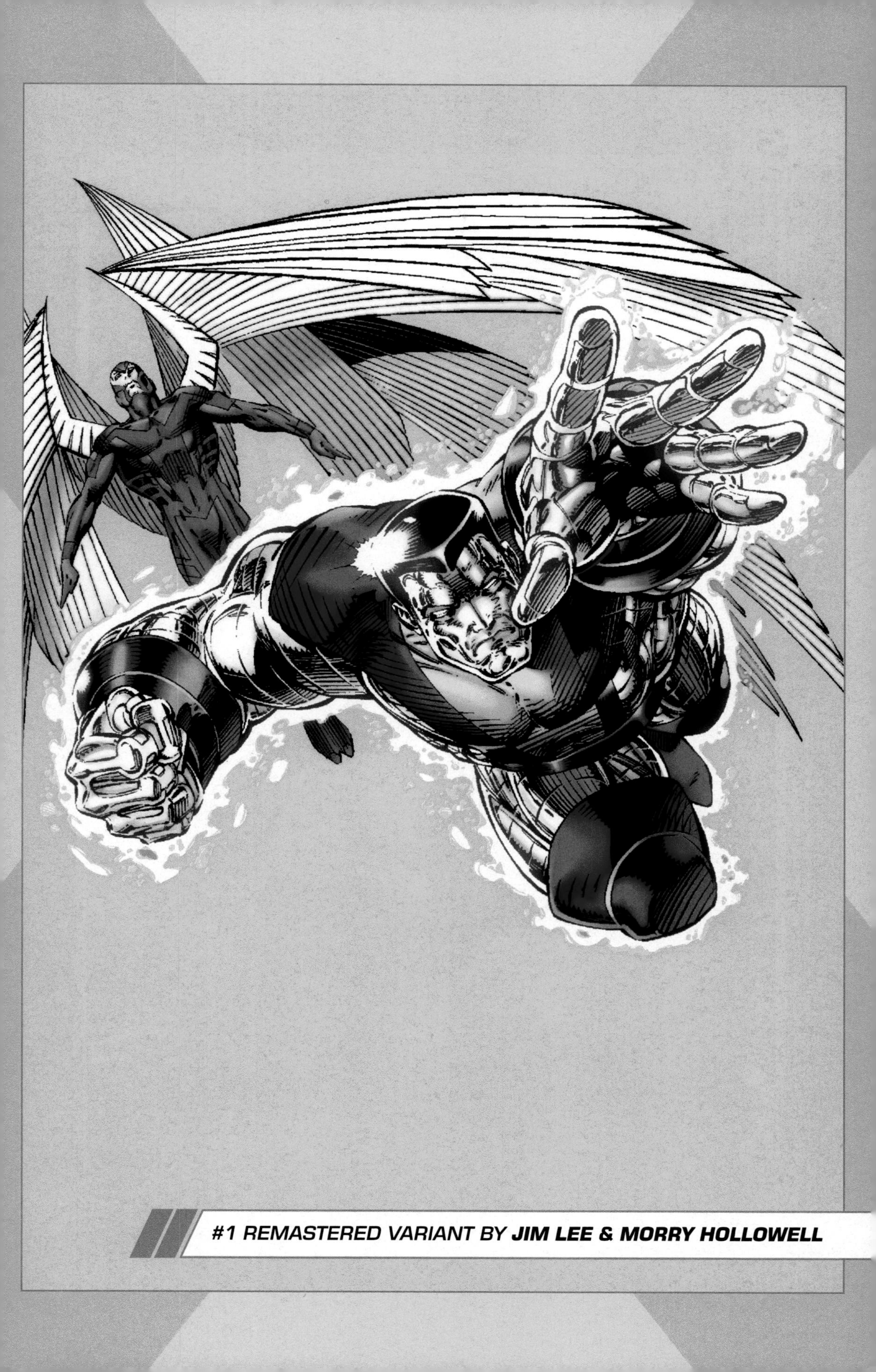

#1 REMASTERED VARIANT BY **JIM LEE & MORRY HOLLOWELL**

3

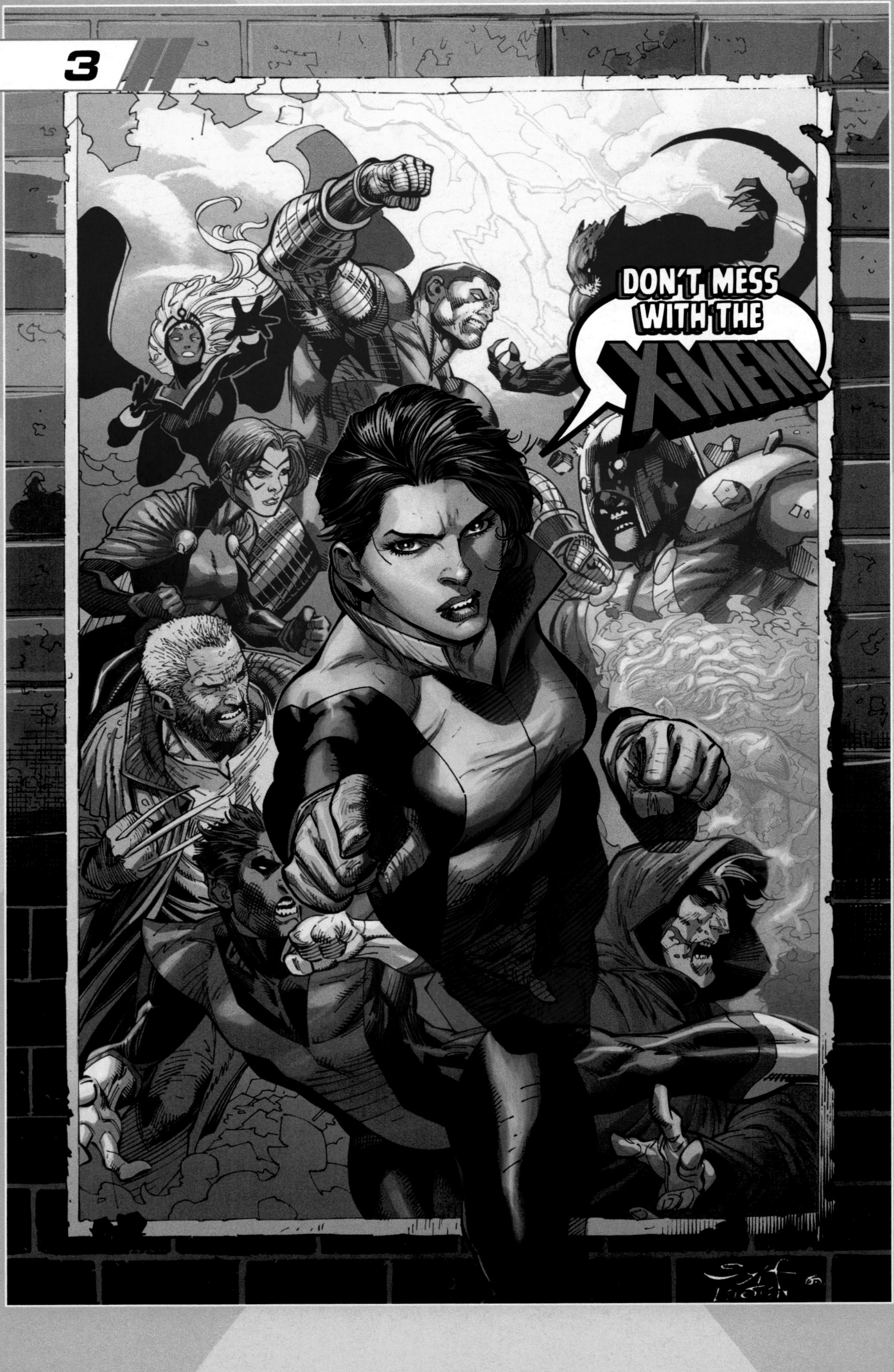

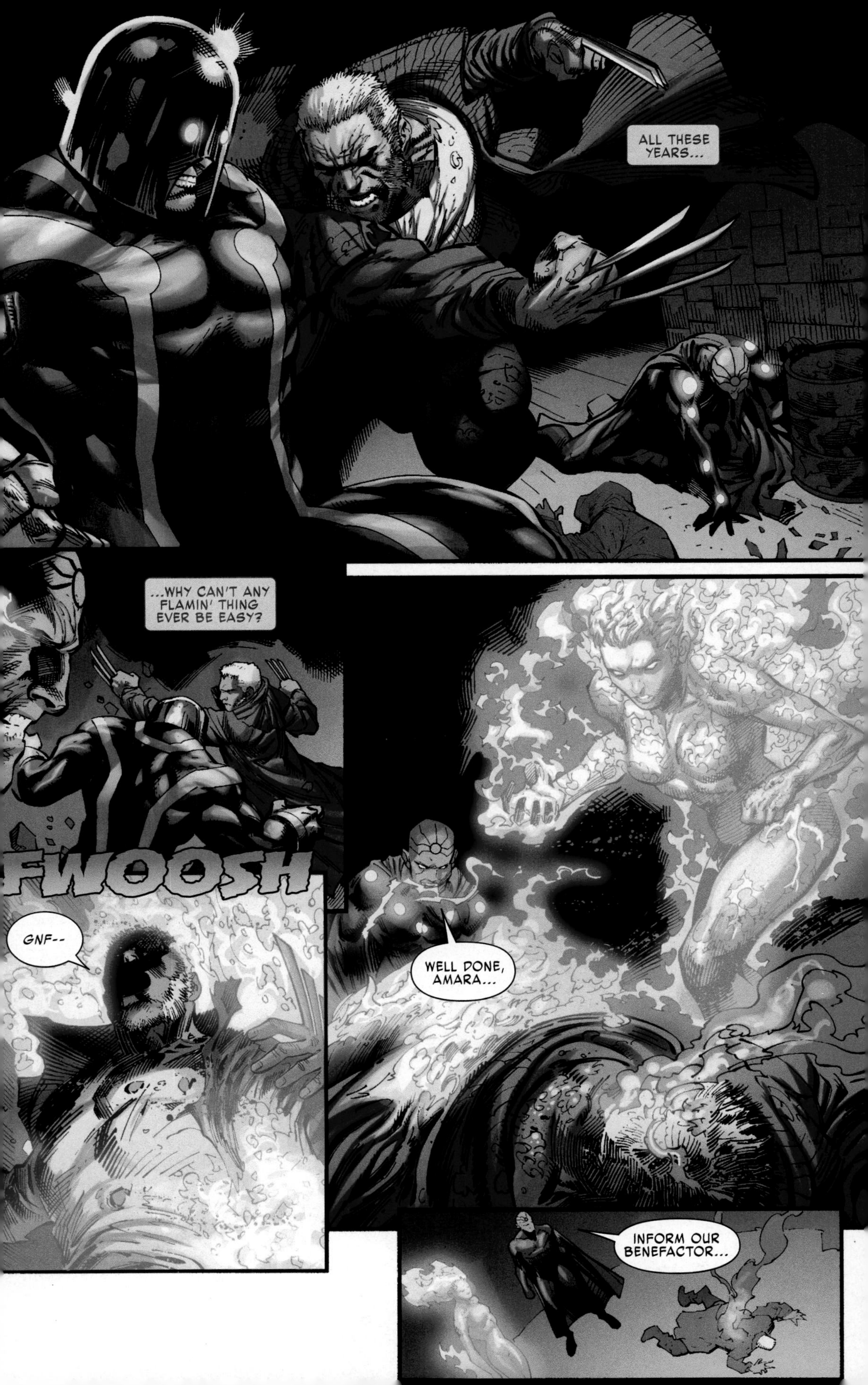
ALL THESE YEARS...
...WHY CAN'T ANY FLAMIN' THING EVER BE EASY?
FWOOSH
GNF--
WELL DONE, AMARA...
INFORM OUR BENEFACTOR...

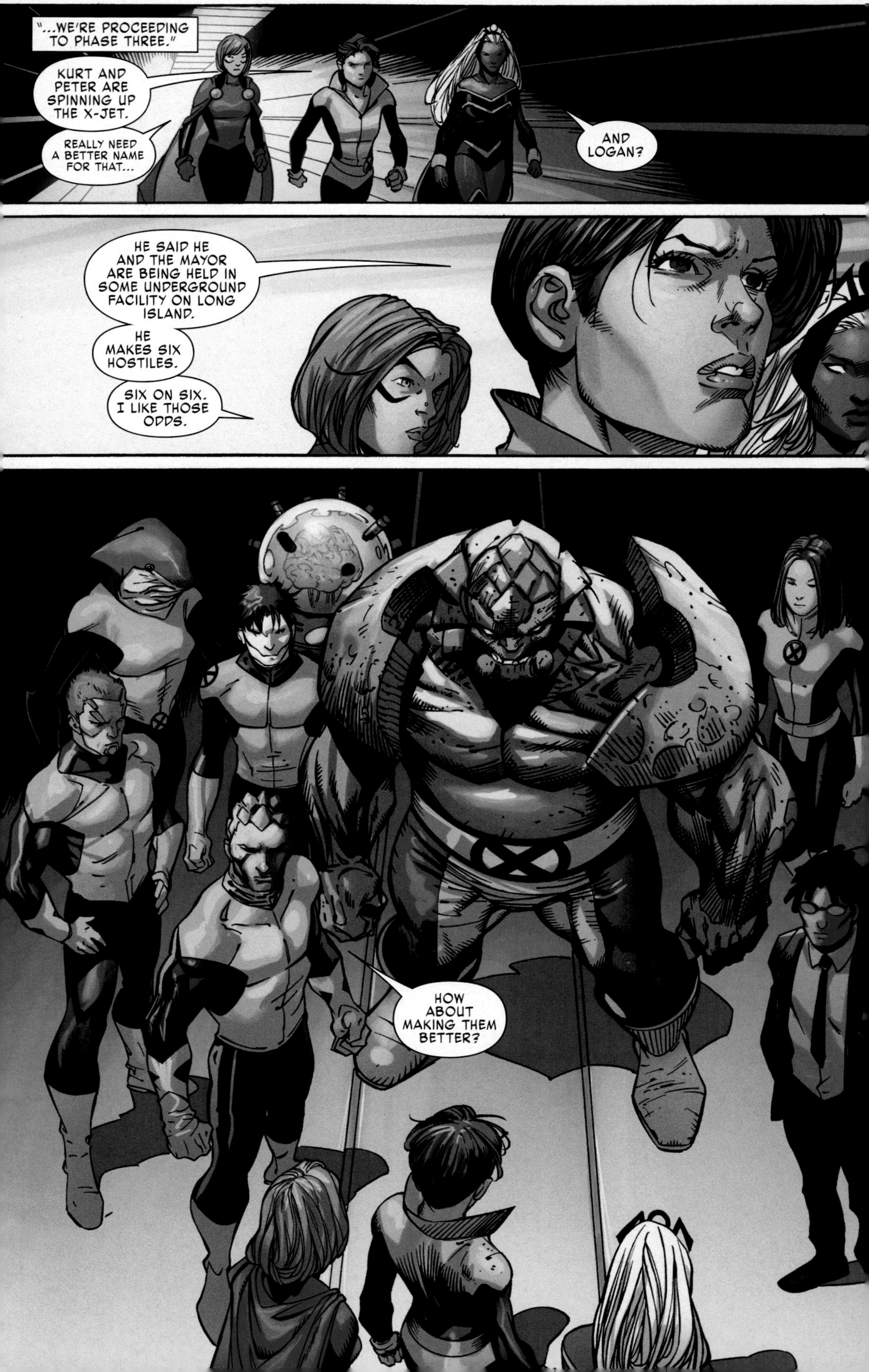
"...WE'RE PROCEEDING TO PHASE THREE."
KURT AND PETER ARE SPINNING UP THE X-JET.
REALLY NEED A BETTER NAME FOR THAT...
AND LOGAN?
HE SAID HE AND THE MAYOR ARE BEING HELD IN SOME UNDERGROUND FACILITY ON LONG ISLAND.
HE MAKES SIX HOSTILES.
SIX ON SIX. I LIKE THOSE ODDS.
HOW ABOUT MAKING THEM BETTER?

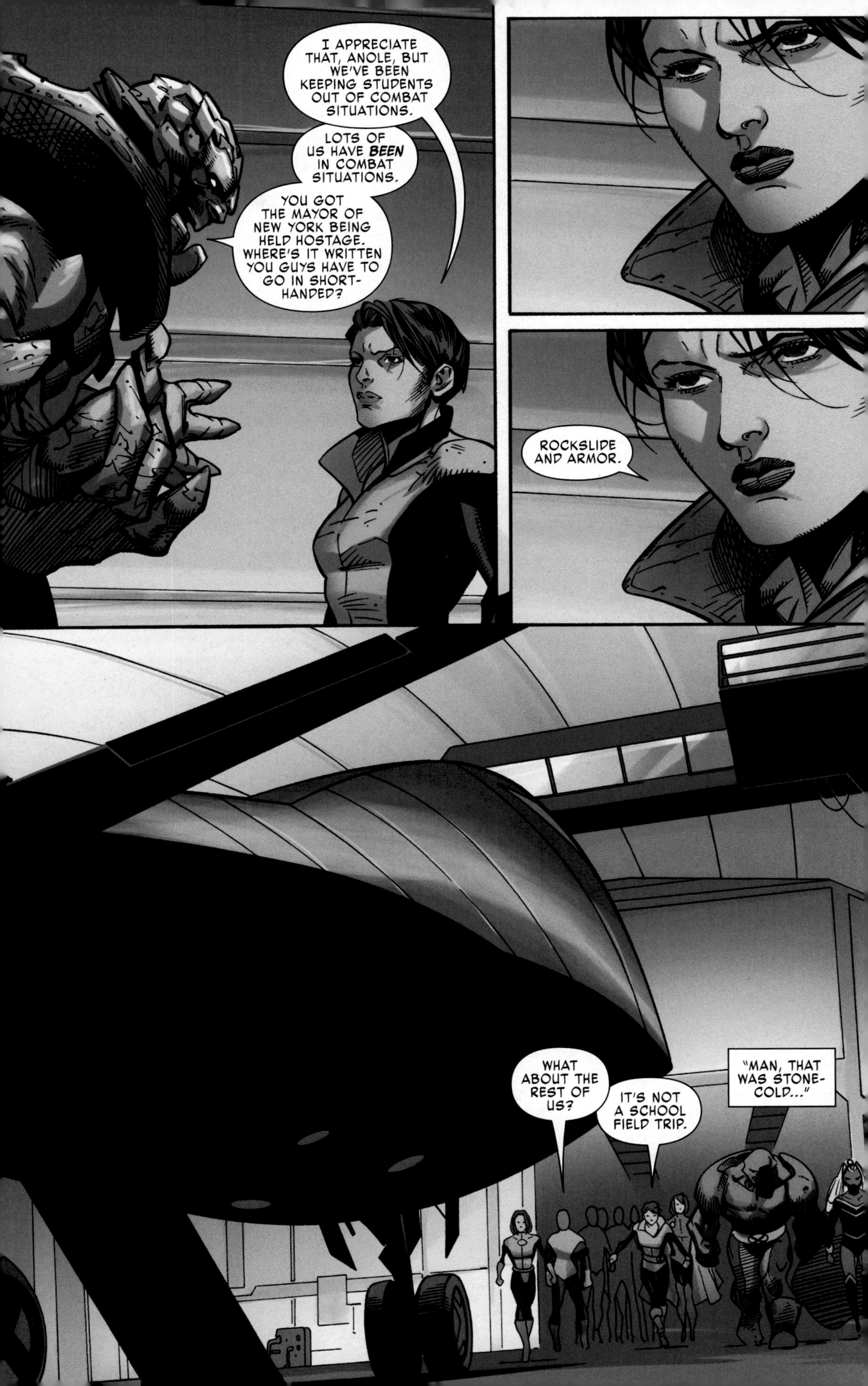
I APPRECIATE THAT, ANOLE, BUT WE'VE BEEN KEEPING STUDENTS OUT OF COMBAT SITUATIONS.
LOTS OF US HAVE *BEEN* IN COMBAT SITUATIONS.
YOU GOT THE MAYOR OF NEW YORK BEING HELD HOSTAGE. WHERE'S IT WRITTEN YOU GUYS HAVE TO GO IN SHORT-HANDED?
ROCKSLIDE AND ARMOR.
WHAT ABOUT THE REST OF US?
IT'S NOT A SCHOOL FIELD TRIP.
"MAN, THAT WAS STONE-COLD..."

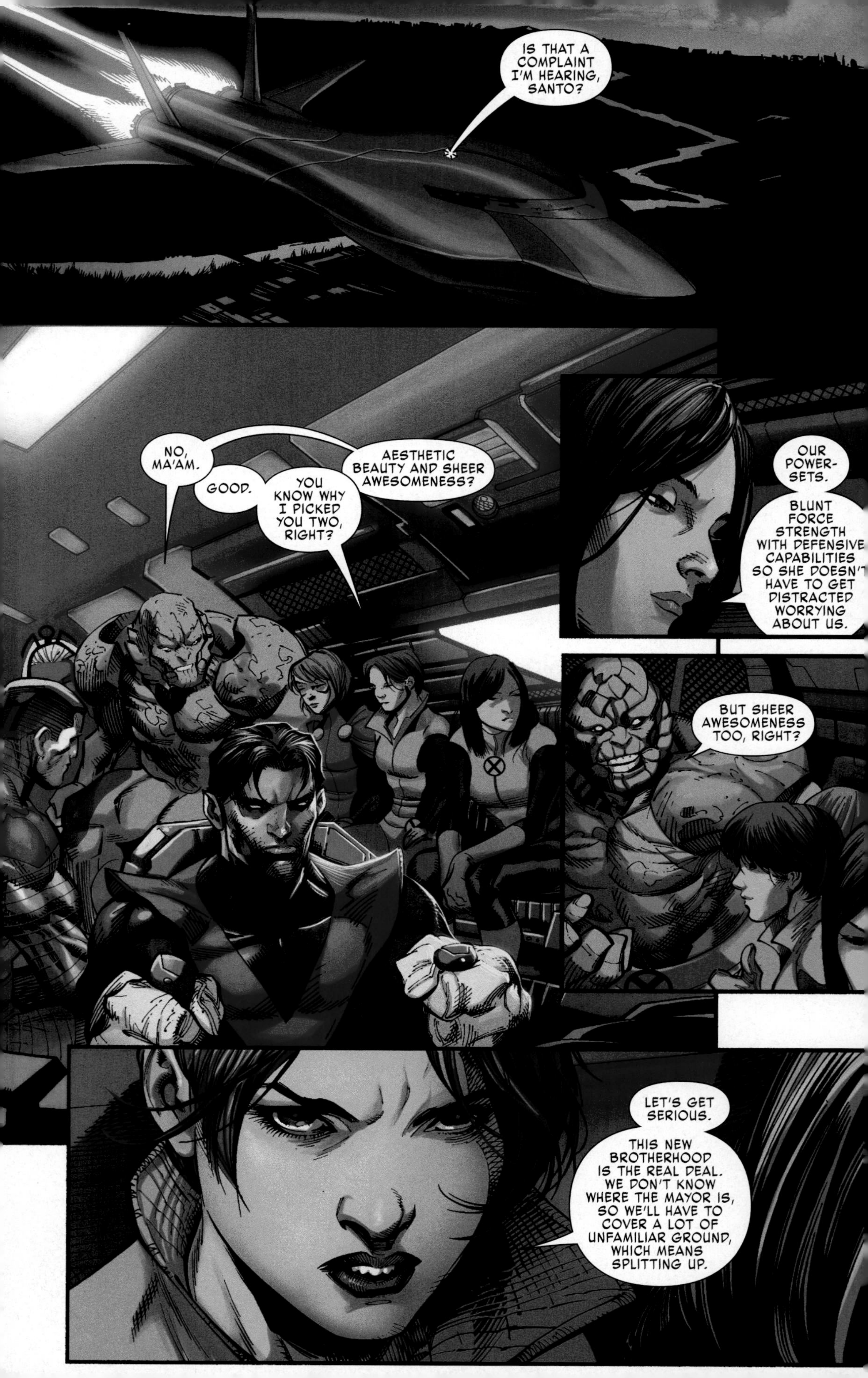
IS THAT A COMPLAINT I'M HEARING, SANTO?
NO, MA'AM.
GOOD.
YOU KNOW WHY I PICKED YOU TWO, RIGHT?
AESTHETIC BEAUTY AND SHEER AWESOMENESS?
OUR POWER-SETS.
BLUNT FORCE STRENGTH WITH DEFENSIVE CAPABILITIES SO SHE DOESN'T HAVE TO GET DISTRACTED WORRYING ABOUT US.
BUT SHEER AWESOMENESS TOO, RIGHT?
LET'S GET SERIOUS.
THIS NEW BROTHERHOOD IS THE REAL DEAL. WE DON'T KNOW WHERE THE MAYOR IS, SO WE'LL HAVE TO COVER A LOT OF UNFAMILIAR GROUND, WHICH MEANS SPLITTING UP.

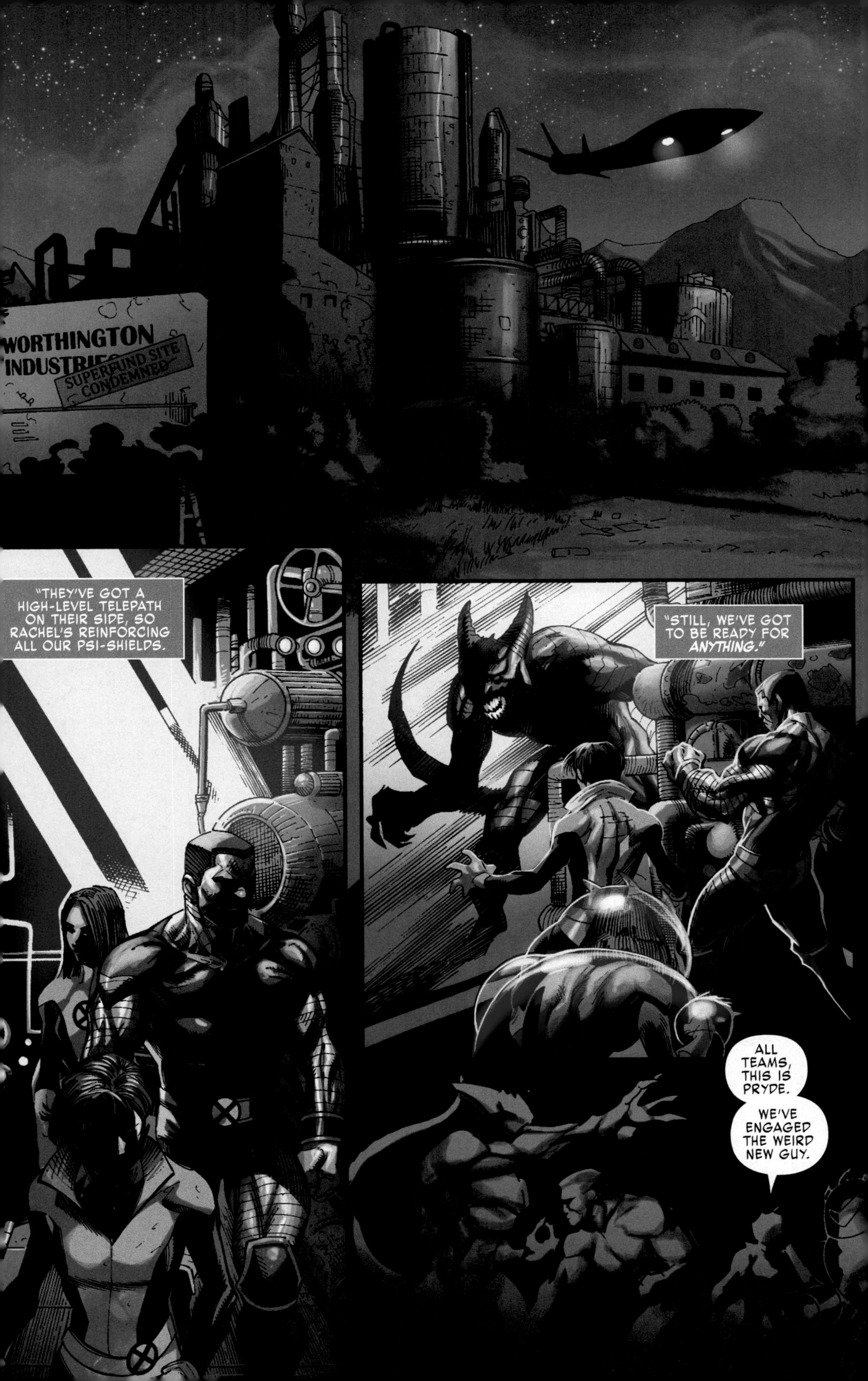
WORTHINGTON INDUSTRIES
SUPERFUND SITE CONDEMNED
"THEY'VE GOT A HIGH-LEVEL TELEPATH ON THEIR SIDE, SO RACHEL'S REINFORCING ALL OUR PSI-SHIELDS.
"STILL, WE'VE GOT TO BE READY FOR *ANYTHING.*"
ALL TEAMS, THIS IS PRYDE.
WE'VE ENGAGED THE WEIRD NEW GUY.

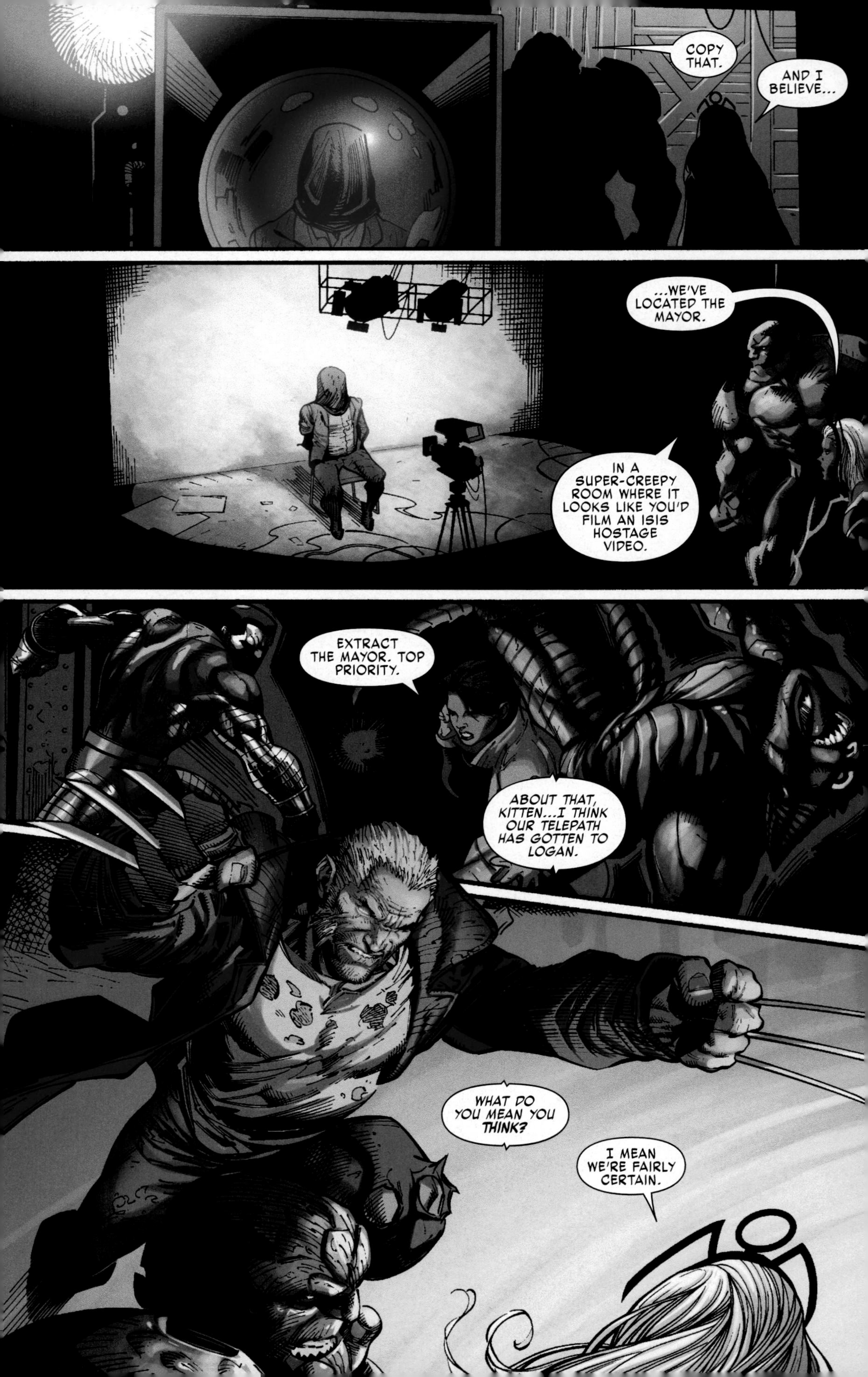
COPY THAT.
AND I BELIEVE...
...WE'VE LOCATED THE MAYOR.
IN A SUPER-CREEPY ROOM WHERE IT LOOKS LIKE YOU'D FILM AN ISIS HOSTAGE VIDEO.
EXTRACT THE MAYOR. TOP PRIORITY.
ABOUT THAT, KITTEN...I THINK OUR TELEPATH HAS GOTTEN TO LOGAN.
WHAT DO YOU MEAN YOU THINK?
I MEAN WE'RE FAIRLY CERTAIN.

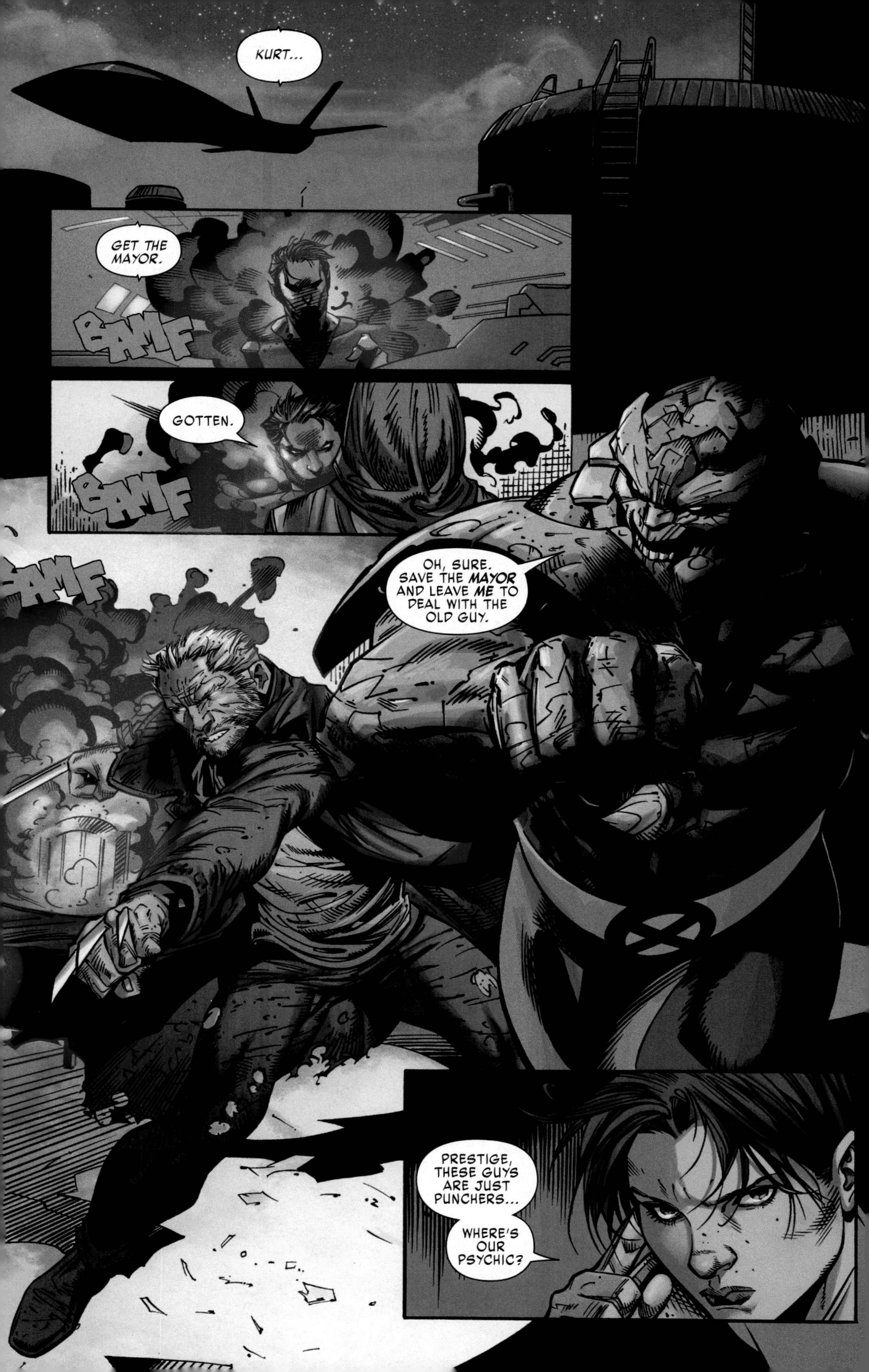
KURT...
GET THE MAYOR.
BAMF
GOTTEN.
BAMF
BAMF
OH, SURE. SAVE THE *MAYOR* AND LEAVE *ME* TO DEAL WITH THE OLD GUY.
PRESTIGE, THESE GUYS ARE JUST PUNCHERS...
WHERE'S OUR PSYCHIC?

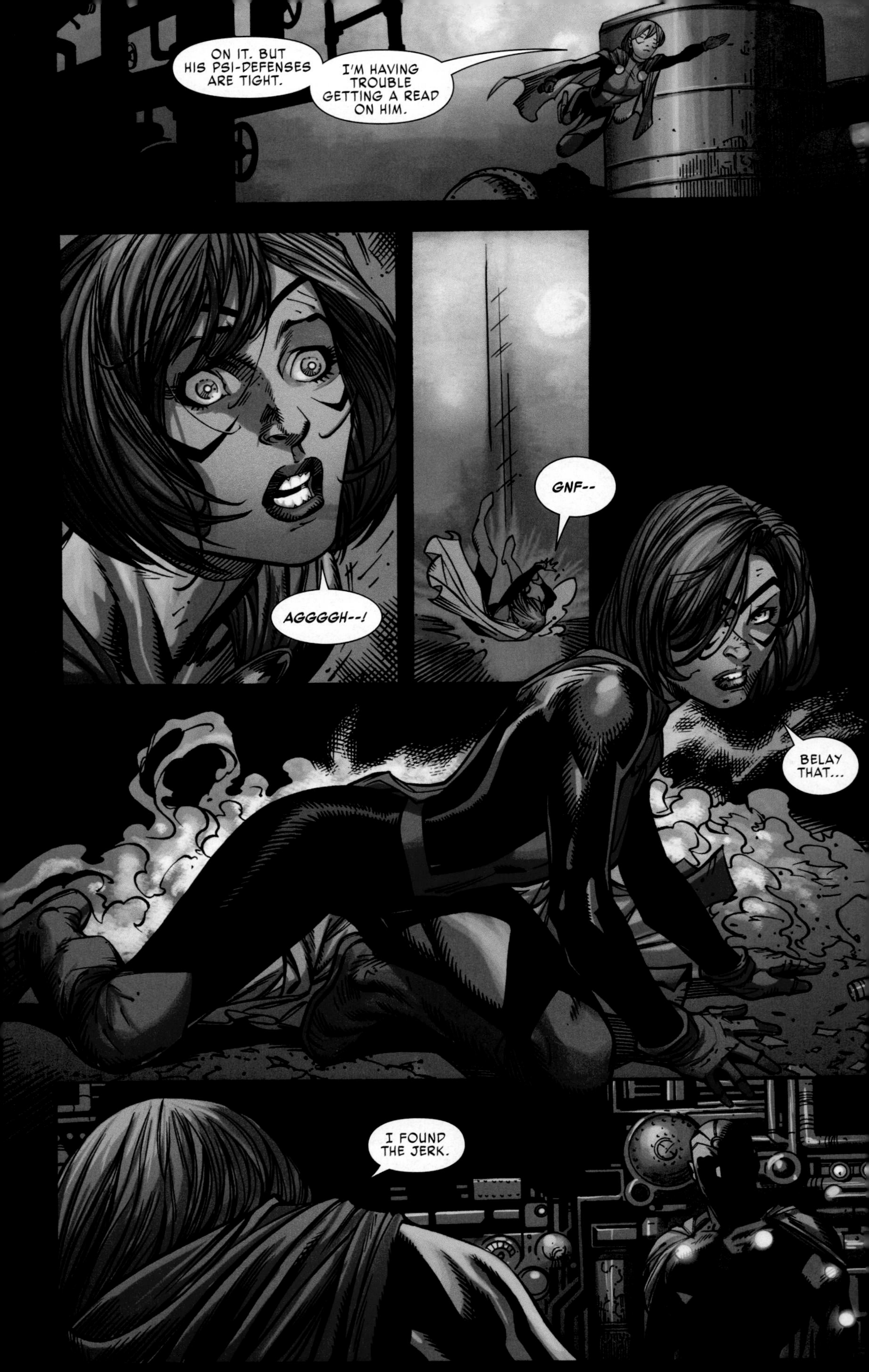
ON IT. BUT HIS PSI-DEFENSES ARE TIGHT.
I'M HAVING TROUBLE GETTING A READ ON HIM.
AGGGGH--!
GNF--
BELAY THAT...
I FOUND THE JERK.

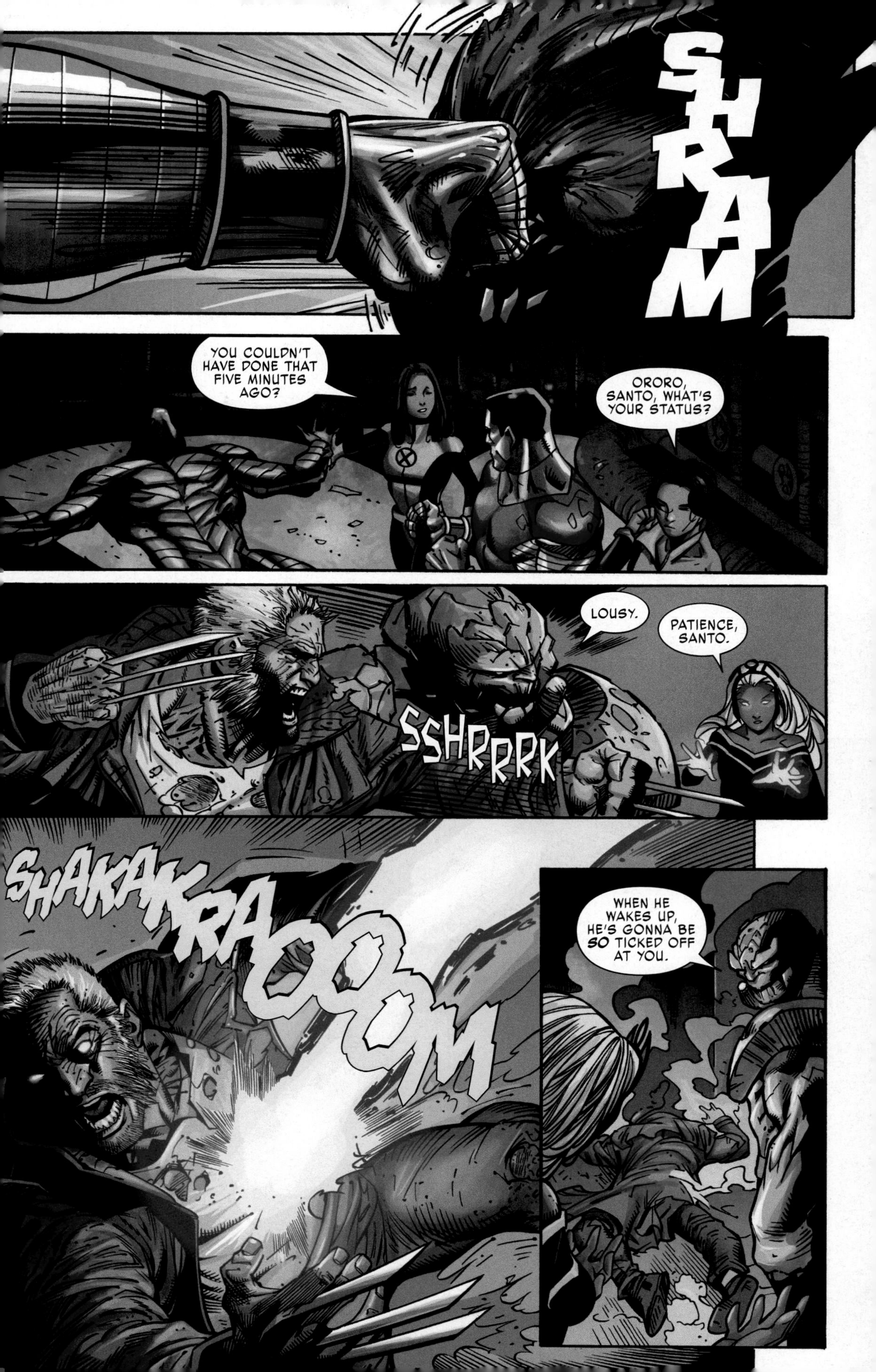
SHRAM
YOU COULDN'T HAVE DONE THAT FIVE MINUTES AGO?
ORORO, SANTO, WHAT'S YOUR STATUS?
LOUSY.
PATIENCE, SANTO.
SSHRRRK
SHAKAKRAOOOM
WHEN HE WAKES UP, HE'S GONNA BE SO TICKED OFF AT YOU.

LOOKS LIKE MR. LOGAN'S BEEN HERE...

LOOKS LIKE.

STILL NEED TO FIND AMARA, THOUGH.

RACHEL?

HANG ON I'M PSI-FIGH THE TELEPA IT'S MESMER

DONE.

THAT WAS FAST.

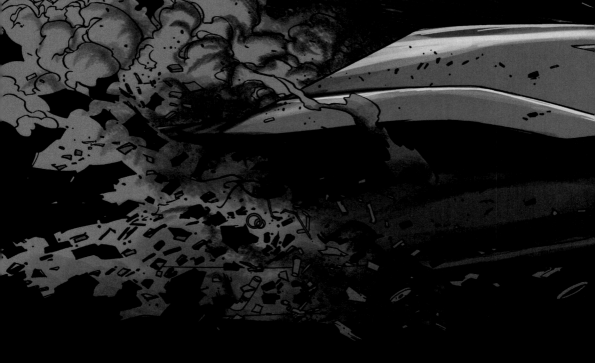

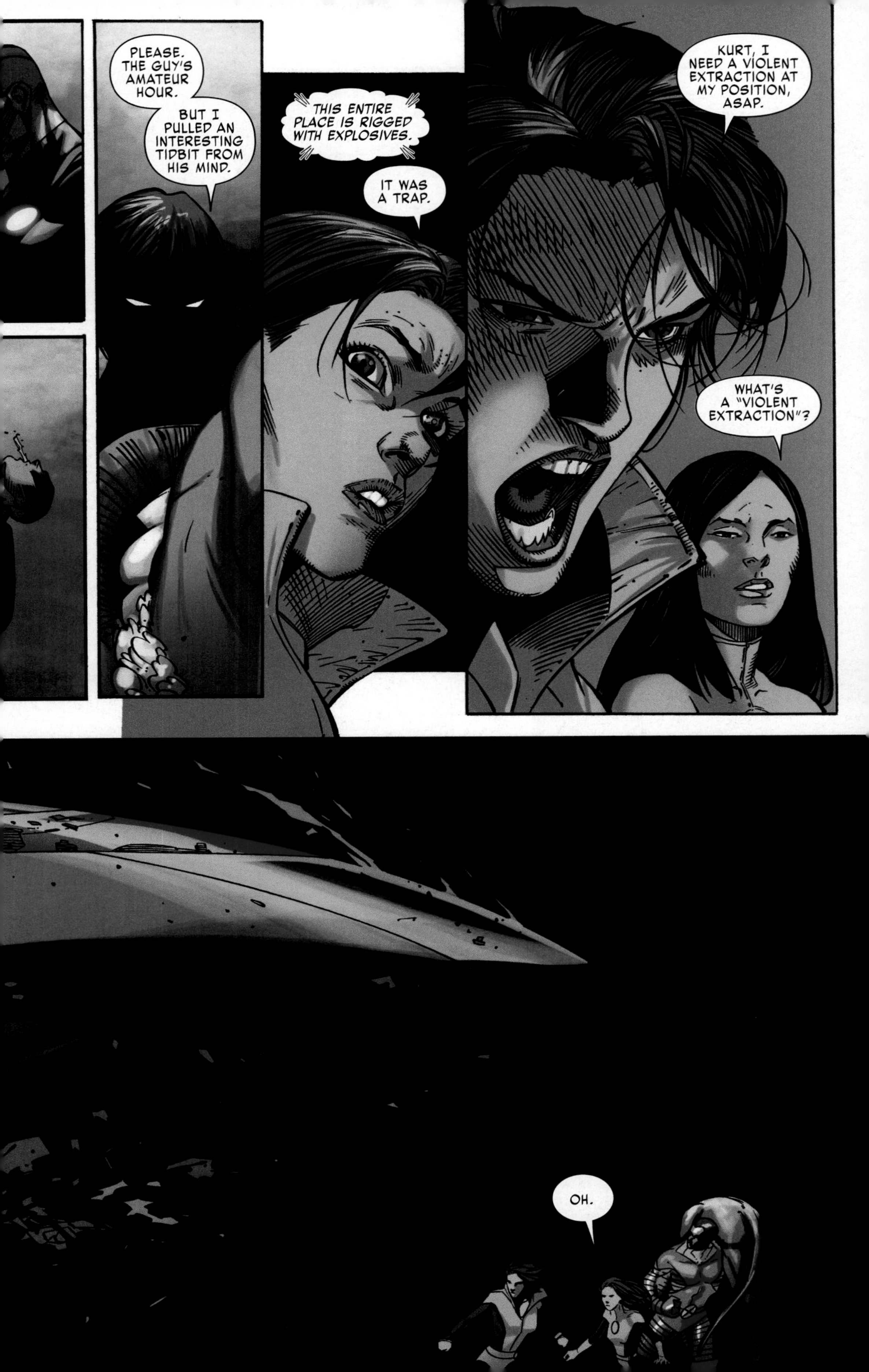
PLEASE. THE GUY'S AMATEUR HOUR.
BUT I PULLED AN INTERESTING TIDBIT FROM HIS MIND.
THIS ENTIRE PLACE IS RIGGED WITH EXPLOSIVES.
IT WAS A TRAP.
KURT, I NEED A VIOLENT EXTRACTION AT MY POSITION, ASAP.
WHAT'S A "VIOLENT EXTRACTION"?
OH.

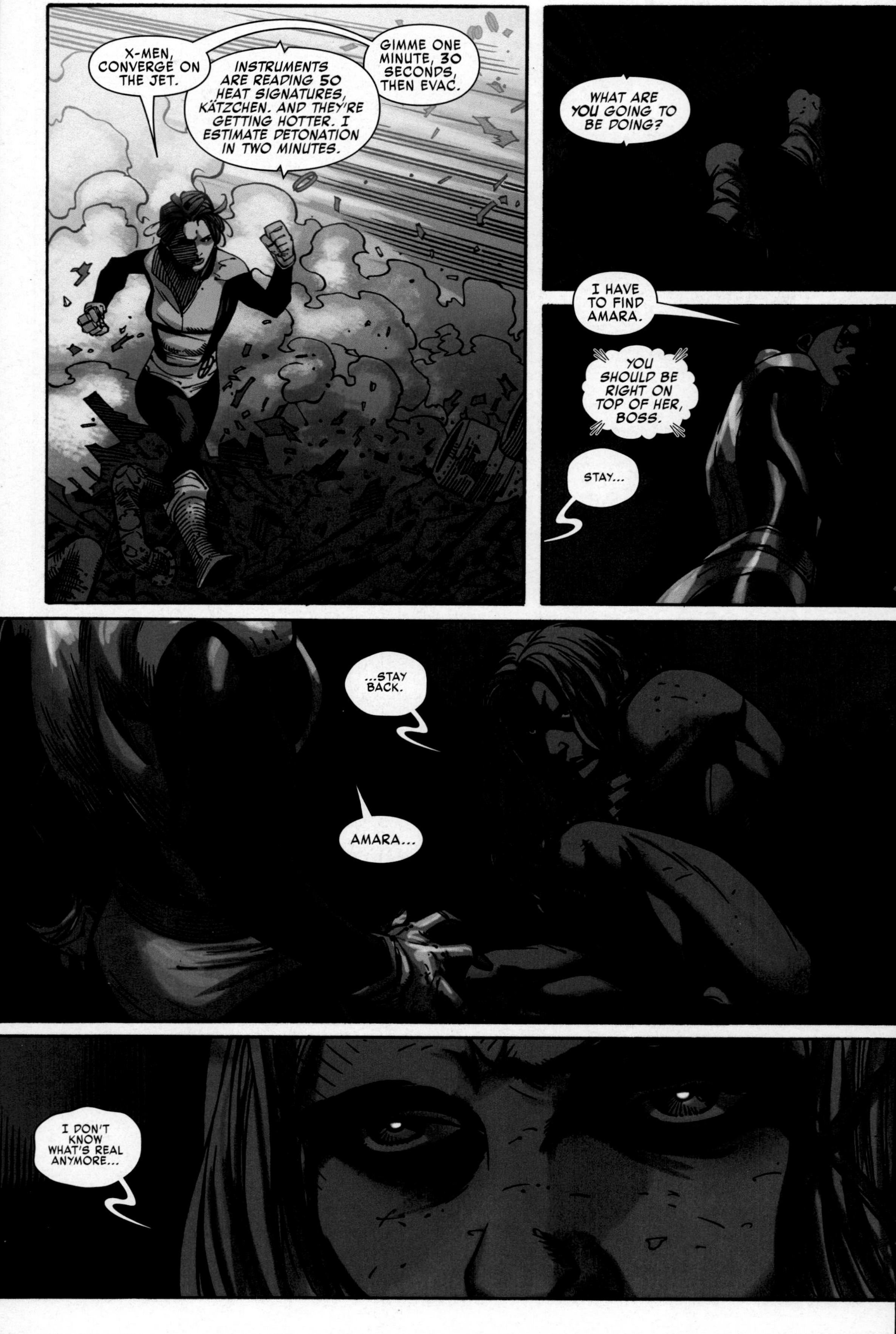
X-MEN, CONVERGE ON THE JET.
INSTRUMENTS ARE READING 50 HEAT SIGNATURES, KÄTZCHEN. AND THEY'RE GETTING HOTTER. I ESTIMATE DETONATION IN TWO MINUTES.
GIMME ONE MINUTE, 30 SECONDS, THEN EVAC.
WHAT ARE YOU GOING TO BE DOING?
I HAVE TO FIND AMARA.
YOU SHOULD BE RIGHT ON TOP OF HER, BOSS.
STAY...
...STAY BACK.
AMARA...
I DON'T KNOW WHAT'S REAL ANYMORE...

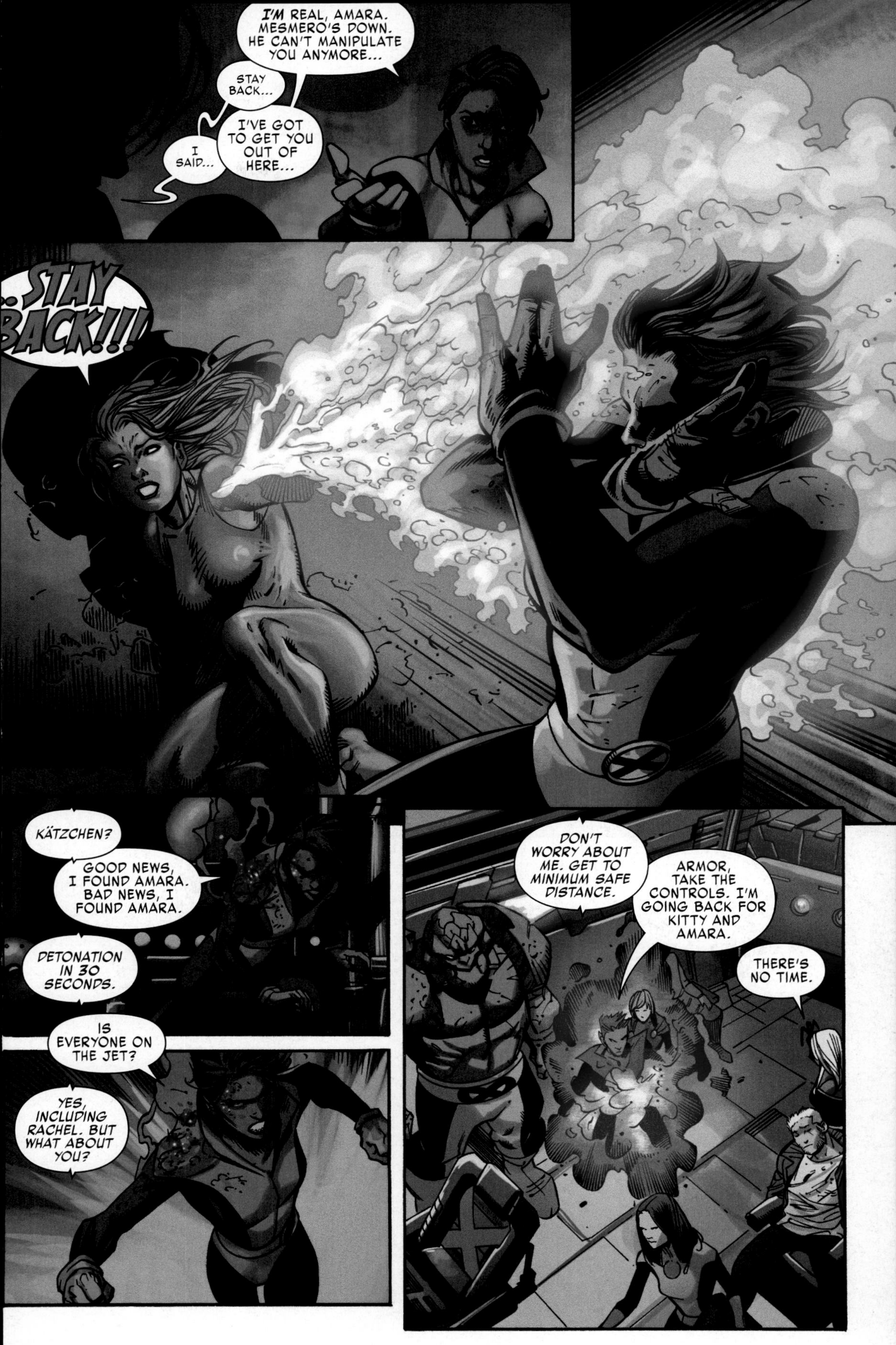
I'M REAL, AMARA. MESMERO'S DOWN. HE CAN'T MANIPULATE YOU ANYMORE...
STAY BACK...
I'VE GOT TO GET YOU OUT OF HERE...
I SAID...
...STAY BACK!!!
KÄTZCHEN?
GOOD NEWS, I FOUND AMARA. BAD NEWS, I FOUND AMARA.
DETONATION IN 30 SECONDS.
IS EVERYONE ON THE JET?
YES, INCLUDING RACHEL. BUT WHAT ABOUT YOU?
DON'T WORRY ABOUT ME. GET TO MINIMUM SAFE DISTANCE.
ARMOR, TAKE THE CONTROLS. I'M GOING BACK FOR KITTY AND AMARA.
THERE'S NO TIME.

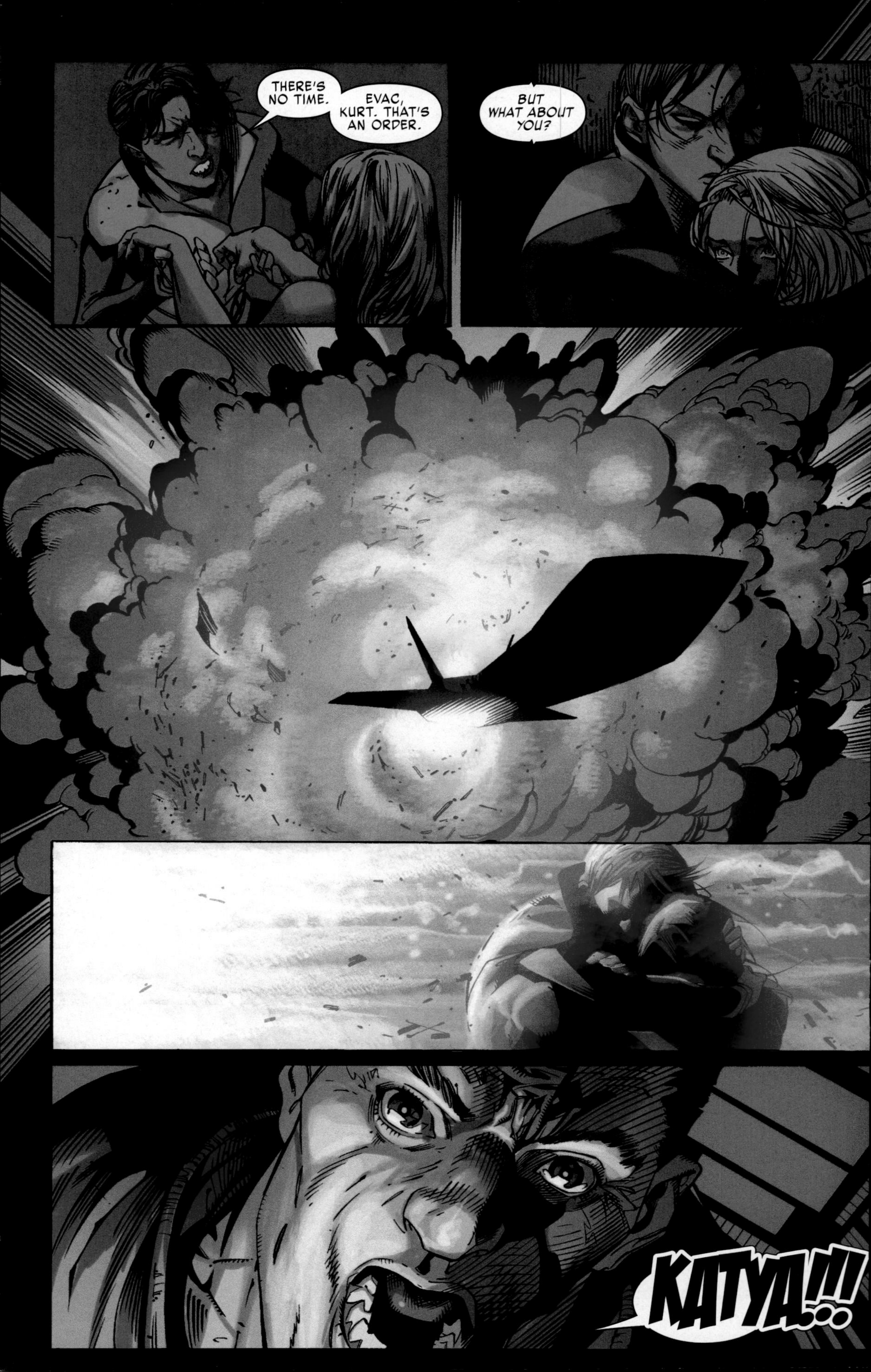

THERE'S NO TIME.
EVAC, KURT. THAT'S AN ORDER.
BUT WHAT ABOUT YOU?
KATYA!!!...

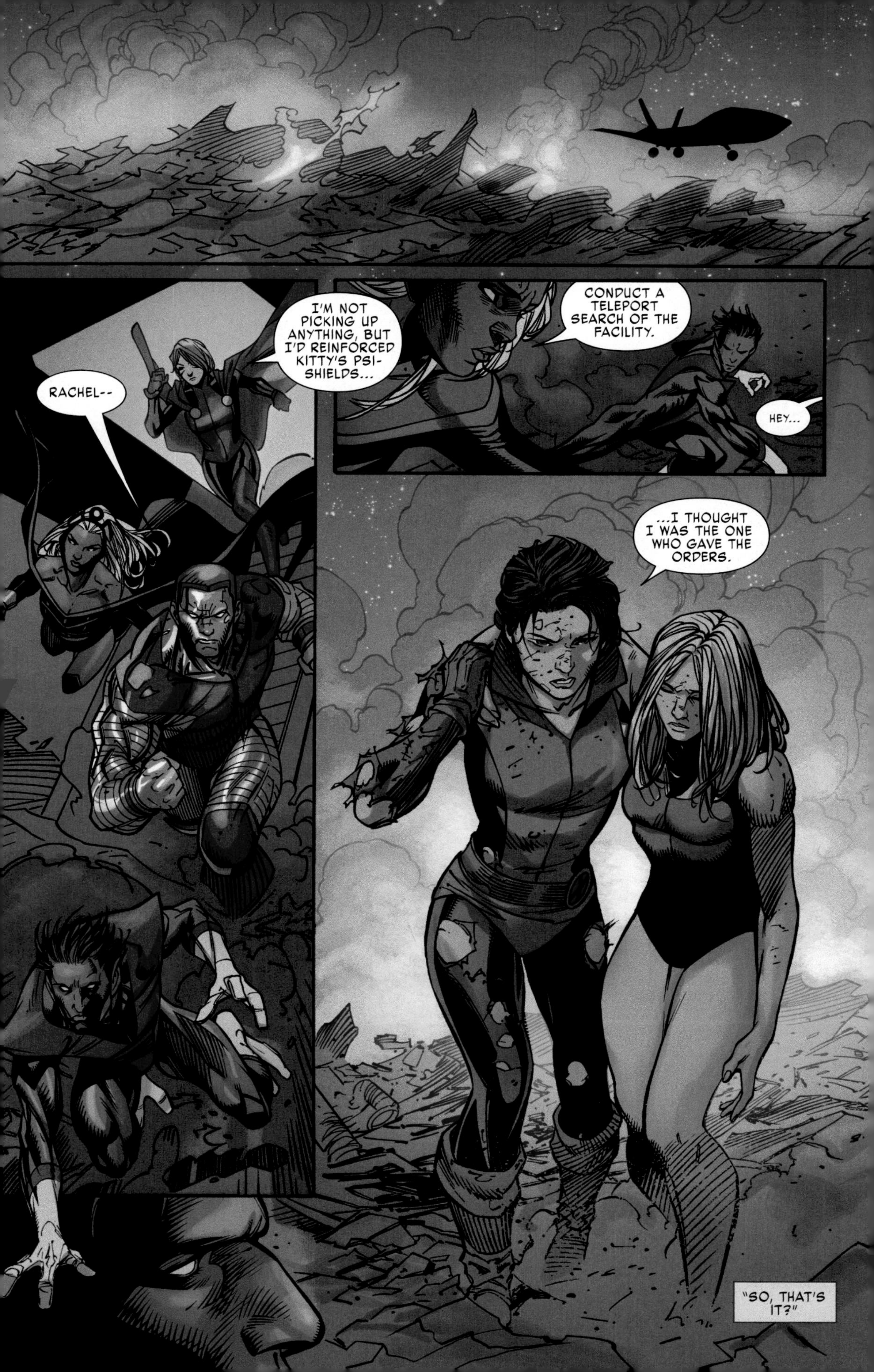
RACHEL--
I'M NOT PICKING UP ANYTHING, BUT I'D REINFORCED KITTY'S PSI-SHIELDS...
CONDUCT A TELEPORT SEARCH OF THE FACILITY.
HEY...
...I THOUGHT I WAS THE ONE WHO GAVE THE ORDERS.
"SO, THAT'S IT?"

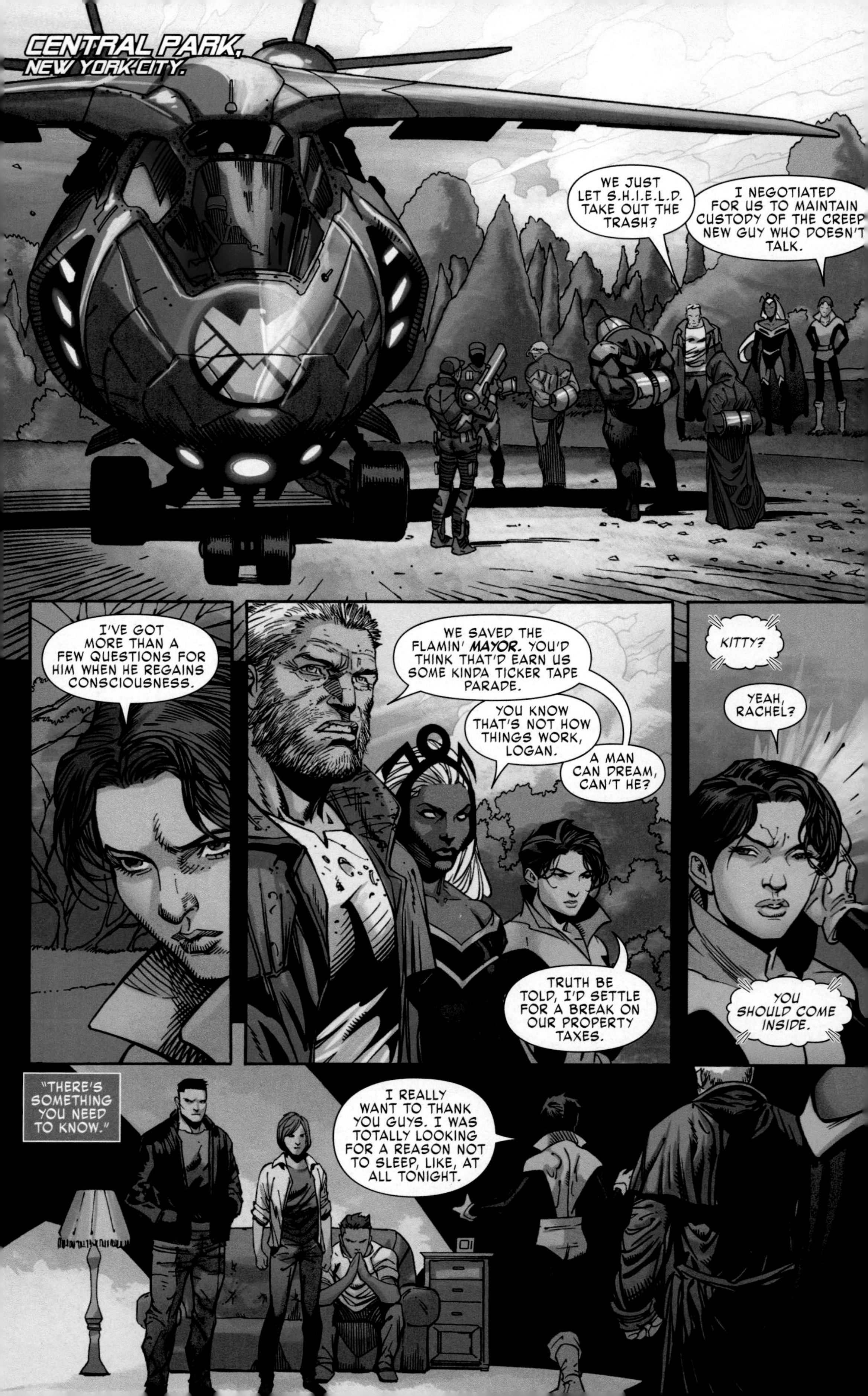
CENTRAL PARK, NEW YORK CITY.
WE JUST LET S.H.I.E.L.D. TAKE OUT THE TRASH?
I NEGOTIATED FOR US TO MAINTAIN CUSTODY OF THE CREEP NEW GUY WHO DOESN'T TALK.
I'VE GOT MORE THAN A FEW QUESTIONS FOR HIM WHEN HE REGAINS CONSCIOUSNESS.
WE SAVED THE FLAMIN' MAYOR. YOU'D THINK THAT'D EARN US SOME KINDA TICKER TAPE PARADE.
YOU KNOW THAT'S NOT HOW THINGS WORK, LOGAN.
A MAN CAN DREAM, CAN'T HE?
TRUTH BE TOLD, I'D SETTLE FOR A BREAK ON OUR PROPERTY TAXES.
KITTY?
YEAH, RACHEL?
YOU SHOULD COME INSIDE.
"THERE'S SOMETHING YOU NEED TO KNOW."
I REALLY WANT TO THANK YOU GUYS. I WAS TOTALLY LOOKING FOR A REASON NOT TO SLEEP, LIKE, AT ALL TONIGHT.

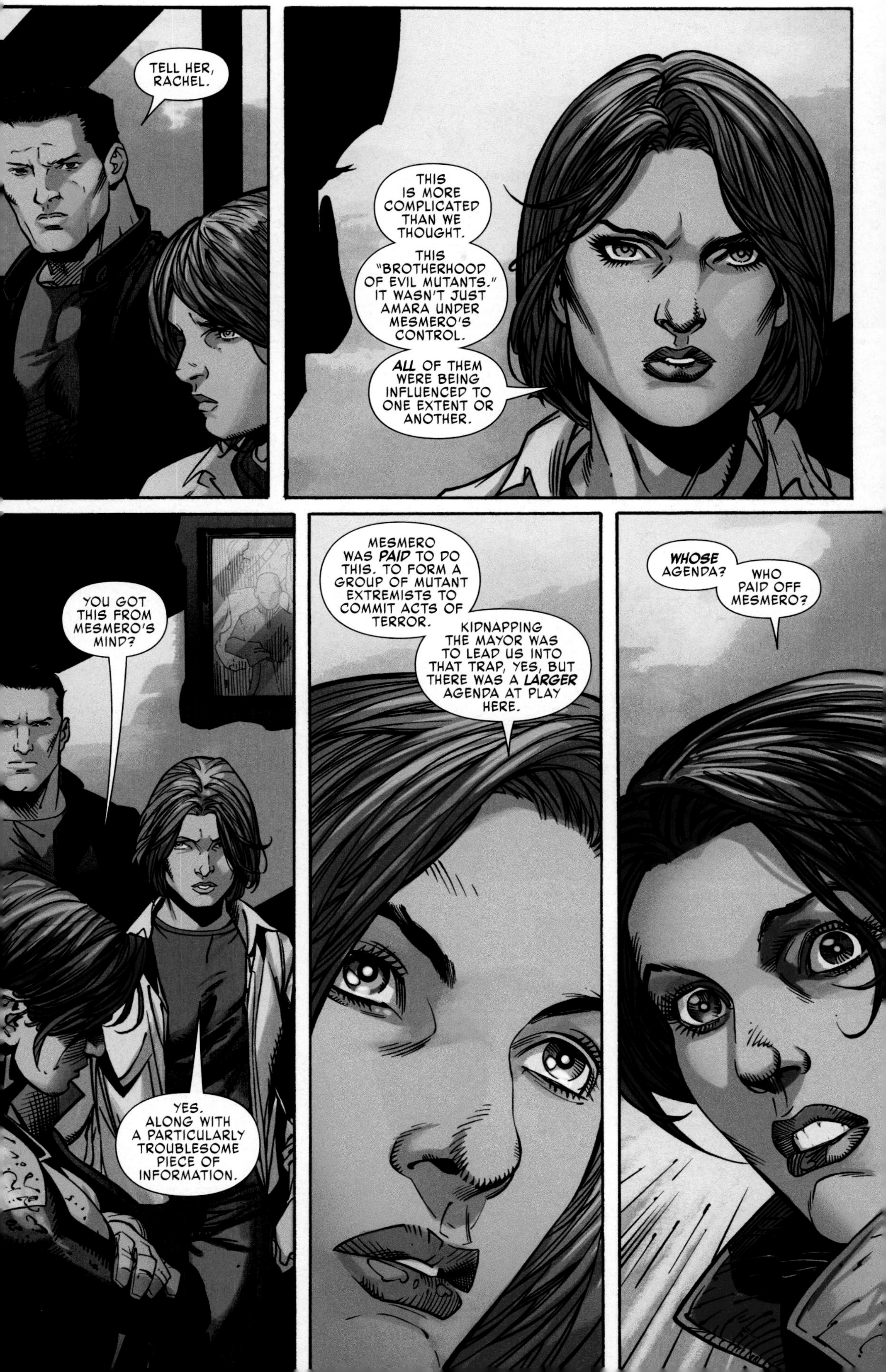
TELL HER, RACHEL.
THIS IS MORE COMPLICATED THAN WE THOUGHT.
THIS "BROTHERHOOD OF EVIL MUTANTS." IT WASN'T JUST AMARA UNDER MESMERO'S CONTROL.
ALL OF THEM WERE BEING INFLUENCED TO ONE EXTENT OR ANOTHER.
YOU GOT THIS FROM MESMERO'S MIND?
YES. ALONG WITH A PARTICULARLY TROUBLESOME PIECE OF INFORMATION.
MESMERO WAS PAID TO DO THIS. TO FORM A GROUP OF MUTANT EXTREMISTS TO COMMIT ACTS OF TERROR.
KIDNAPPING THE MAYOR WAS TO LEAD US INTO THAT TRAP, YES, BUT THERE WAS A LARGER AGENDA AT PLAY HERE.
WHOSE AGENDA?
WHO PAID OFF MESMERO?

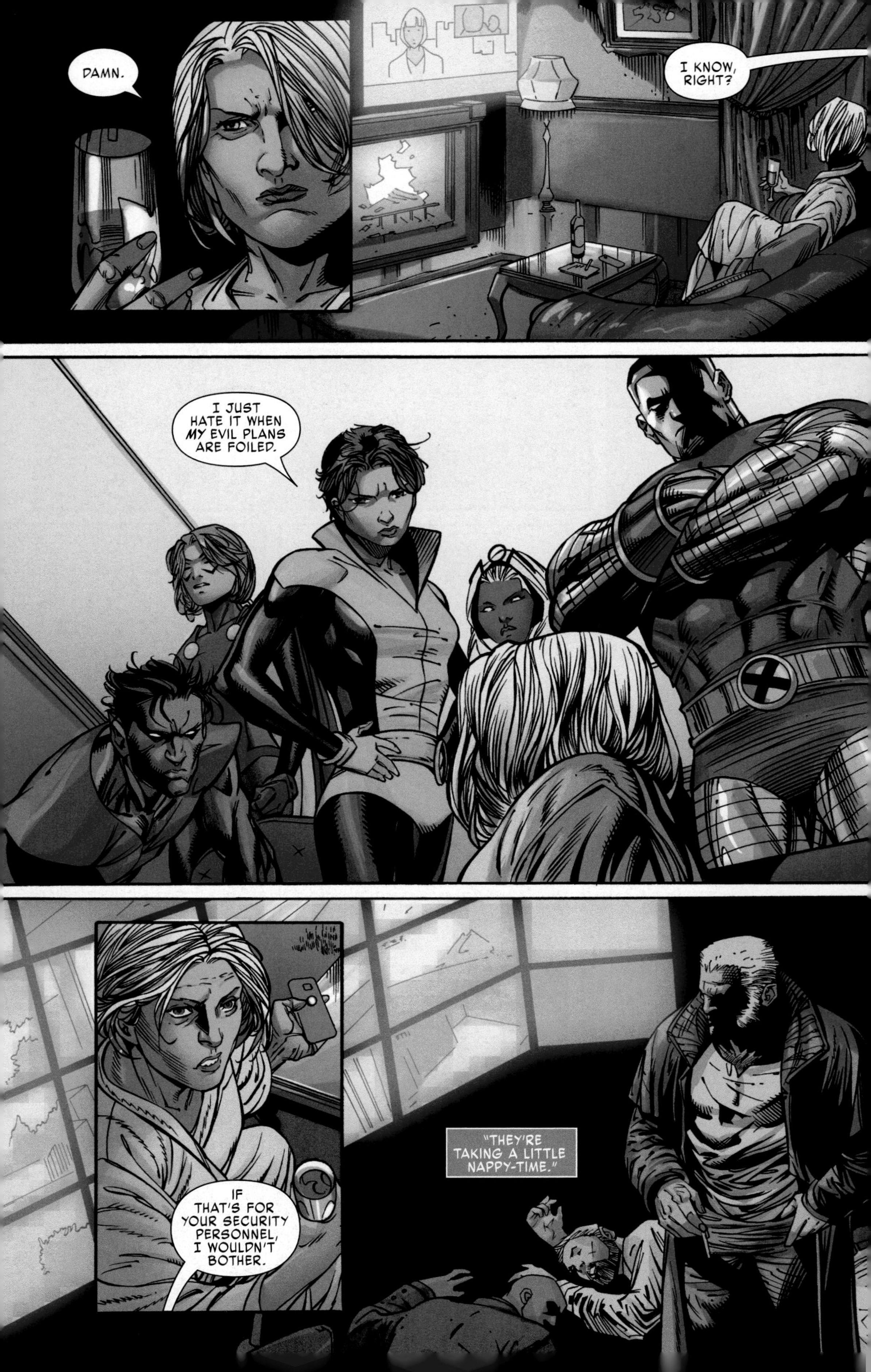
DAMN.
I KNOW, RIGHT?
I JUST HATE IT WHEN MY EVIL PLANS ARE FOILED.
IF THAT'S FOR YOUR SECURITY PERSONNEL, I WOULDN'T BOTHER.
"THEY'RE TAKING A LITTLE NAPPY-TIME."

BUT LET'S TALK ABOUT *YOU,* MS. NANCE.

YOU CREATED A GROUP OF MUTANTS TO COMMIT TERRORIST ACTS YOU COULD USE TO JUSTIFY YOUR ANTI-MUTANT POLITICS.

"BROTHERHOOD OF *EVIL* MUTANTS." GOD, YOU WEREN'T EVEN SUBTLE.

YOU'RE TRESPASSING.

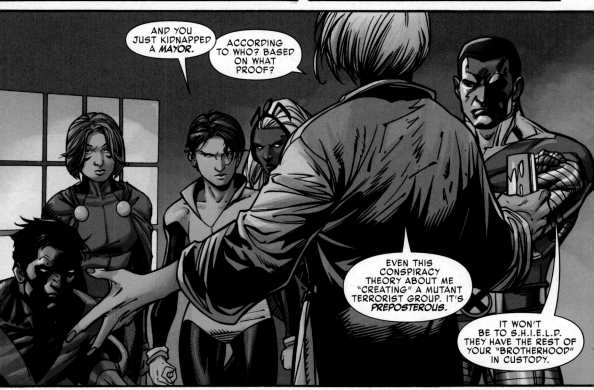

AND YOU JUST KIDNAPPED A *MAYOR.*

ACCORDING TO WHO? BASED ON WHAT PROOF?

EVEN THIS CONSPIRACY THEORY ABOUT ME "CREATING" A MUTANT TERRORIST GROUP. IT'S *PREPOSTEROUS.*

IT WON'T BE TO S.H.I.E.L.D. THEY HAVE THE REST OF YOUR "BROTHERHOOD" IN CUSTODY.

I THINK YOU'LL FIND THEY DON'T HAVE MUCH MEMORY OF THEIR ACTIONS.

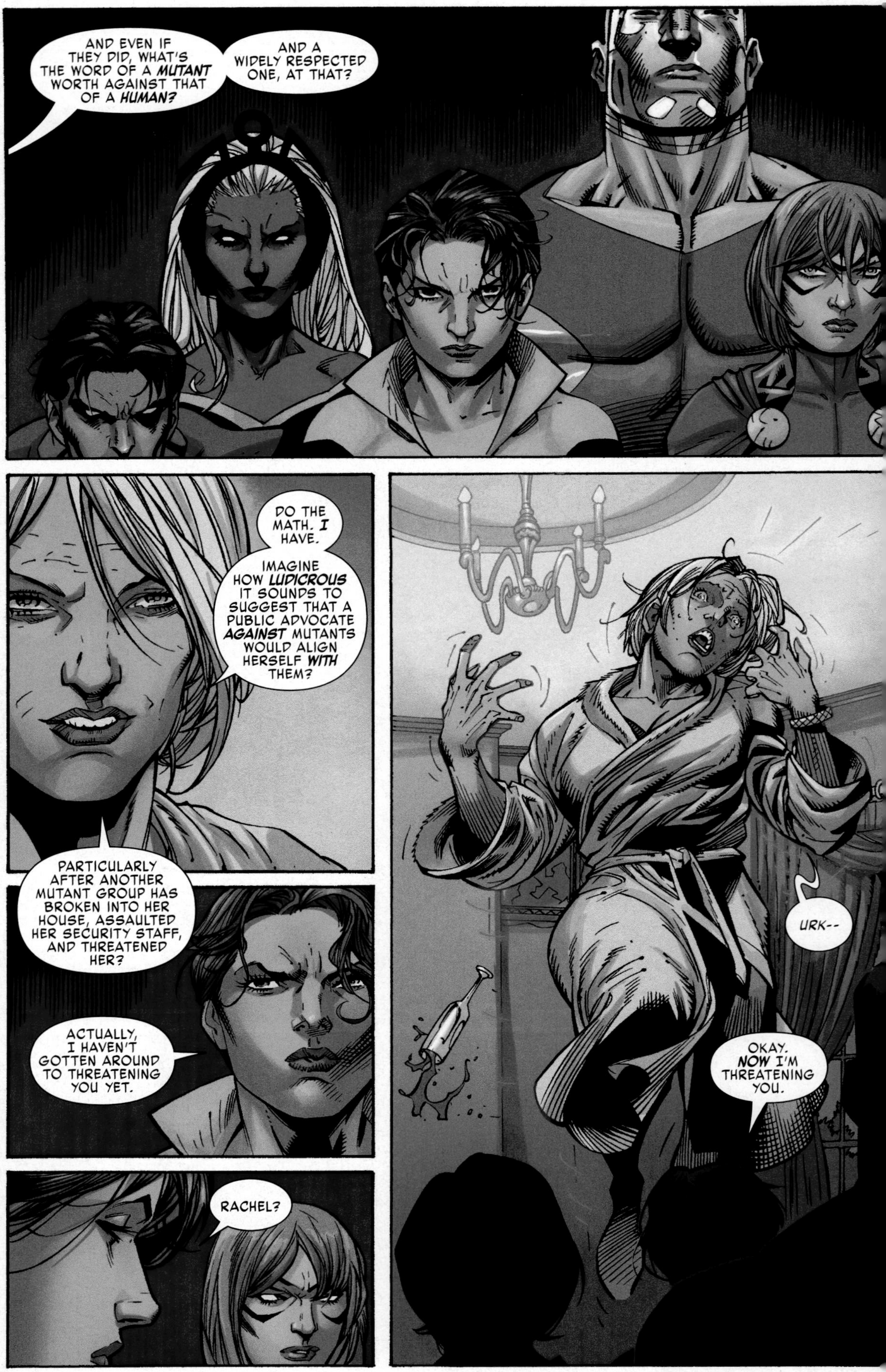
AND EVEN IF THEY DID, WHAT'S THE WORD OF A MUTANT WORTH AGAINST THAT OF A HUMAN?
AND A WIDELY RESPECTED ONE, AT THAT?
DO THE MATH. I HAVE.
IMAGINE HOW LUDICROUS IT SOUNDS TO SUGGEST THAT A PUBLIC ADVOCATE AGAINST MUTANTS WOULD ALIGN HERSELF WITH THEM?
PARTICULARLY AFTER ANOTHER MUTANT GROUP HAS BROKEN INTO HER HOUSE, ASSAULTED HER SECURITY STAFF, AND THREATENED HER?
ACTUALLY, I HAVEN'T GOTTEN AROUND TO THREATENING YOU YET.
RACHEL?
URK--
OKAY. NOW I'M THREATENING YOU.

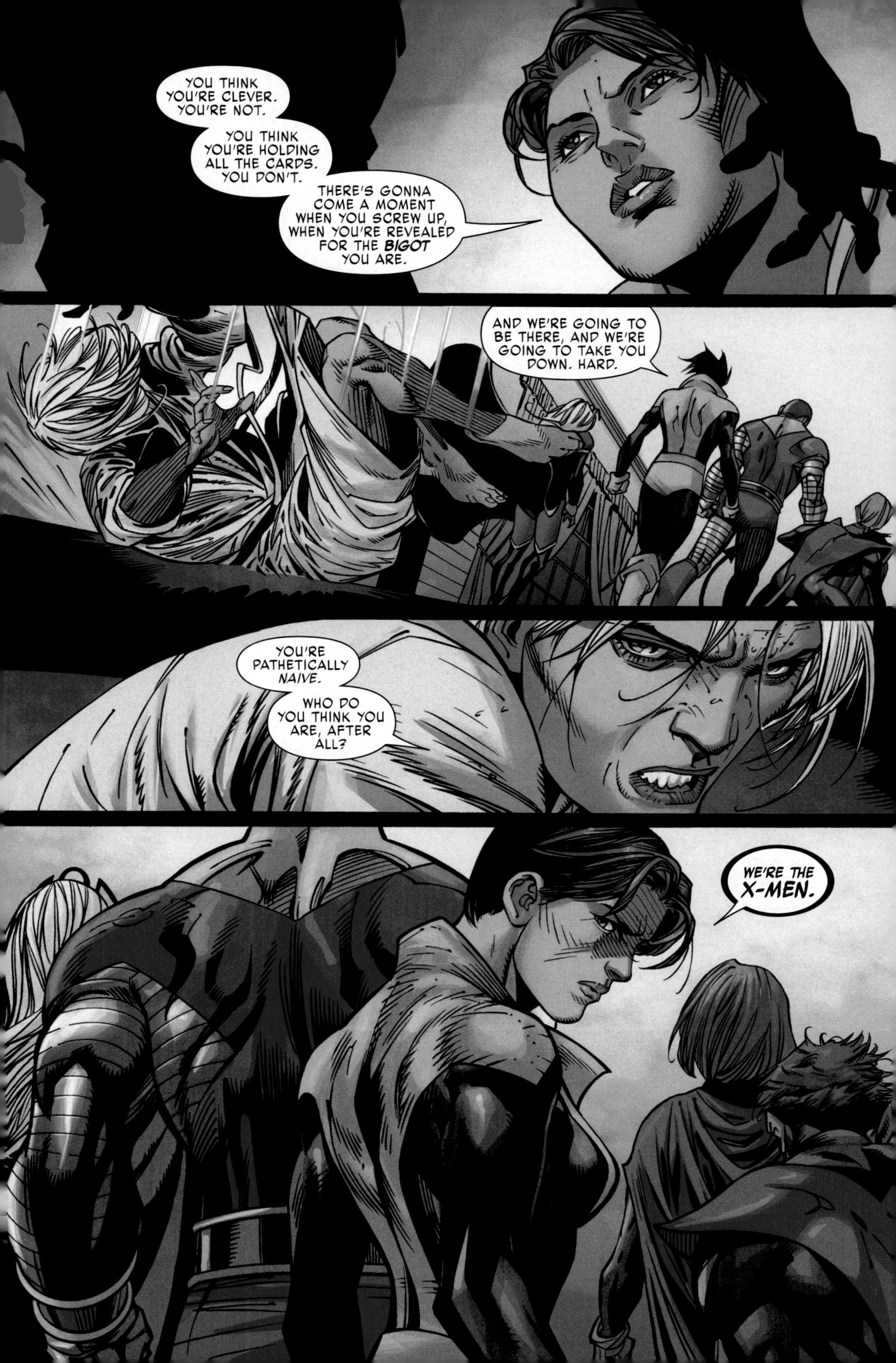
YOU THINK YOU'RE CLEVER. YOU'RE NOT.
YOU THINK YOU'RE HOLDING ALL THE CARDS. YOU DON'T.
THERE'S GONNA COME A MOMENT WHEN YOU SCREW UP, WHEN YOU'RE REVEALED FOR THE *BIGOT* YOU ARE.
AND WE'RE GOING TO BE THERE, AND WE'RE GOING TO TAKE YOU DOWN. HARD.
YOU'RE PATHETICALLY *NAIVE.*
WHO DO YOU THINK YOU ARE, AFTER ALL?
WE'RE THE X-MEN.

4

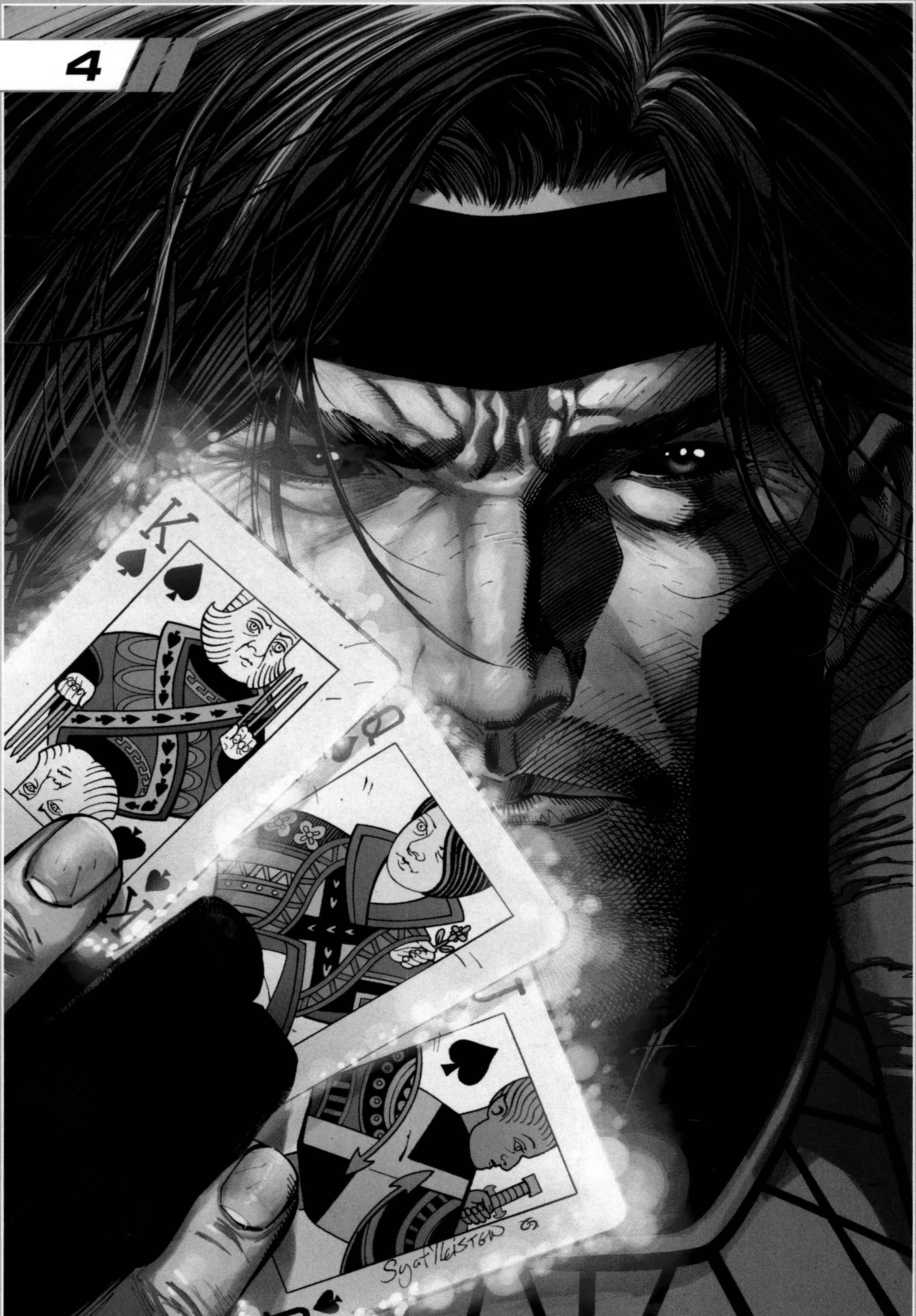

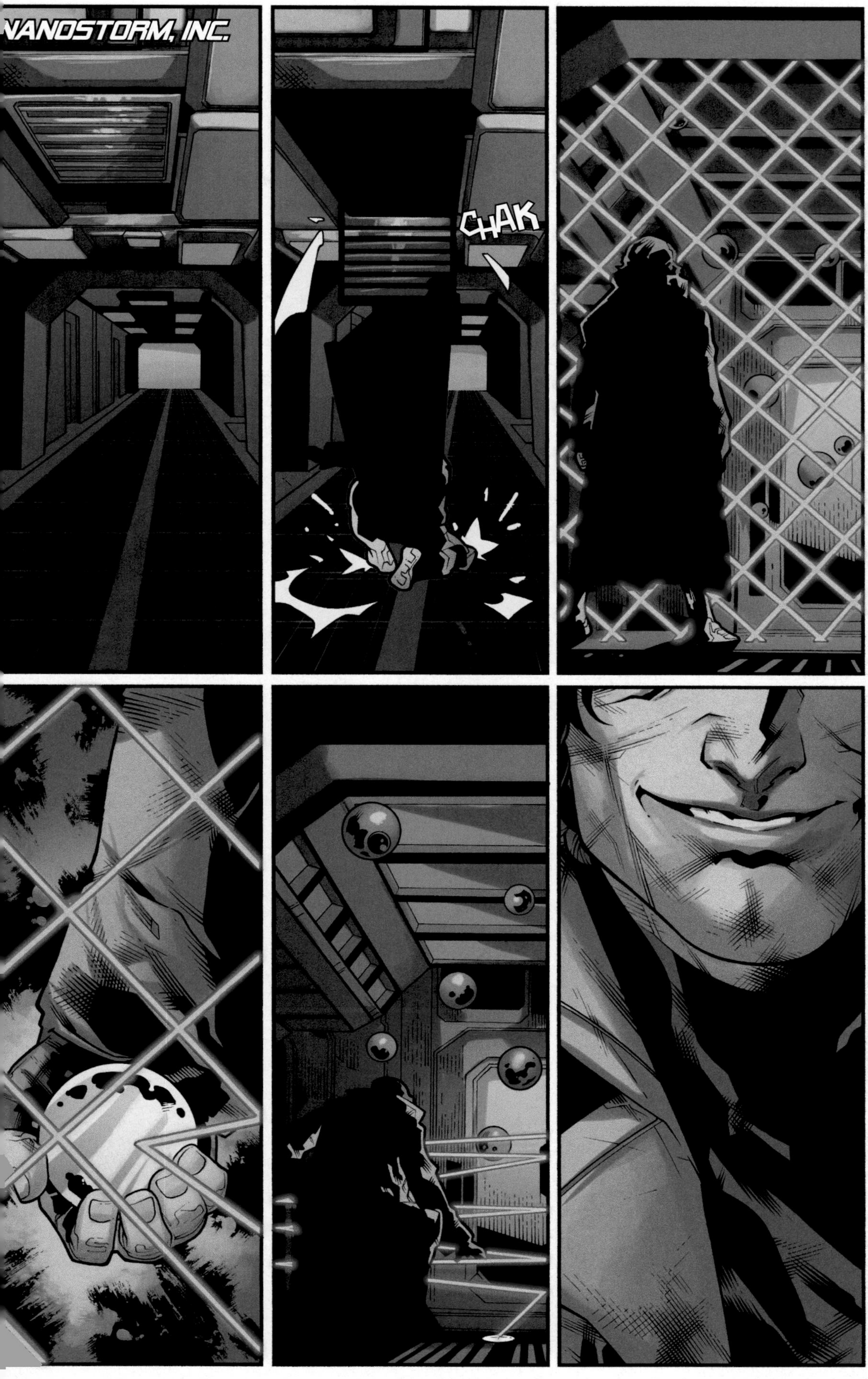
NANOSTORM, INC.
CHAK

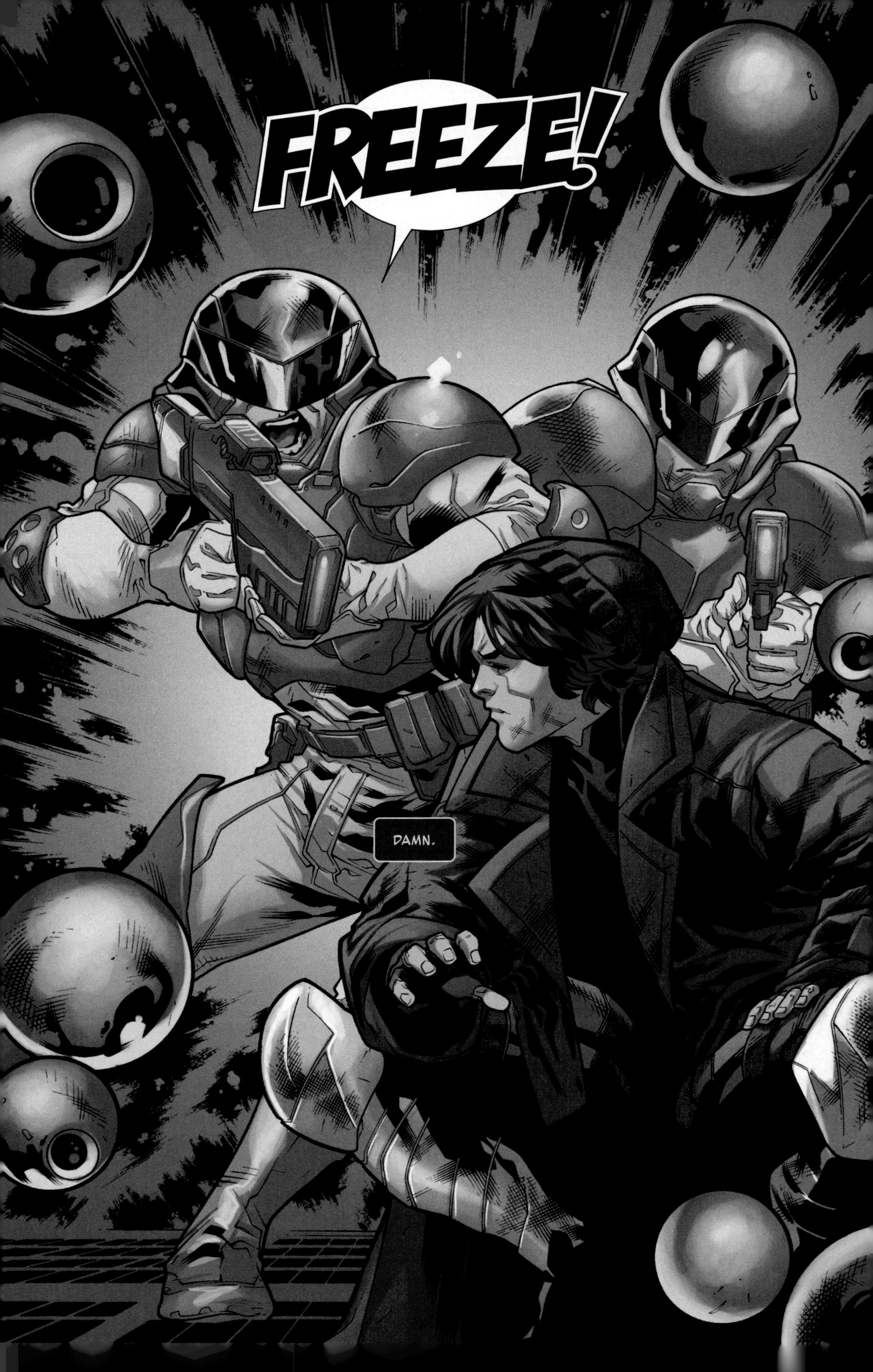
FREEZE!
DAMN.

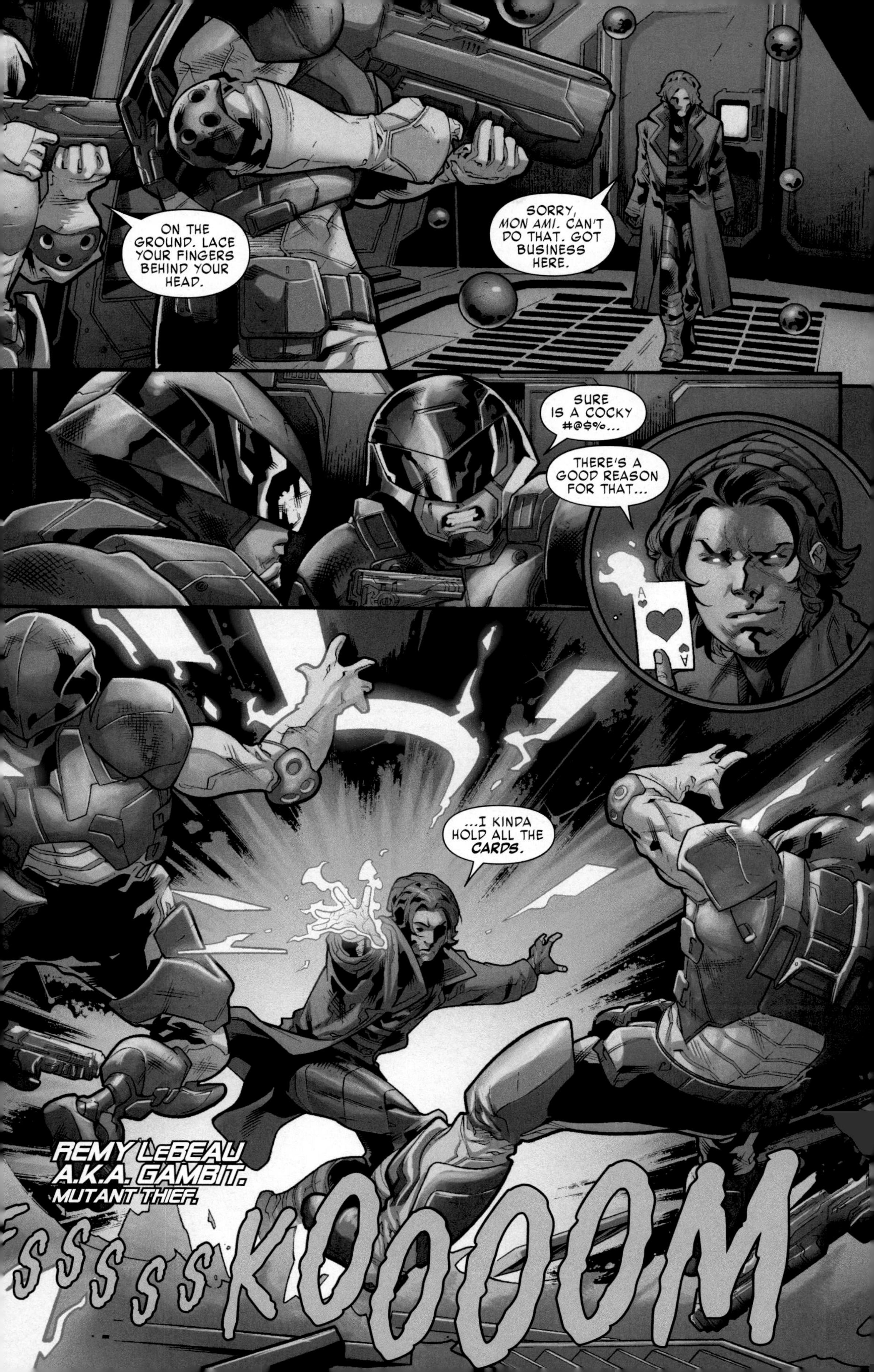
ON THE GROUND. LACE YOUR FINGERS BEHIND YOUR HEAD.
SORRY, MON AMI. CAN'T DO THAT. GOT BUSINESS HERE.
SURE IS A COCKY #@$%...
THERE'S A GOOD REASON FOR THAT...
...I KINDA HOLD ALL THE CARDS.
REMY LeBEAU A.K.A. GAMBIT. MUTANT THIEF.
SSSSSSKOOOOM

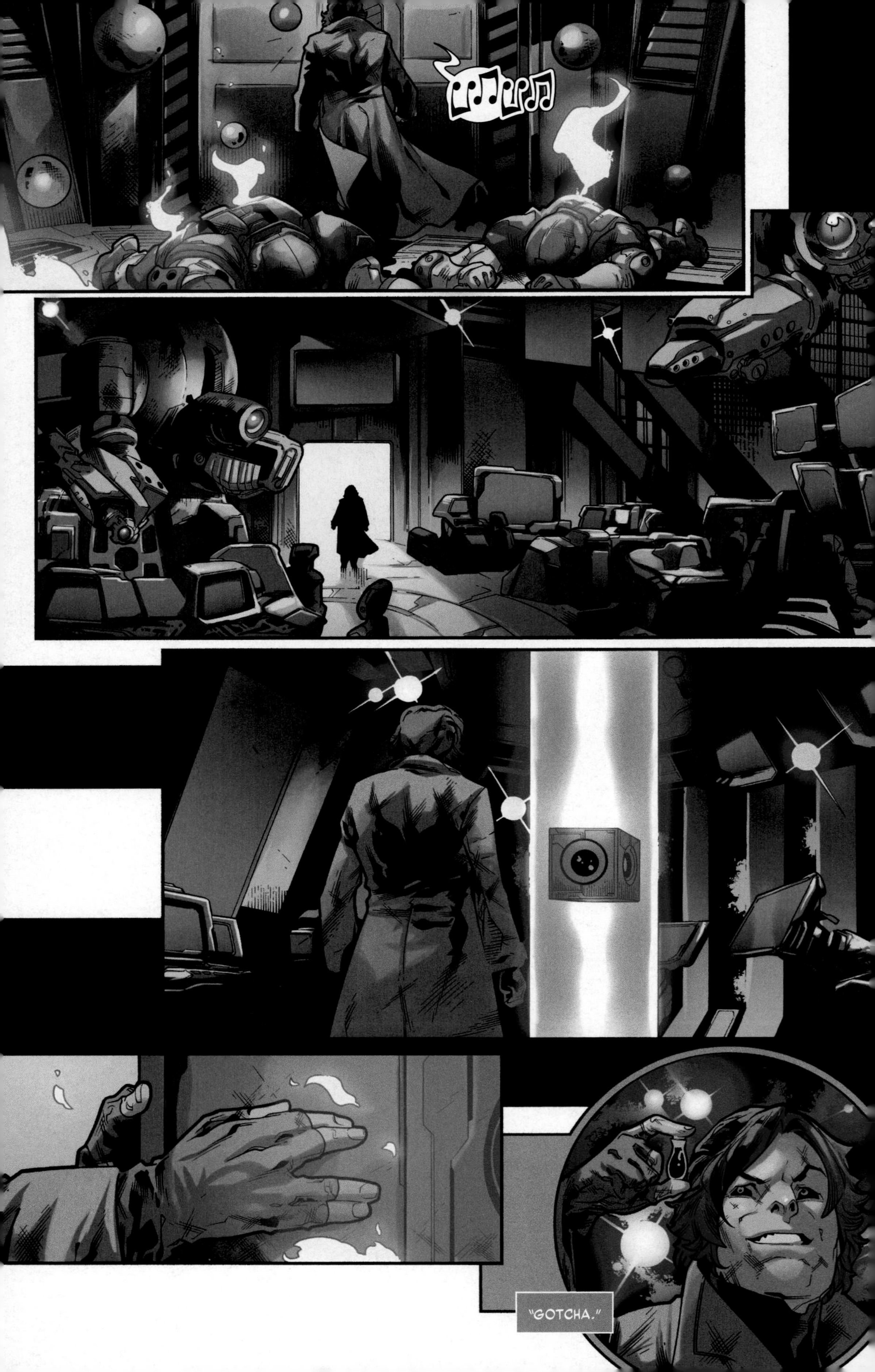
"GOTCHA."

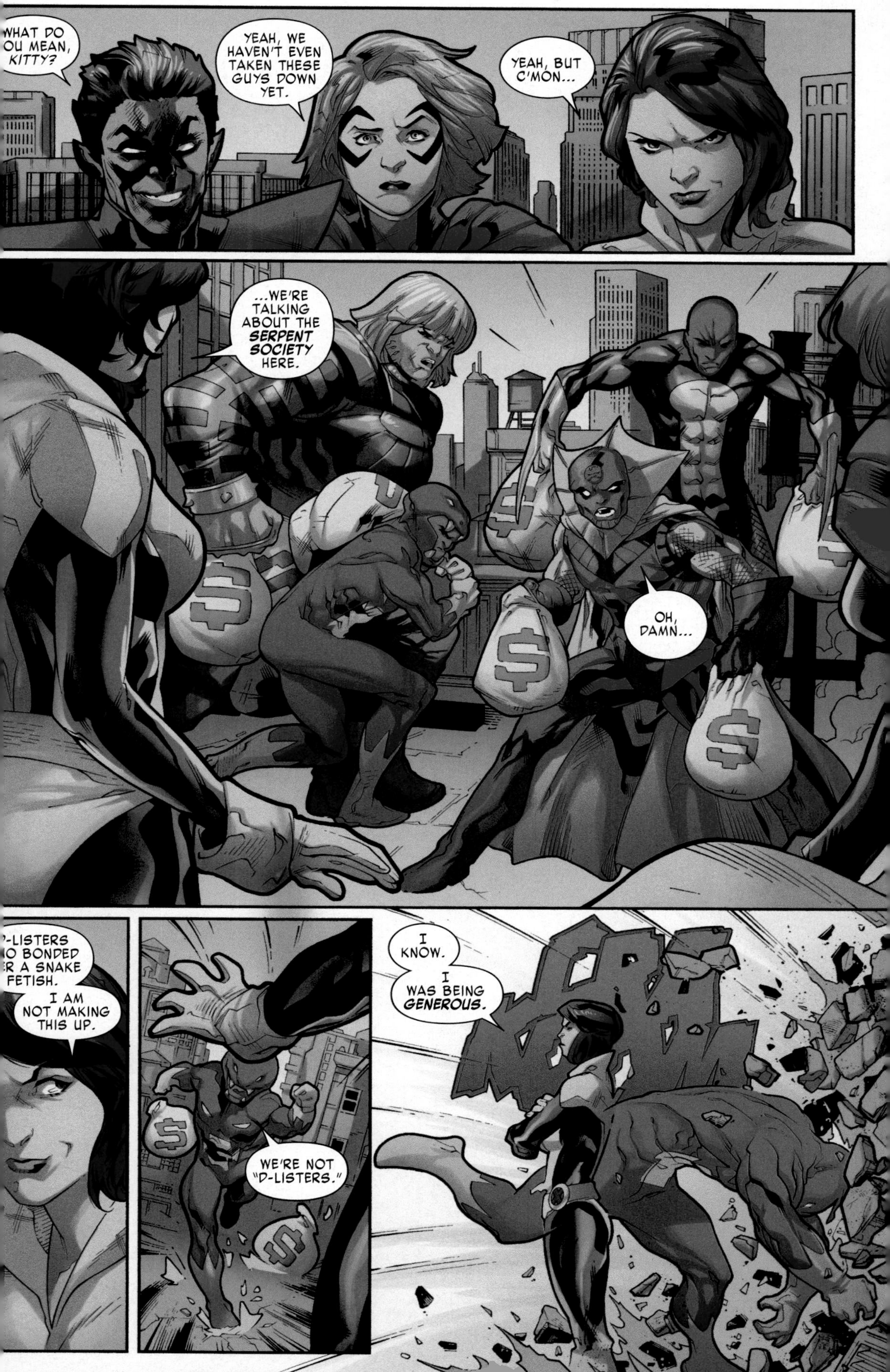
WHAT DO OU MEAN, KITTY?
YEAH, WE HAVEN'T EVEN TAKEN THESE GUYS DOWN YET.
YEAH, BUT C'MON...
...WE'RE TALKING ABOUT THE SERPENT SOCIETY HERE.
OH, DAMN...
-LISTERS O BONDED R A SNAKE FETISH.
I AM NOT MAKING THIS UP.
WE'RE NOT "D-LISTERS."
I KNOW.
I WAS BEING GENEROUS.

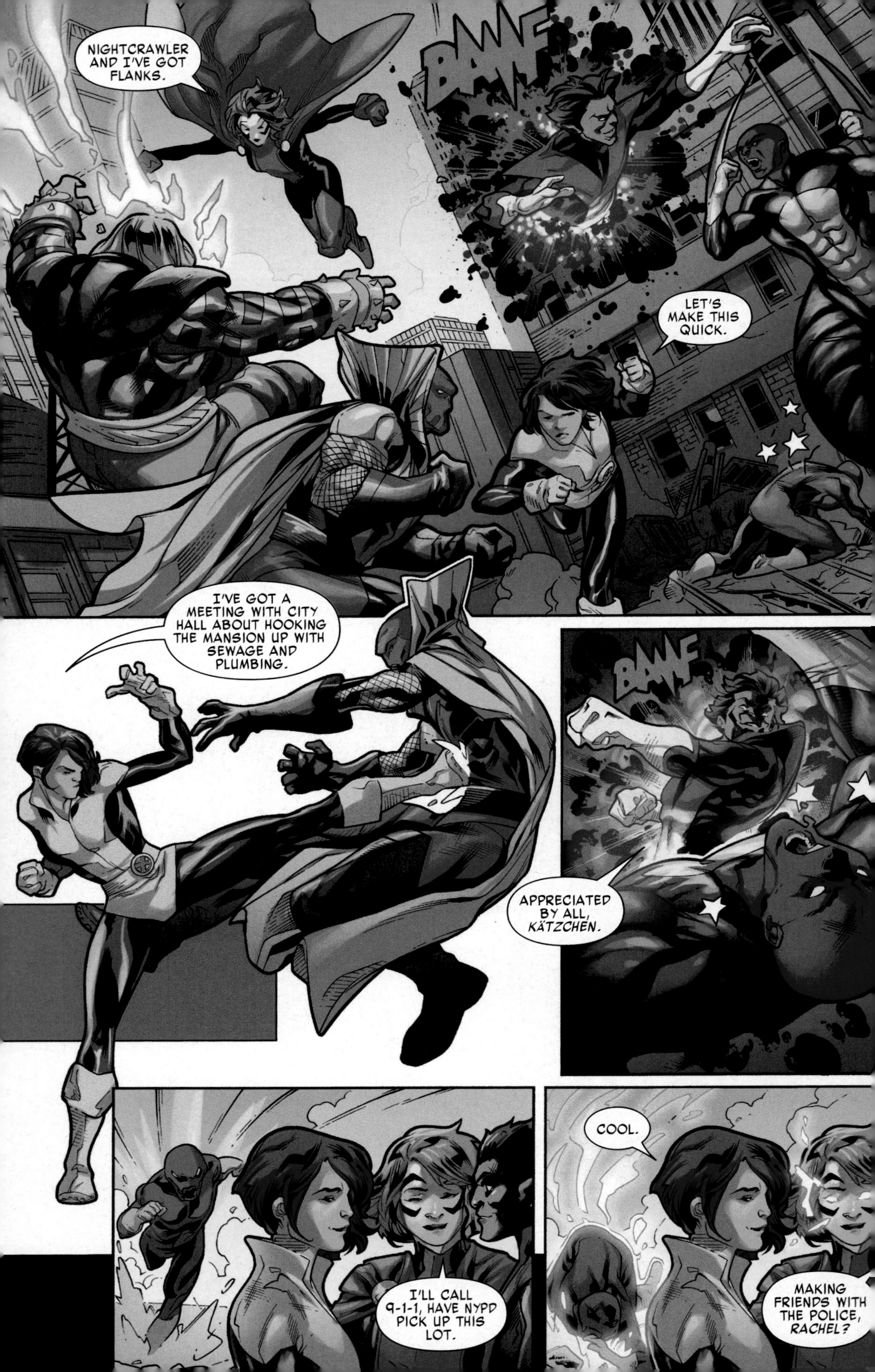
NIGHTCRAWLER AND I'VE GOT FLANKS.
BAMF
LET'S MAKE THIS QUICK.
I'VE GOT A MEETING WITH CITY HALL ABOUT HOOKING THE MANSION UP WITH SEWAGE AND PLUMBING.
BAMF
APPRECIATED BY ALL, KÄTZCHEN.
I'LL CALL 9-1-1, HAVE NYPD PICK UP THIS LOT.
COOL.
MAKING FRIENDS WITH THE POLICE, RACHEL?

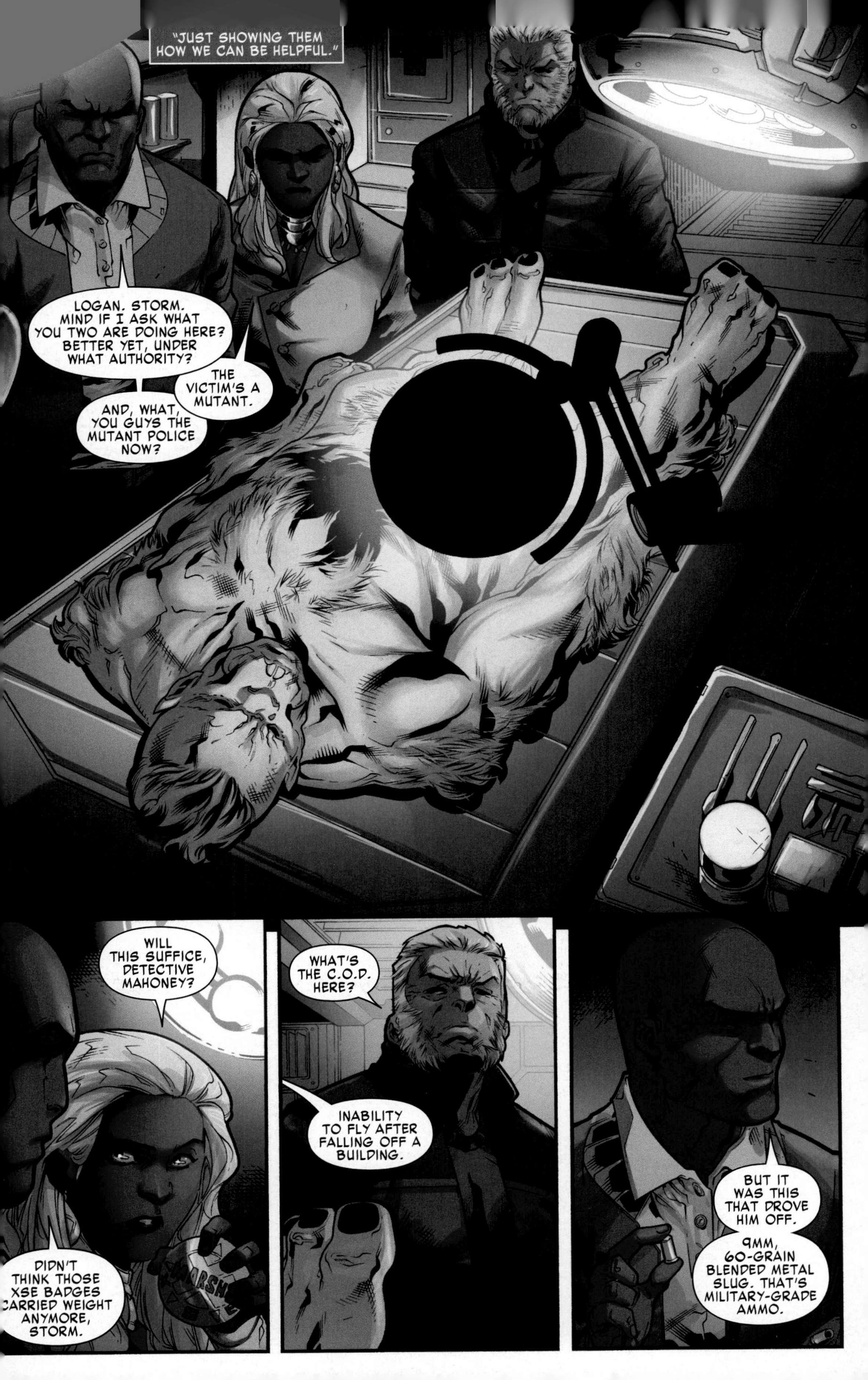
"JUST SHOWING THEM HOW WE CAN BE HELPFUL."
LOGAN. STORM. MIND IF I ASK WHAT YOU TWO ARE DOING HERE? BETTER YET, UNDER WHAT AUTHORITY?
THE VICTIM'S A MUTANT.
AND, WHAT, YOU GUYS THE MUTANT POLICE NOW?
WILL THIS SUFFICE, DETECTIVE MAHONEY?
DIDN'T THINK THOSE XSE BADGES CARRIED WEIGHT ANYMORE, STORM.
WHAT'S THE C.O.D. HERE?
INABILITY TO FLY AFTER FALLING OFF A BUILDING.
BUT IT WAS THIS THAT DROVE HIM OFF.
9MM, 60-GRAIN BLENDED METAL SLUG. THAT'S MILITARY-GRADE AMMO.

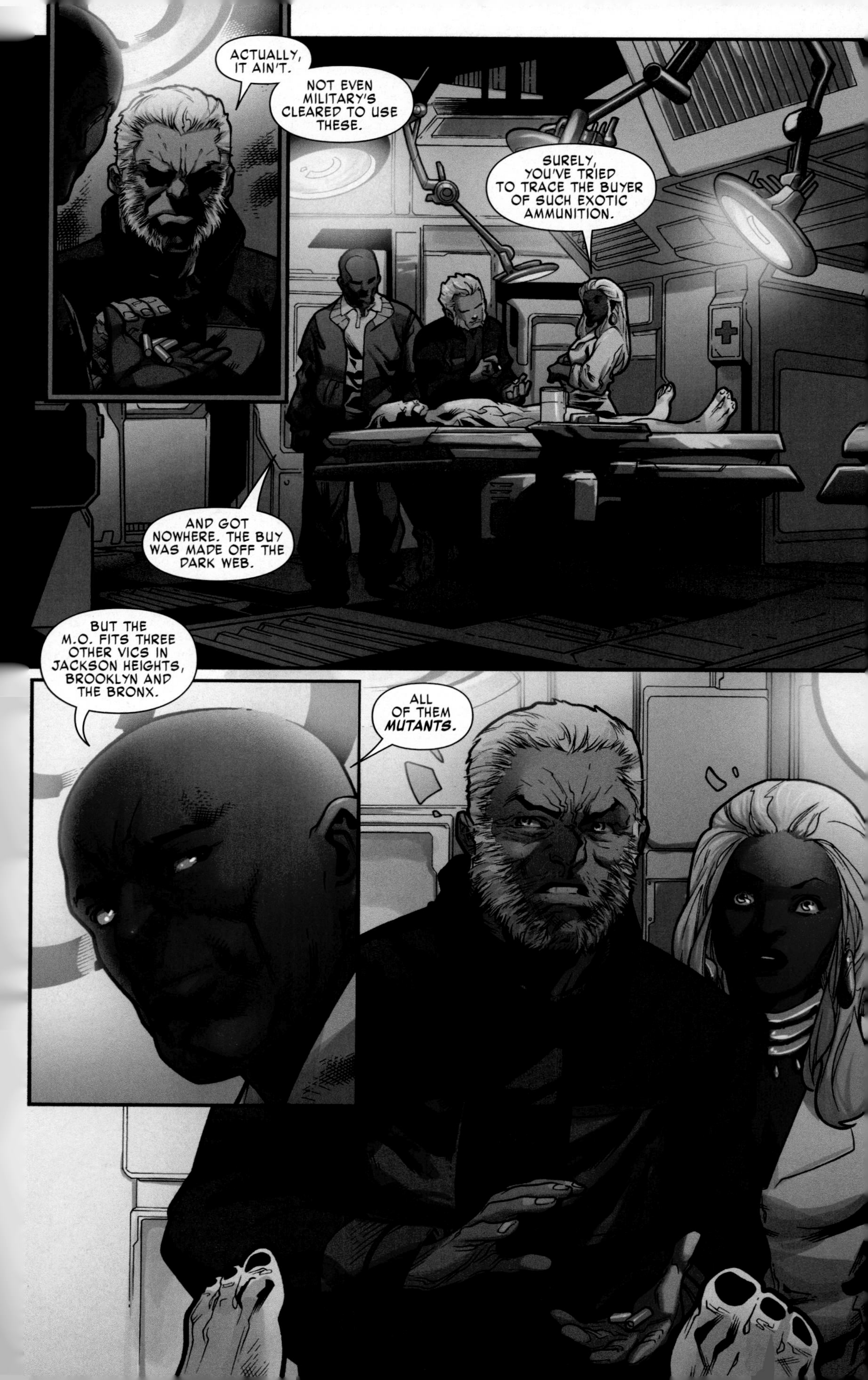
ACTUALLY, IT AIN'T.
NOT EVEN MILITARY'S CLEARED TO USE THESE.
SURELY, YOU'VE TRIED TO TRACE THE BUYER OF SUCH EXOTIC AMMUNITION.
AND GOT NOWHERE. THE BUY WAS MADE OFF THE DARK WEB.
BUT THE M.O. FITS THREE OTHER VICS IN JACKSON HEIGHTS, BROOKLYN AND THE BRONX.
ALL OF THEM *MUTANTS.*

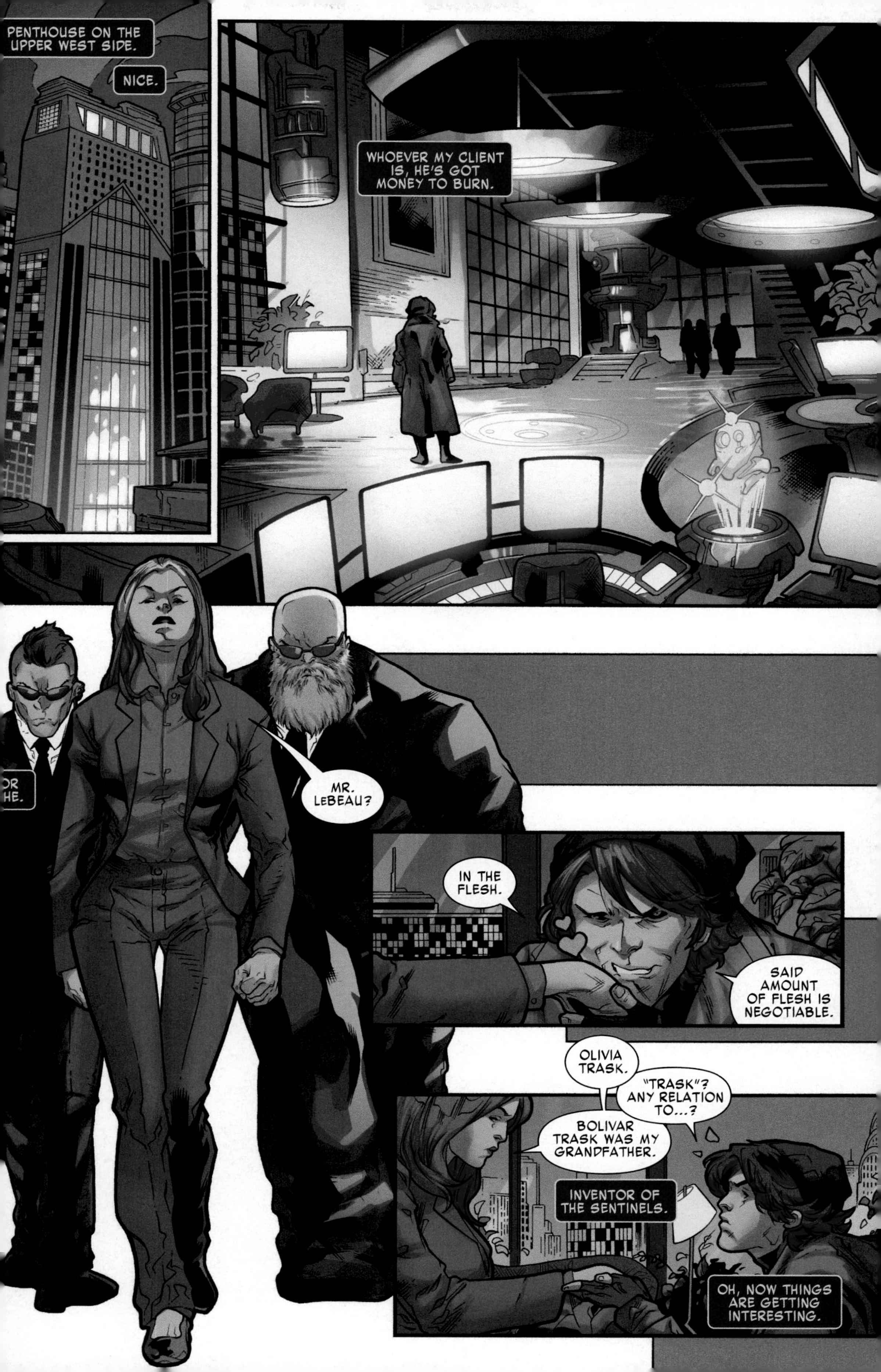
PENTHOUSE ON THE UPPER WEST SIDE.
NICE.
WHOEVER MY CLIENT IS, HE'S GOT MONEY TO BURN.
OR HE.
MR. LeBEAU?
IN THE FLESH.
SAID AMOUNT OF FLESH IS NEGOTIABLE.
OLIVIA TRASK.
"TRASK"? ANY RELATION TO...?
BOLIVAR TRASK WAS MY GRANDFATHER.
INVENTOR OF THE SENTINELS.
OH, NOW THINGS ARE GETTING INTERESTING.

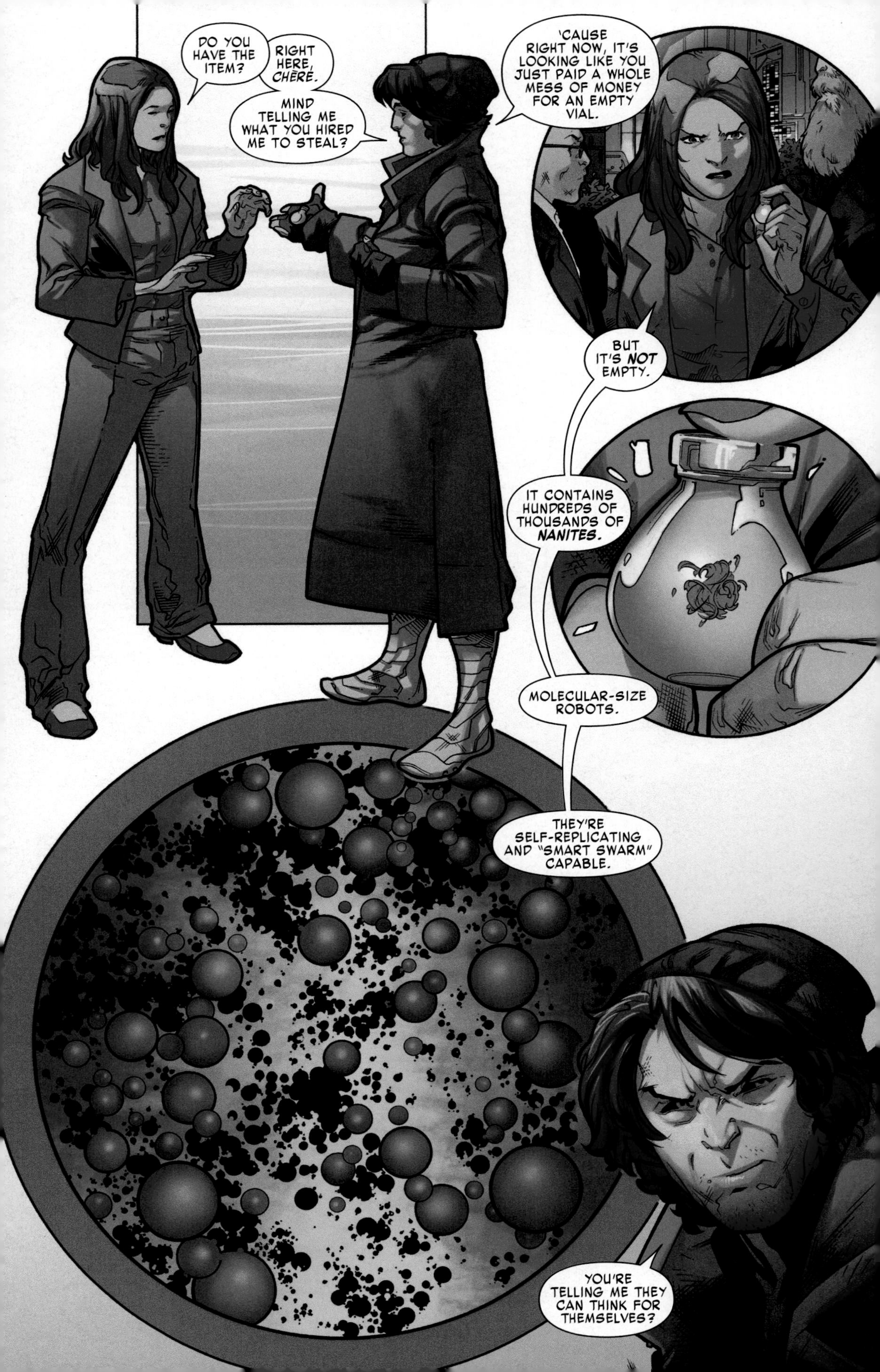
DO YOU HAVE THE ITEM?
RIGHT HERE, CHÈRE.
MIND TELLING ME WHAT YOU HIRED ME TO STEAL?
'CAUSE RIGHT NOW, IT'S LOOKING LIKE YOU JUST PAID A WHOLE MESS OF MONEY FOR AN EMPTY VIAL.
BUT IT'S NOT EMPTY.
IT CONTAINS HUNDREDS OF THOUSANDS OF NANITES.
MOLECULAR-SIZE ROBOTS.
THEY'RE SELF-REPLICATING AND "SMART SWARM" CAPABLE.
YOU'RE TELLING ME THEY CAN THINK FOR THEMSELVES?

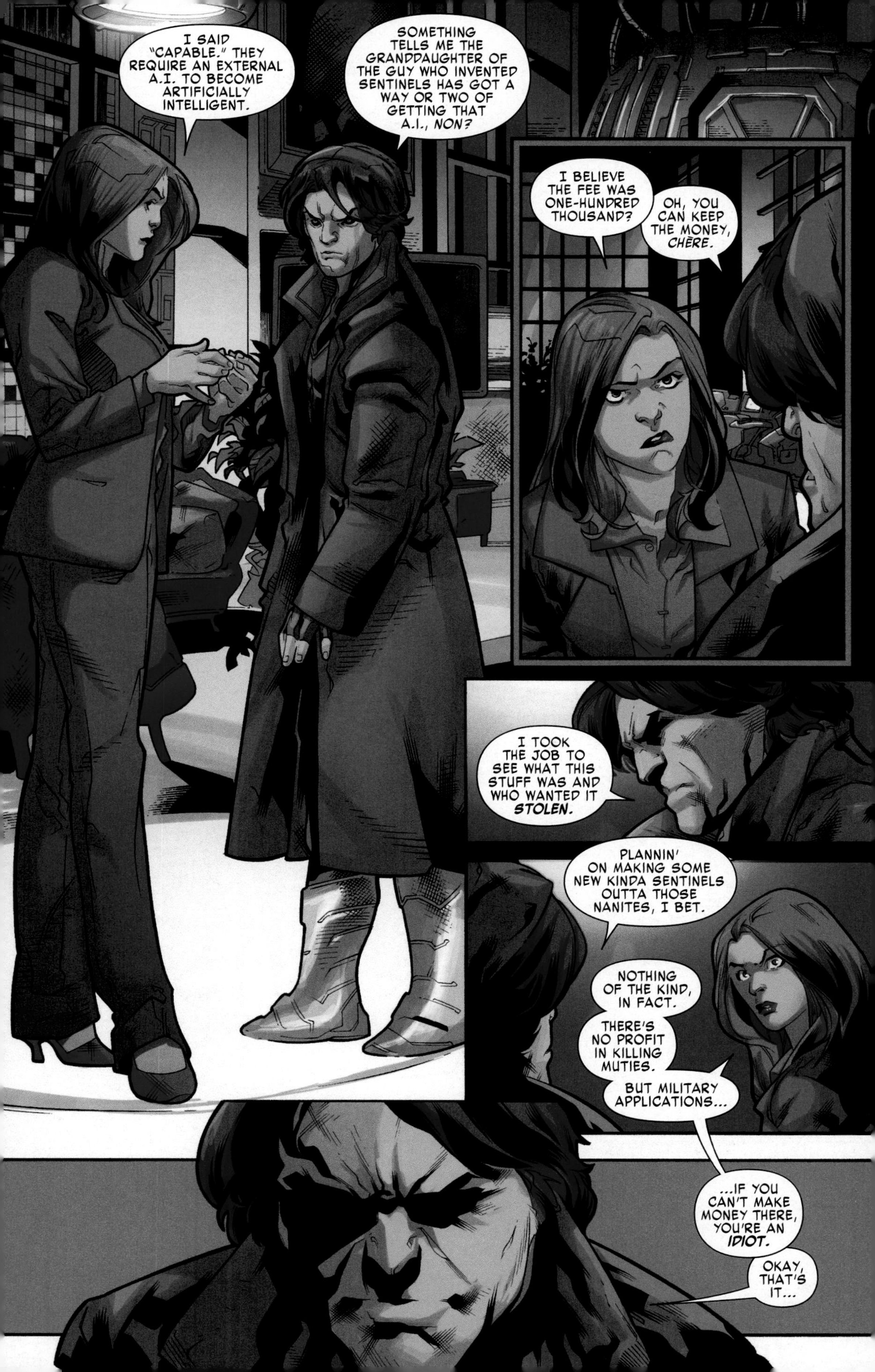
I SAID "CAPABLE." THEY REQUIRE AN EXTERNAL A.I. TO BECOME ARTIFICIALLY INTELLIGENT.
SOMETHING TELLS ME THE GRANDDAUGHTER OF THE GUY WHO INVENTED SENTINELS HAS GOT A WAY OR TWO OF GETTING THAT A.I., *NON?*
I BELIEVE THE FEE WAS ONE-HUNDRED THOUSAND?
OH, YOU CAN KEEP THE MONEY, *CHÈRE.*
I TOOK THE JOB TO SEE WHAT THIS STUFF WAS AND WHO WANTED IT ***STOLEN.***
PLANNIN' ON MAKING SOME NEW KINDA SENTINELS OUTTA THOSE NANITES, I BET.
NOTHING OF THE KIND, IN FACT.
THERE'S NO PROFIT IN KILLING MUTIES.
BUT MILITARY APPLICATIONS...
...IF YOU CAN'T MAKE MONEY THERE, YOU'RE AN ***IDIOT.***
OKAY, THAT'S IT...

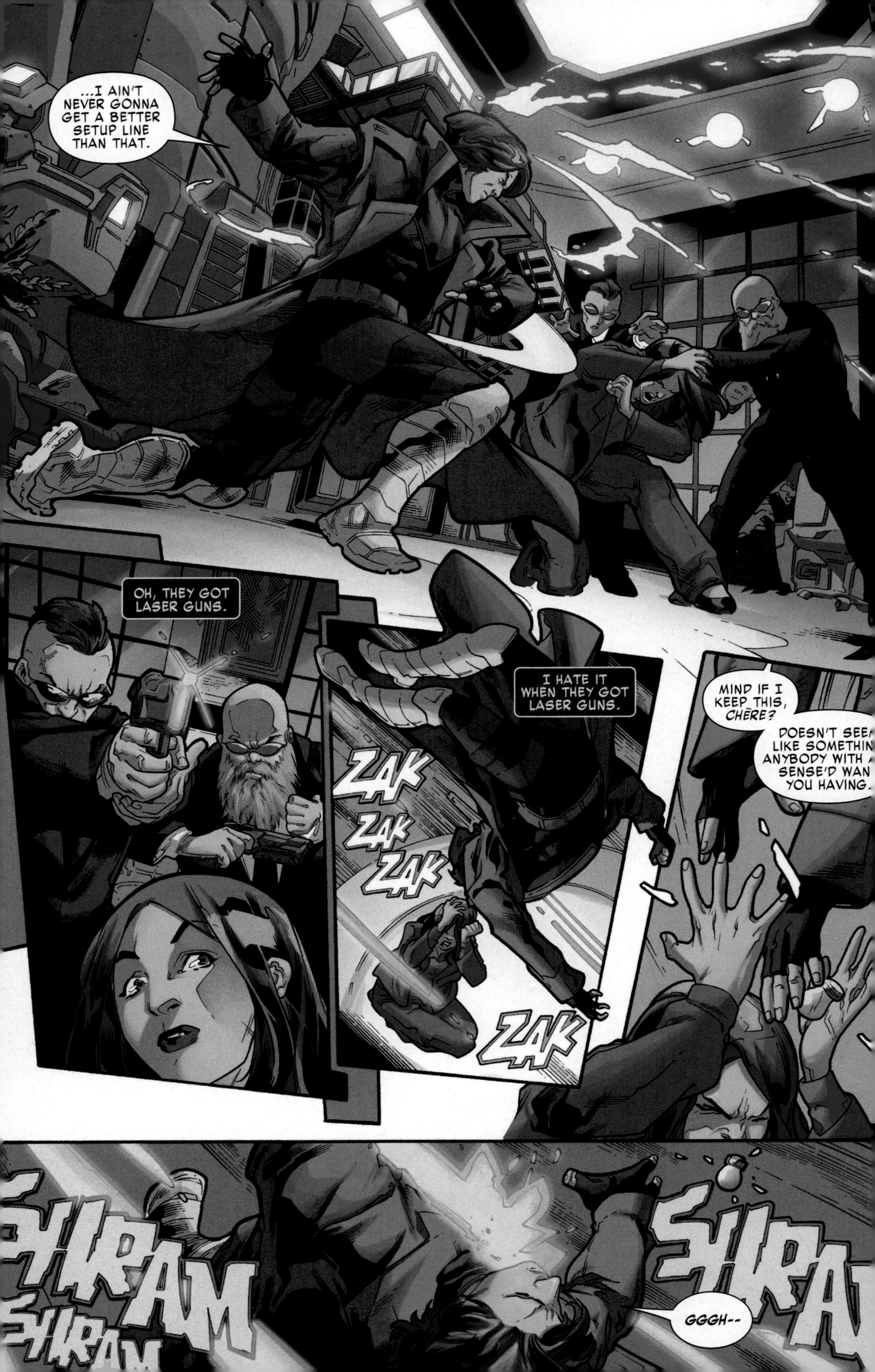
...I AIN'T NEVER GONNA GET A BETTER SETUP LINE THAN THAT.
OH, THEY GOT LASER GUNS.
I HATE IT WHEN THEY GOT LASER GUNS.
ZAK
ZAK
ZAK
ZAK
MIND IF I KEEP THIS, CHÈRE?
SHRAM
SHRAM
GGGH--

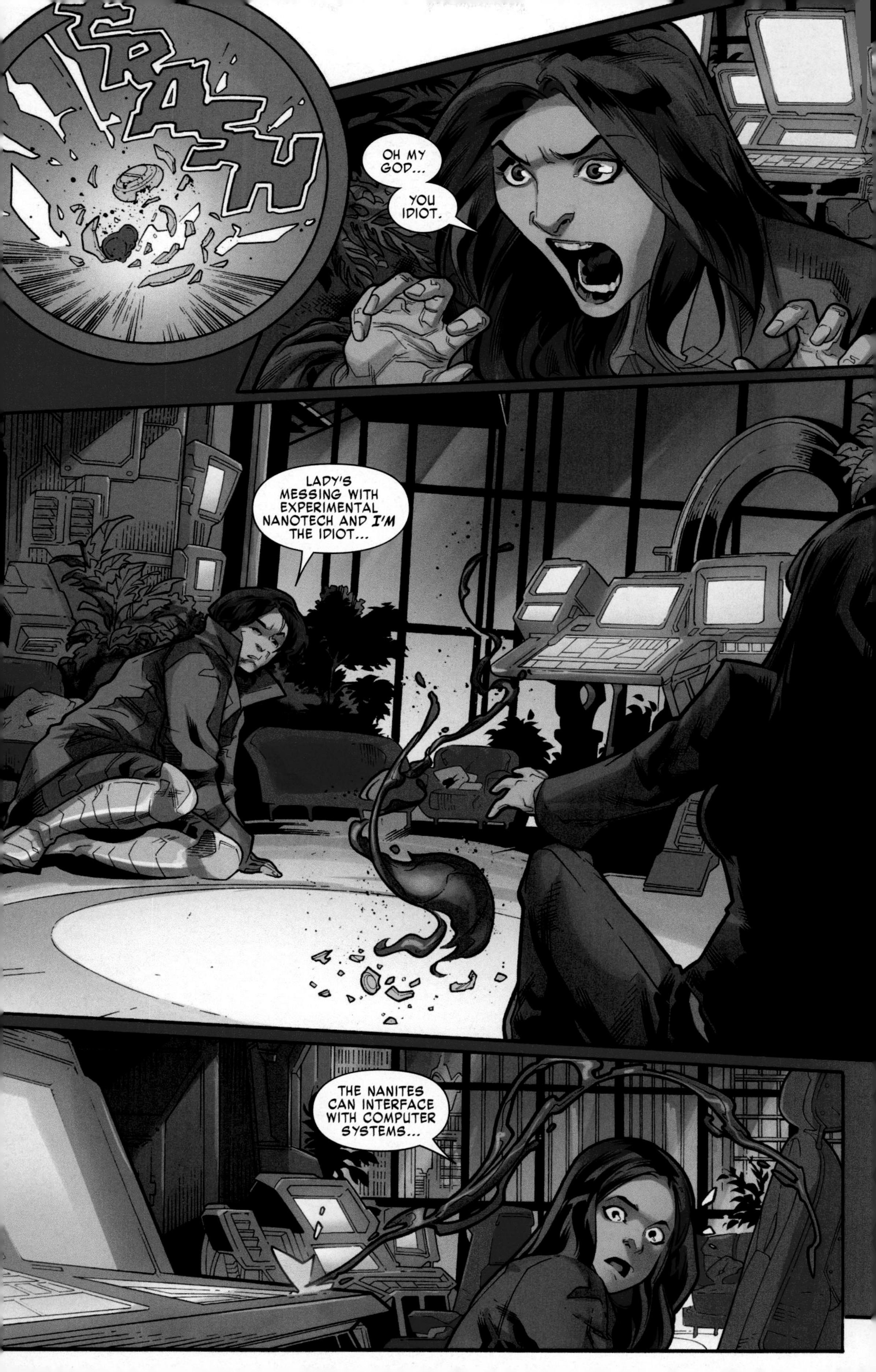
CRAASH
OH MY GOD...
YOU IDIOT.
LADY'S MESSING WITH EXPERIMENTAL NANOTECH AND I'M THE IDIOT...
THE NANITES CAN INTERFACE WITH COMPUTER SYSTEMS...

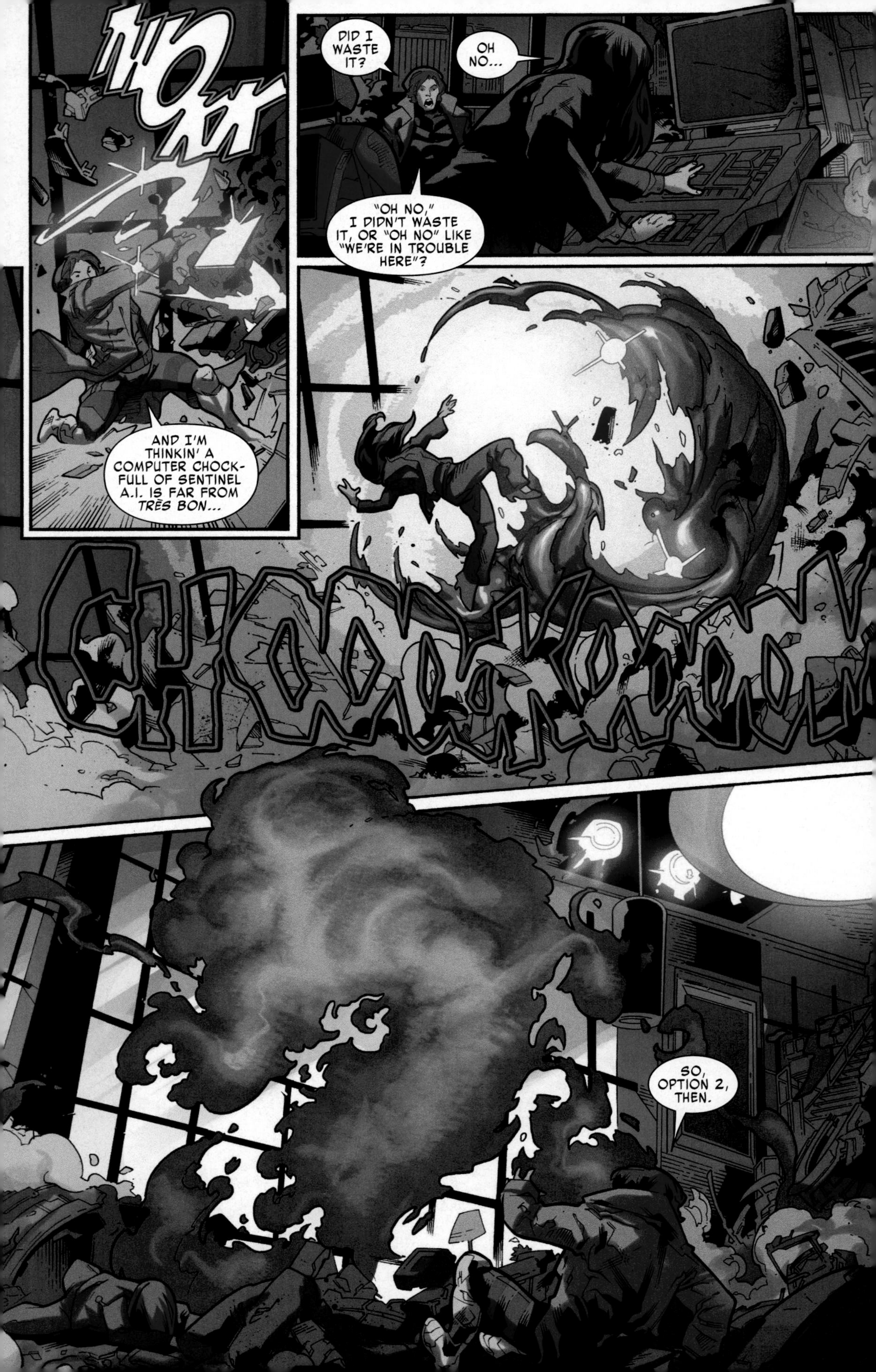
THOOM
DID I WASTE IT?
OH NO...
"OH NO," I DIDN'T WASTE IT, OR "OH NO" LIKE "WE'RE IN TROUBLE HERE"?
AND I'M THINKIN' A COMPUTER CHOCK-FULL OF SENTINEL A.I. IS FAR FROM *TRÈS BON*...
CHKOOOOKOOOOM
SO, OPTION 2, THEN.

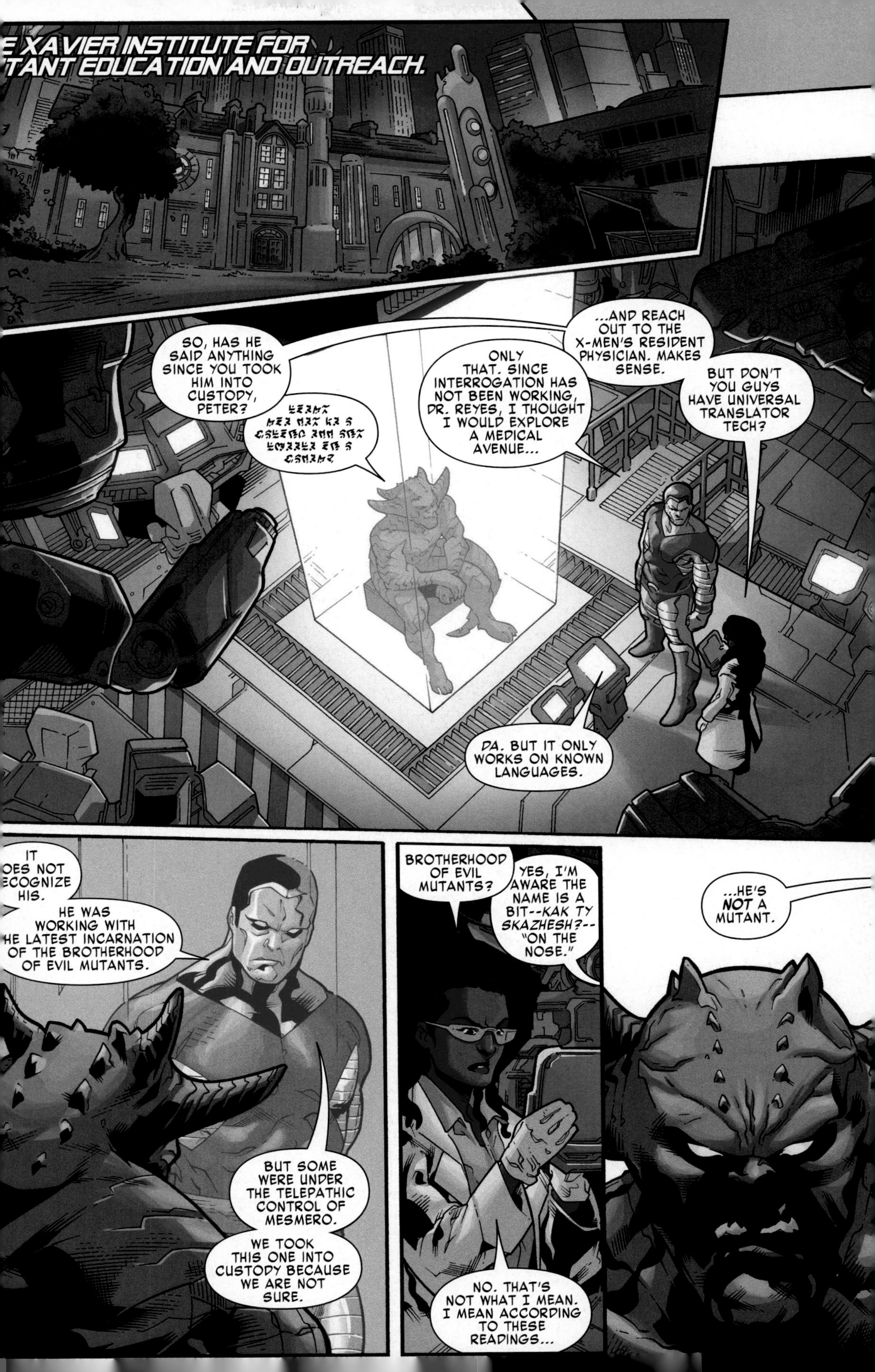
E XAVIER INSTITUTE FOR
TANT EDUCATION AND OUTREACH.
SO, HAS HE SAID ANYTHING SINCE YOU TOOK HIM INTO CUSTODY, PETER?
ONLY THAT. SINCE INTERROGATION HAS NOT BEEN WORKING, DR. REYES, I THOUGHT I WOULD EXPLORE A MEDICAL AVENUE...
...AND REACH OUT TO THE X-MEN'S RESIDENT PHYSICIAN. MAKES SENSE.
BUT DON'T YOU GUYS HAVE UNIVERSAL TRANSLATOR TECH?
DA. BUT IT ONLY WORKS ON KNOWN LANGUAGES.
IT OES NOT ECOGNIZE HIS.
HE WAS WORKING WITH HE LATEST INCARNATION OF THE BROTHERHOOD OF EVIL MUTANTS.
BUT SOME WERE UNDER THE TELEPATHIC CONTROL OF MESMERO.
WE TOOK THIS ONE INTO CUSTODY BECAUSE WE ARE NOT SURE.
BROTHERHOOD OF EVIL MUTANTS?
YES, I'M AWARE THE NAME IS A BIT--KAK TY SKAZHESH?--"ON THE NOSE."
...HE'S NOT A MUTANT.
NO. THAT'S NOT WHAT I MEAN. I MEAN ACCORDING TO THESE READINGS...

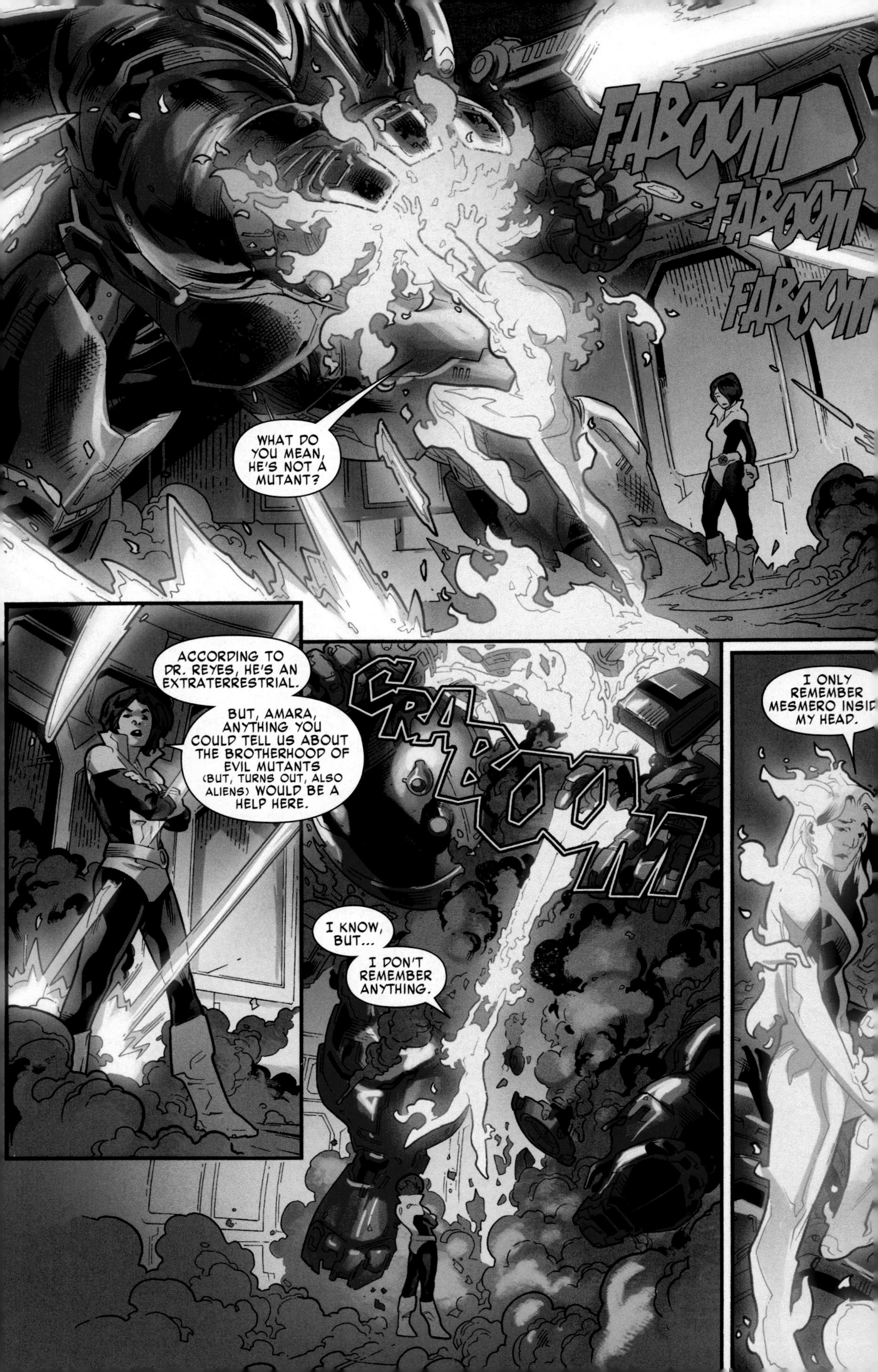
FABOOM
FABOOM
FABOOM
WHAT DO YOU MEAN, HE'S NOT A MUTANT?
ACCORDING TO DR. REYES, HE'S AN EXTRATERRESTRIAL.
BUT, AMARA, ANYTHING YOU COULD TELL US ABOUT THE BROTHERHOOD OF EVIL MUTANTS (BUT, TURNS OUT, ALSO ALIENS) WOULD BE A HELP HERE.
CRA-BOOOM
I KNOW, BUT...
I DON'T REMEMBER ANYTHING.
I ONLY REMEMBER MESMERO INSID MY HEAD.

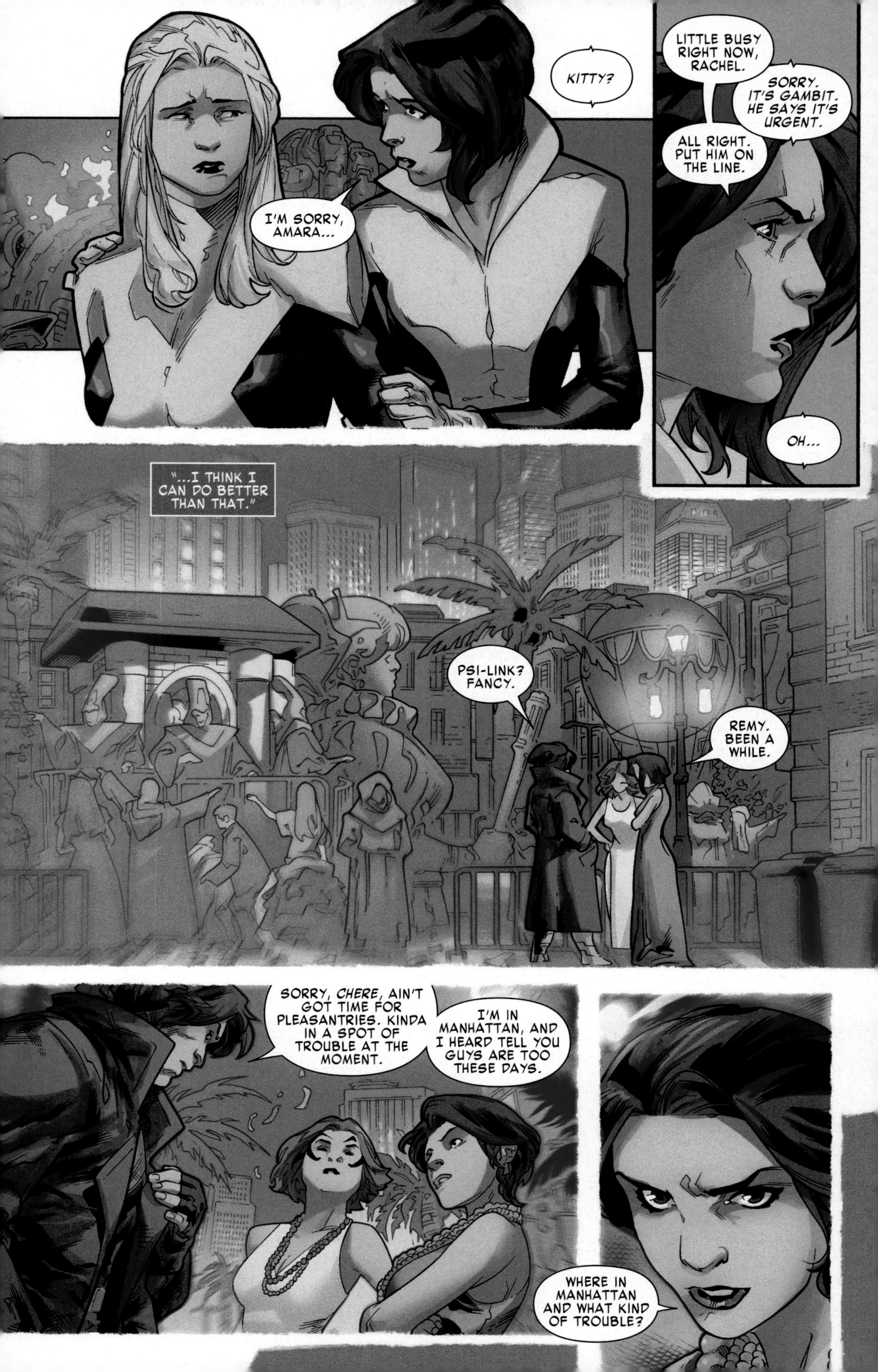
KITTY?
I'M SORRY, AMARA...
LITTLE BUSY RIGHT NOW, RACHEL.
SORRY. IT'S GAMBIT. HE SAYS IT'S URGENT.
ALL RIGHT. PUT HIM ON THE LINE.
OH...
"...I THINK I CAN DO BETTER THAN THAT."
PSI-LINK? FANCY.
REMY. BEEN A WHILE.
SORRY, CHERE, AIN'T GOT TIME FOR PLEASANTRIES. KINDA IN A SPOT OF TROUBLE AT THE MOMENT.
I'M IN MANHATTAN, AND I HEARD TELL YOU GUYS ARE TOO THESE DAYS.
WHERE IN MANHATTAN AND WHAT KIND OF TROUBLE?

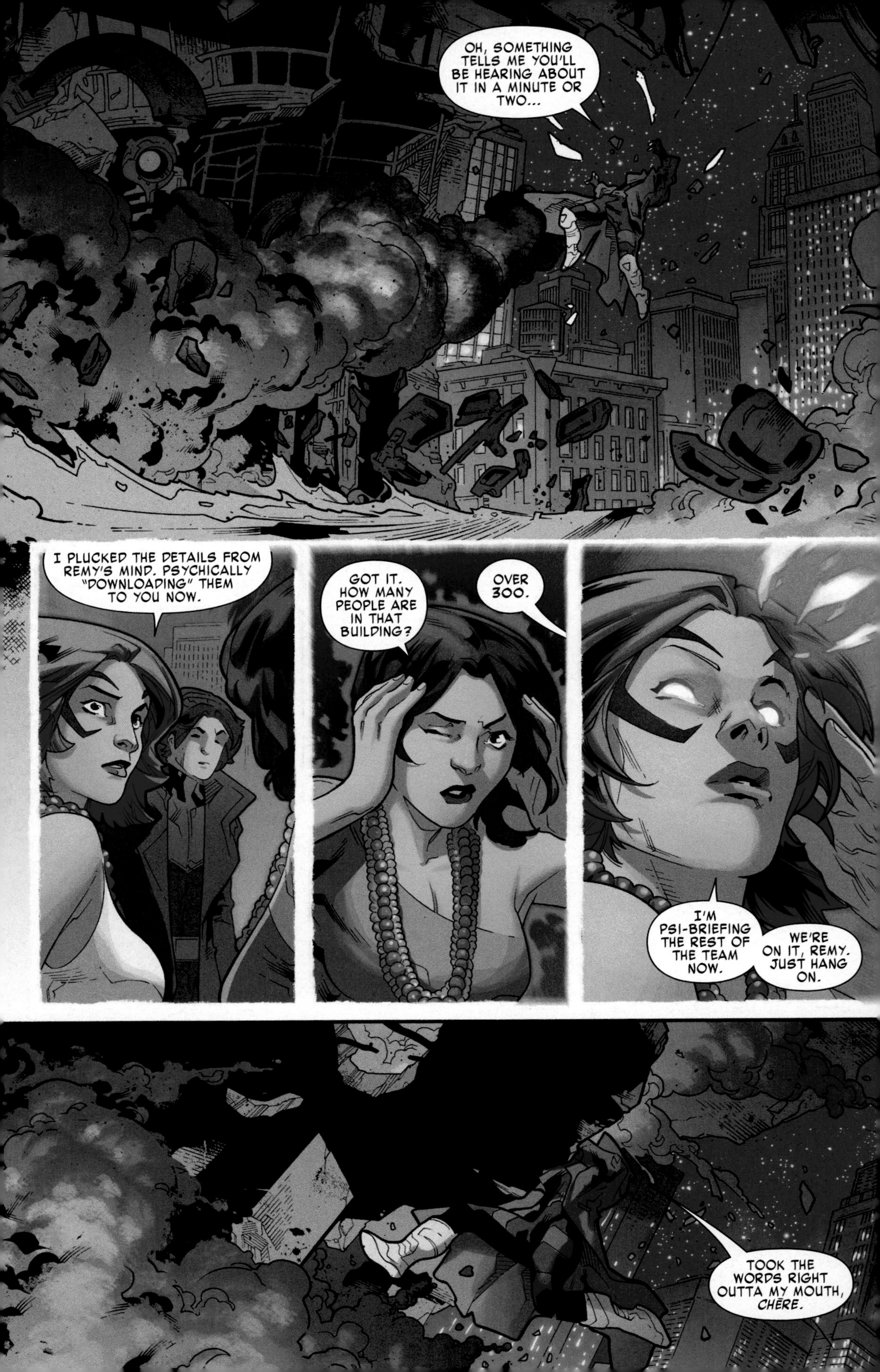
OH, SOMETHING TELLS ME YOU'LL BE HEARING ABOUT IT IN A MINUTE OR TWO...
I PLUCKED THE DETAILS FROM REMY'S MIND. PSYCHICALLY "DOWNLOADING" THEM TO YOU NOW.
GOT IT. HOW MANY PEOPLE ARE IN THAT BUILDING?
OVER 300.
I'M PSI-BRIEFING THE REST OF THE TEAM NOW.
WE'RE ON IT, REMY. JUST HANG ON.
TOOK THE WORDS RIGHT OUTTA MY MOUTH, *CHÈRE.*

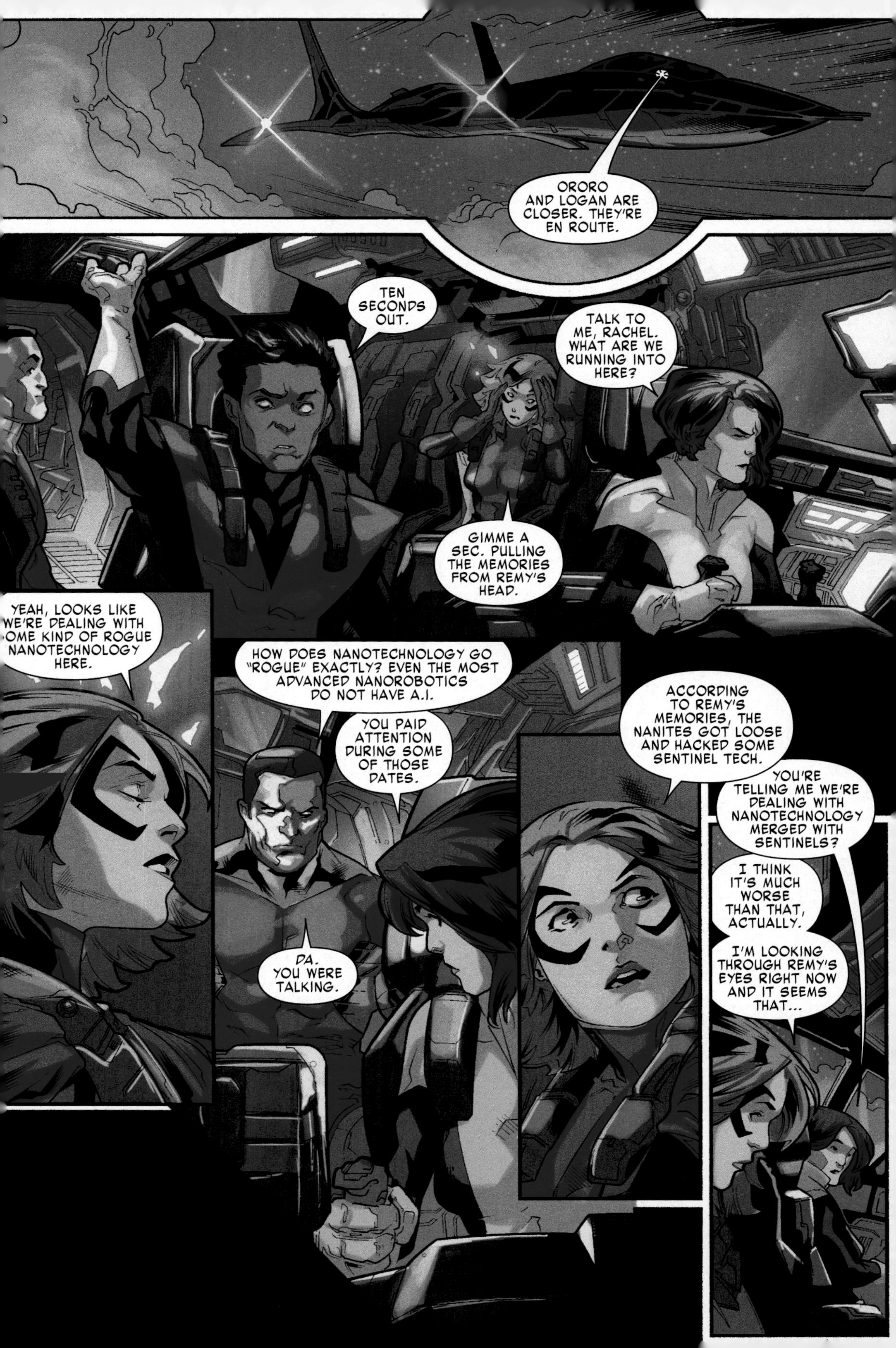
ORORO AND LOGAN ARE CLOSER. THEY'RE EN ROUTE.
TEN SECONDS OUT.
TALK TO ME, RACHEL. WHAT ARE WE RUNNING INTO HERE?
GIMME A SEC. PULLING THE MEMORIES FROM REMY'S HEAD.
YEAH, LOOKS LIKE WE'RE DEALING WITH SOME KIND OF ROGUE NANOTECHNOLOGY HERE.
HOW DOES NANOTECHNOLOGY GO "ROGUE" EXACTLY? EVEN THE MOST ADVANCED NANOROBOTICS DO NOT HAVE A.I.
YOU PAID ATTENTION DURING SOME OF THOSE DATES.
DA. YOU WERE TALKING.
ACCORDING TO REMY'S MEMORIES, THE NANITES GOT LOOSE AND HACKED SOME SENTINEL TECH.
YOU'RE TELLING ME WE'RE DEALING WITH NANOTECHNOLOGY MERGED WITH SENTINELS?
I THINK IT'S MUCH WORSE THAN THAT, ACTUALLY.
I'M LOOKING THROUGH REMY'S EYES RIGHT NOW AND IT SEEMS THAT...

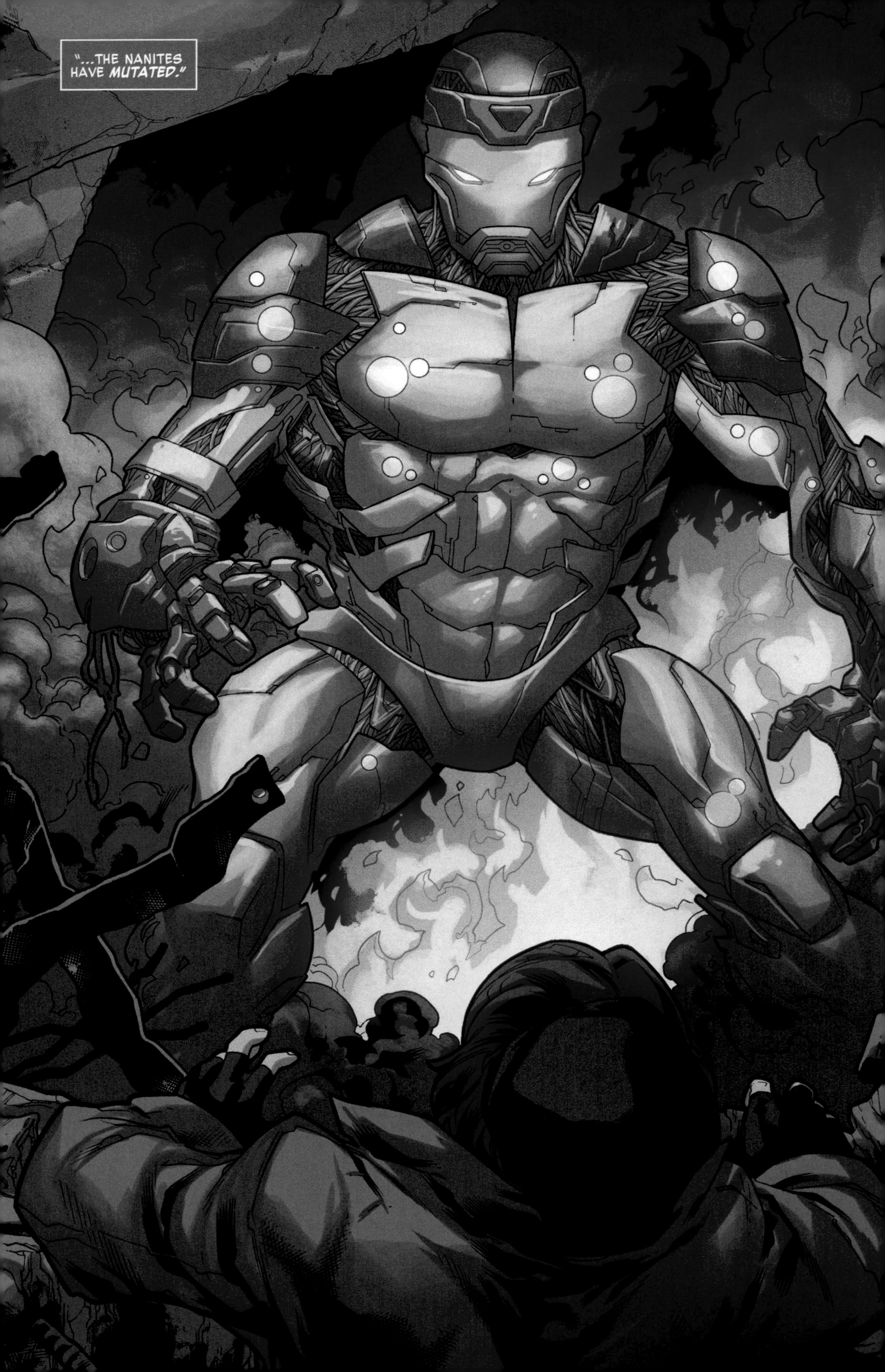
"...THE NANITES HAVE *MUTATED*."

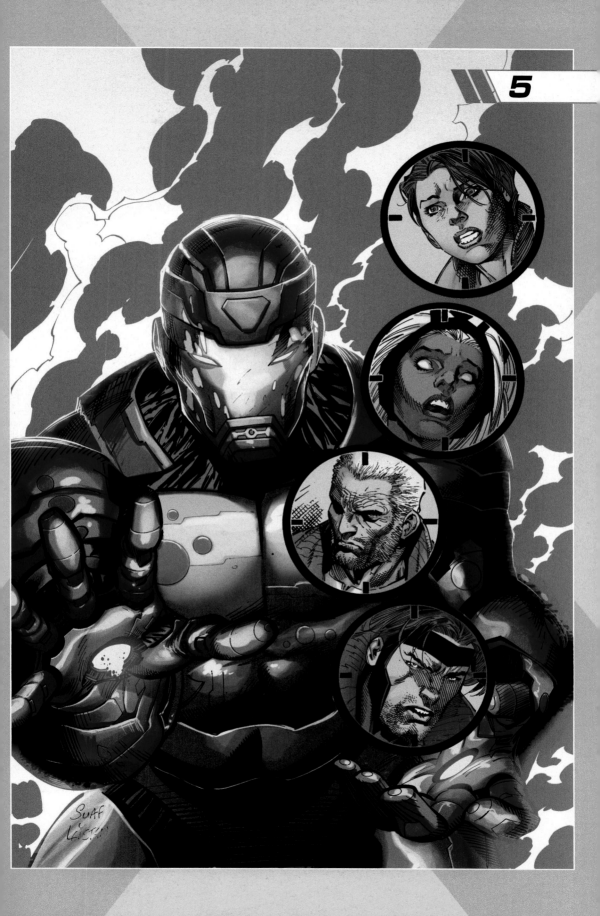

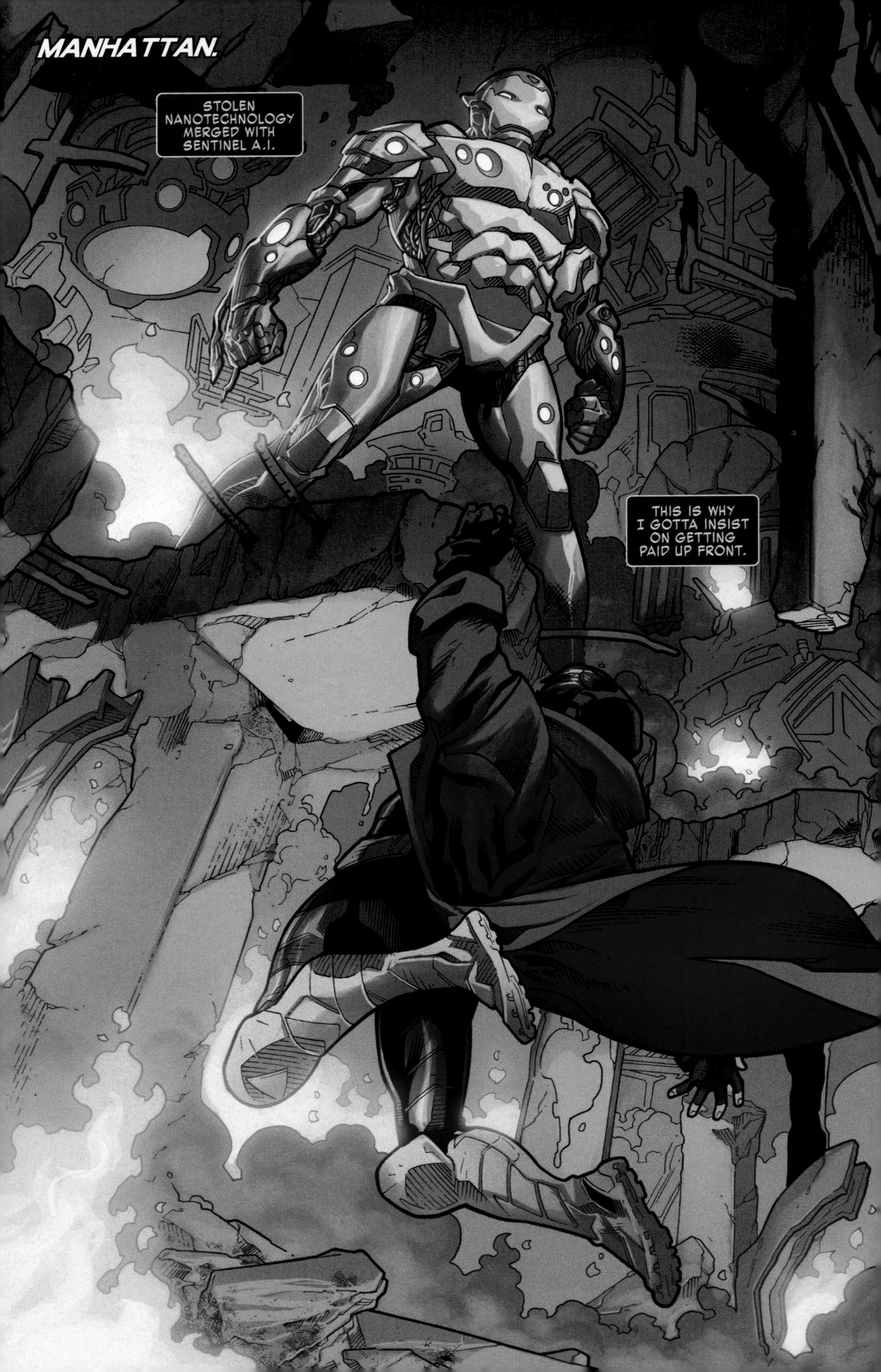
MANHATTAN.
STOLEN NANOTECHNOLOGY MERGED WITH SENTINEL A.I.
THIS IS WHY I GOTTA INSIST ON GETTING PAID UP FRONT.

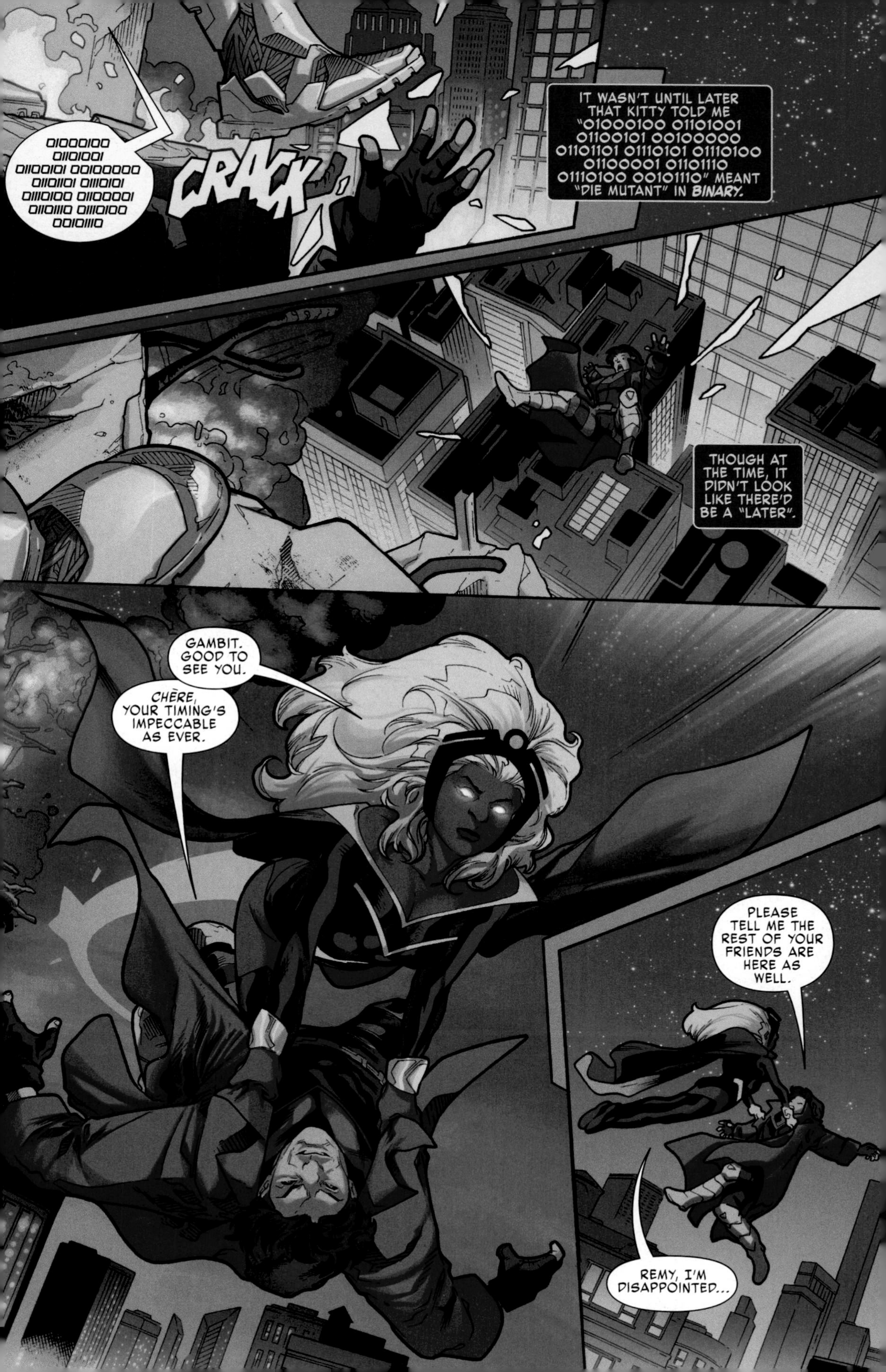

01000100 01101001 01100101 00100000 01101101 01110101 01110100 01100001 01101110 01110100 00101110
CRACK
IT WASN'T UNTIL LATER THAT KITTY TOLD ME "01000100 01101001 01100101 00100000 01101101 01110101 01110100 01100001 01101110 01110100 00101110" MEANT "DIE MUTANT" IN BINARY.
THOUGH AT THE TIME, IT DIDN'T LOOK LIKE THERE'D BE A "LATER".
GAMBIT. GOOD TO SEE YOU.
CHÈRE, YOUR TIMING'S IMPECCABLE AS EVER.
PLEASE TELL ME THE REST OF YOUR FRIENDS ARE HERE AS WELL.
REMY, I'M DISAPPOINTED...

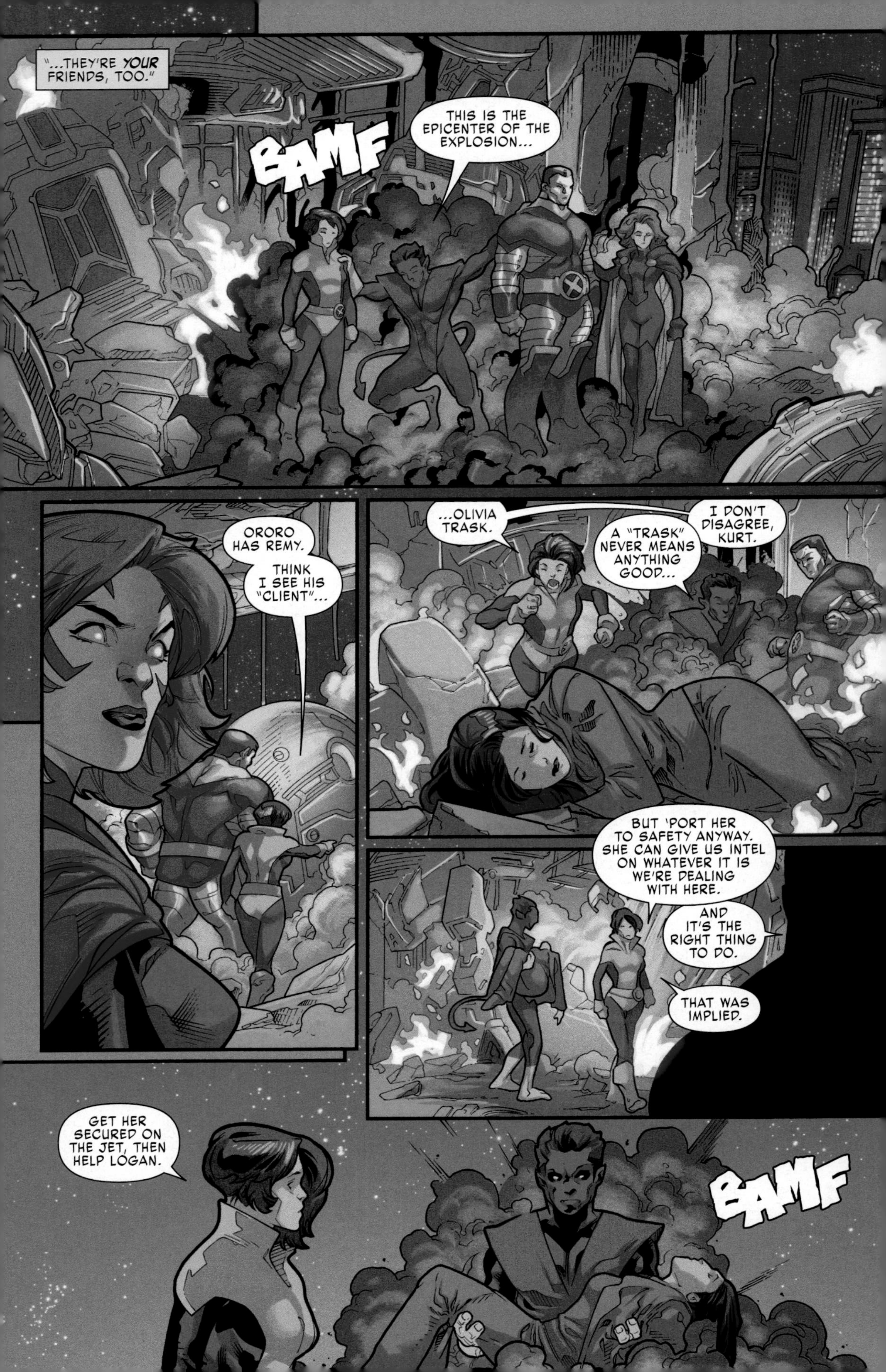
"...THEY'RE YOUR FRIENDS, TOO."
BAMF
THIS IS THE EPICENTER OF THE EXPLOSION...
ORORO HAS REMY.
THINK I SEE HIS "CLIENT"...
...OLIVIA TRASK.
A "TRASK" NEVER MEANS ANYTHING GOOD...
I DON'T DISAGREE, KURT.
BUT 'PORT HER TO SAFETY ANYWAY. SHE CAN GIVE US INTEL ON WHATEVER IT IS WE'RE DEALING WITH HERE.
AND IT'S THE RIGHT THING TO DO.
THAT WAS IMPLIED.
GET HER SECURED ON THE JET, THEN HELP LOGAN.
BAMF

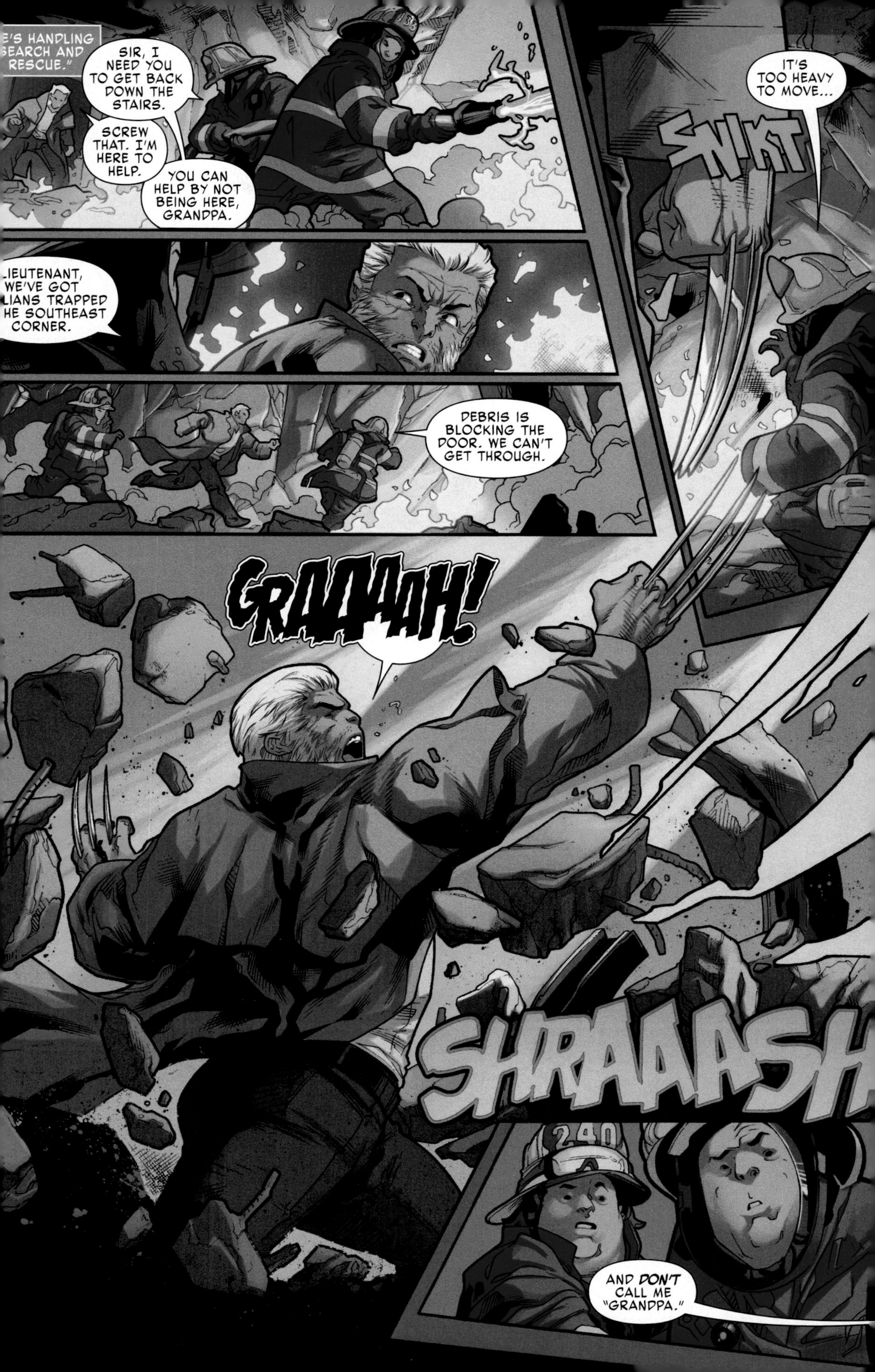
E'S HANDLING
SEARCH AND RESCUE."
SIR, I NEED YOU TO GET BACK DOWN THE STAIRS.
SCREW THAT. I'M HERE TO HELP.
YOU CAN HELP BY NOT BEING HERE, GRANDPA.
LIEUTENANT, WE'VE GOT
LIANS TRAPPED
HE SOUTHEAST CORNER.
DEBRIS IS BLOCKING THE DOOR. WE CAN'T GET THROUGH.
IT'S TOO HEAVY TO MOVE...
SNIKT
GRAAAAH!
SHRAAASH
AND DON'T CALL ME "GRANDPA."

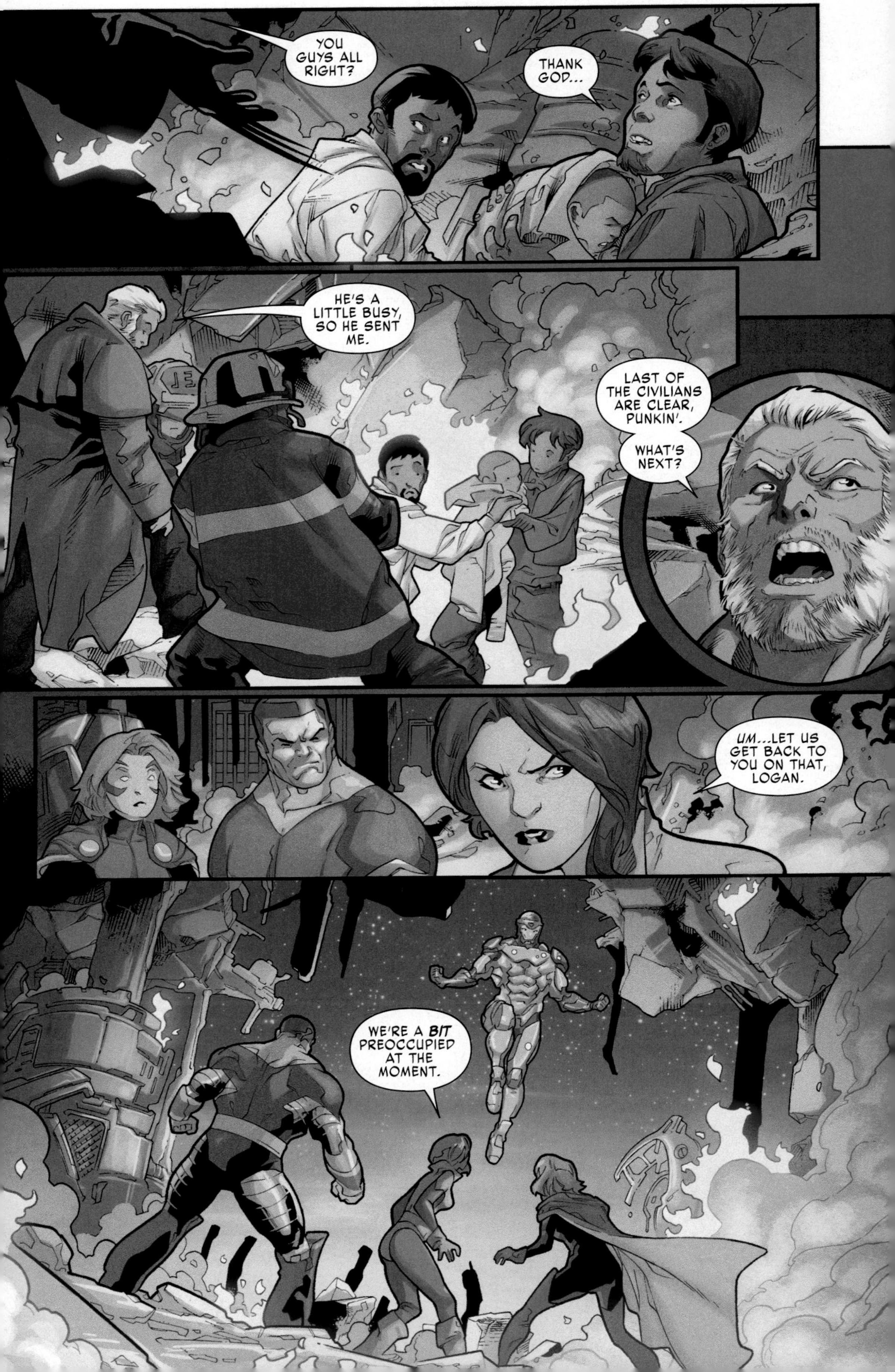
YOU GUYS ALL RIGHT?
THANK GOD...
HE'S A LITTLE BUSY, SO HE SENT ME.
LAST OF THE CIVILIANS ARE CLEAR, PUNKIN'.
WHAT'S NEXT?
UM...LET US GET BACK TO YOU ON THAT, LOGAN.
WE'RE A BIT PREOCCUPIED AT THE MOMENT.

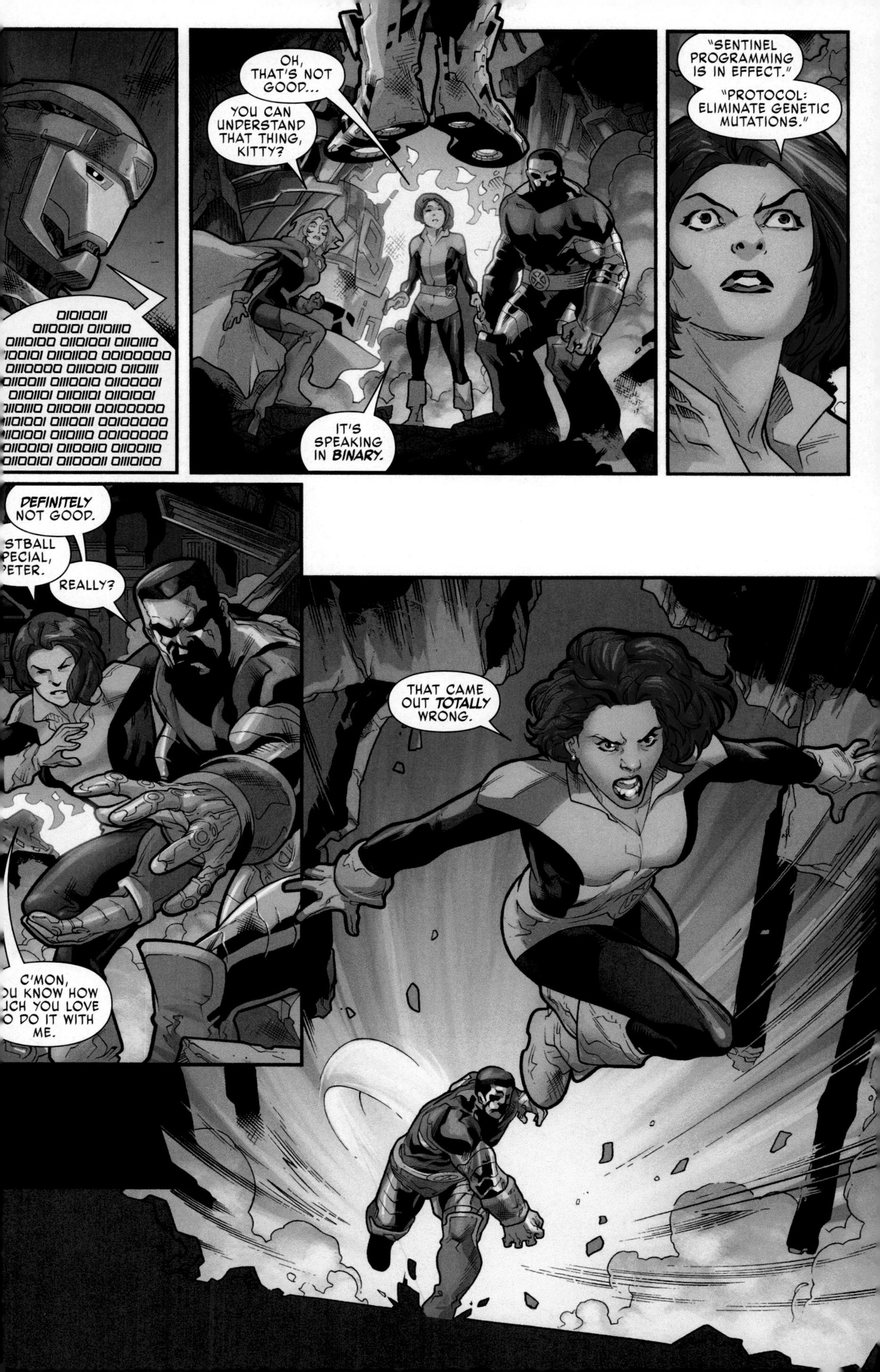
01010011
01100101 01101110
01110100 01101001 01101110
100101 01101100 00100000
01110000 01110010 01101111
01100111 01110010 01100001
01101101 01101101 01101001
1101110 01100111 00100000
1101001 01110011 00100000
1101001 01101110 00100000
01100101 01100110 01100110
01100101 01100011 01110100
OH, THAT'S NOT GOOD...
YOU CAN UNDERSTAND THAT THING, KITTY?
IT'S SPEAKING IN *BINARY*.
"SENTINEL PROGRAMMING IS IN EFFECT."
"PROTOCOL: ELIMINATE GENETIC MUTATIONS."
DEFINITELY NOT GOOD.
STBALL PECIAL, PETER.
REALLY?
C'MON, OU KNOW HOW UCH YOU LOVE O DO IT WITH ME.
THAT CAME OUT *TOTALLY* WRONG.

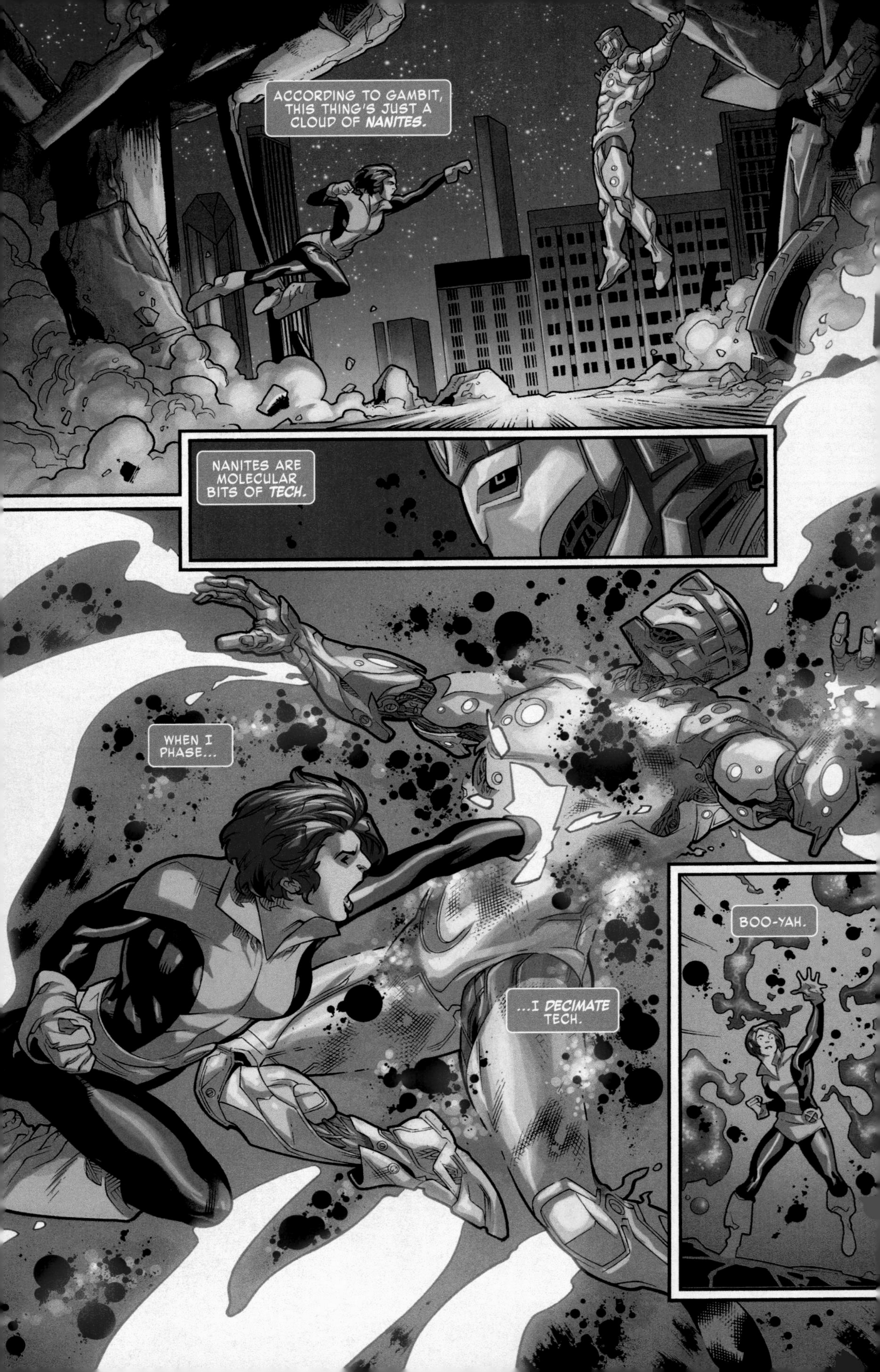
ACCORDING TO GAMBIT, THIS THING'S JUST A CLOUD OF *NANITES.*
NANITES ARE MOLECULAR BITS OF *TECH.*
WHEN I PHASE...
...I *DECIMATE* TECH.
BOO-YAH.

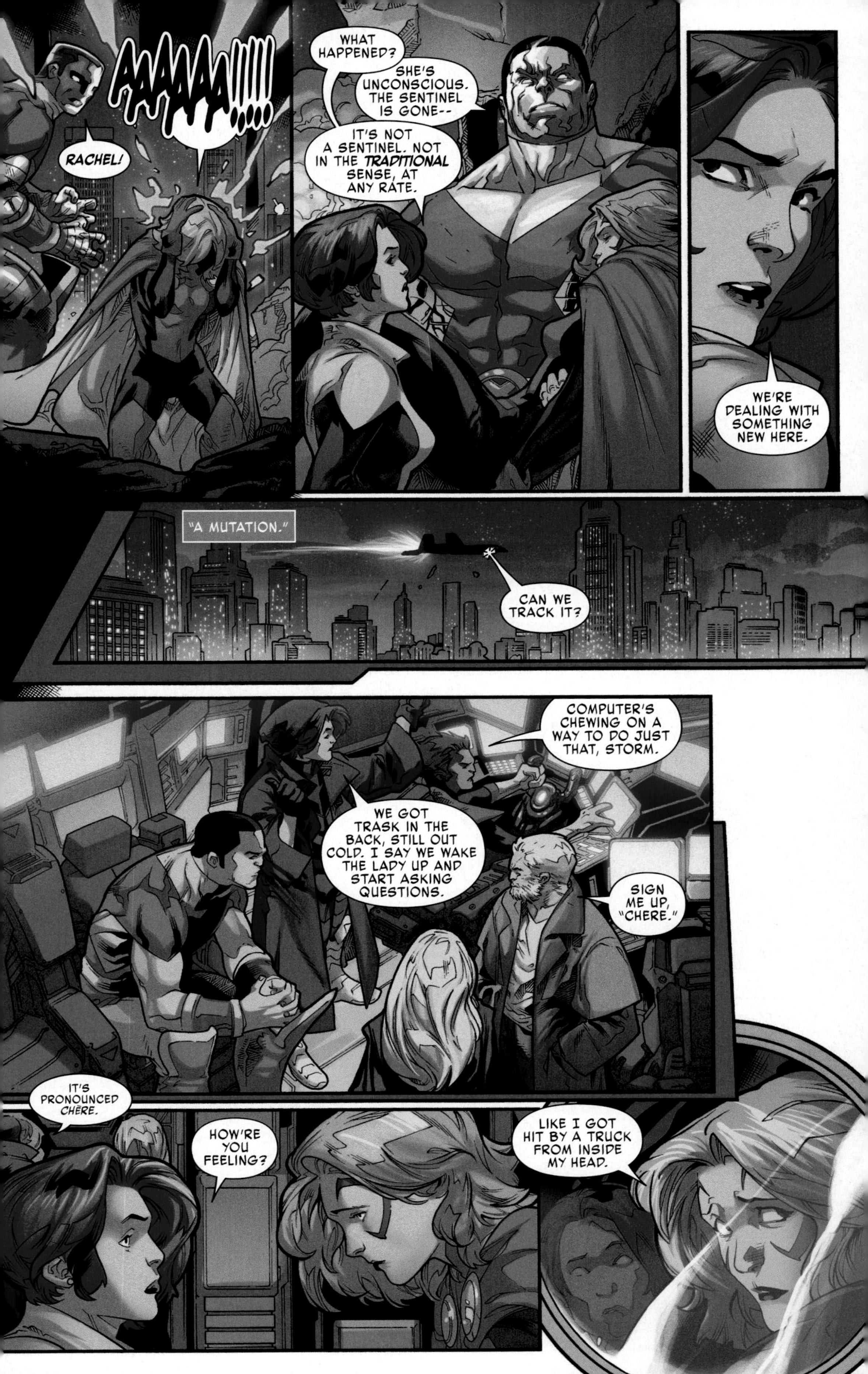
RACHEL!
AAAAAA!!!!!!
WHAT HAPPENED?
SHE'S UNCONSCIOUS. THE SENTINEL IS GONE--
IT'S NOT A SENTINEL. NOT IN THE TRADITIONAL SENSE, AT ANY RATE.
WE'RE DEALING WITH SOMETHING NEW HERE.
"A MUTATION."
CAN WE TRACK IT?
COMPUTER'S CHEWING ON A WAY TO DO JUST THAT, STORM.
WE GOT TRASK IN THE BACK, STILL OUT COLD. I SAY WE WAKE THE LADY UP AND START ASKING QUESTIONS.
SIGN ME UP, "CHERE."
IT'S PRONOUNCED CHÈRE.
HOW'RE YOU FEELING?
LIKE I GOT HIT BY A TRUCK FROM INSIDE MY HEAD.

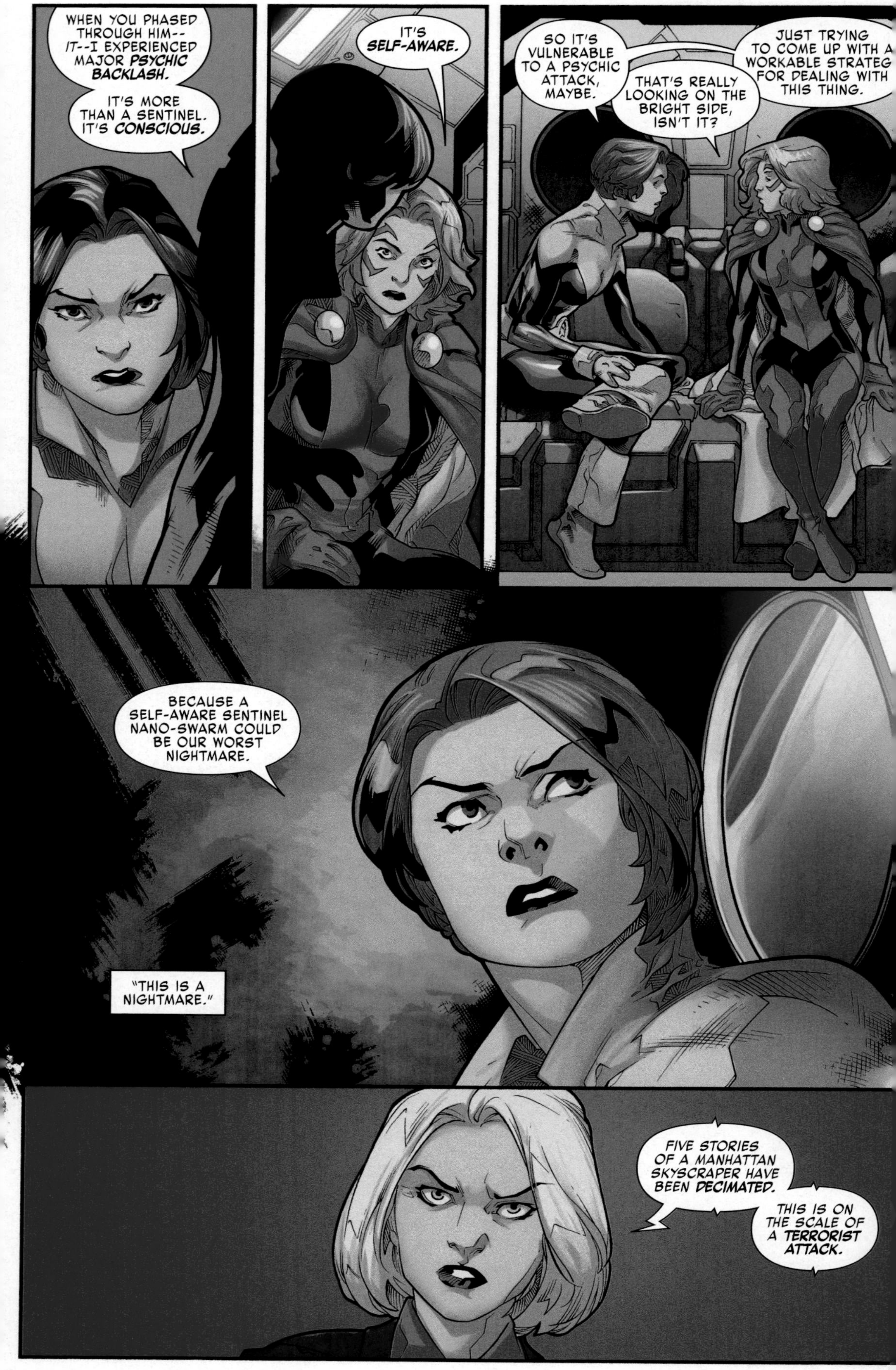
WHEN YOU PHASED THROUGH HIM-- IT--I EXPERIENCED MAJOR PSYCHIC BACKLASH.
IT'S MORE THAN A SENTINEL. IT'S CONSCIOUS.
IT'S SELF-AWARE.
SO IT'S VULNERABLE TO A PSYCHIC ATTACK, MAYBE.
THAT'S REALLY LOOKING ON THE BRIGHT SIDE, ISN'T IT?
JUST TRYING TO COME UP WITH A WORKABLE STRATEG FOR DEALING WITH THIS THING.
BECAUSE A SELF-AWARE SENTINEL NANO-SWARM COULD BE OUR WORST NIGHTMARE.
"THIS IS A NIGHTMARE."
FIVE STORIES OF A MANHATTAN SKYSCRAPER HAVE BEEN DECIMATED.
THIS IS ON THE SCALE OF A TERRORIST ATTACK.

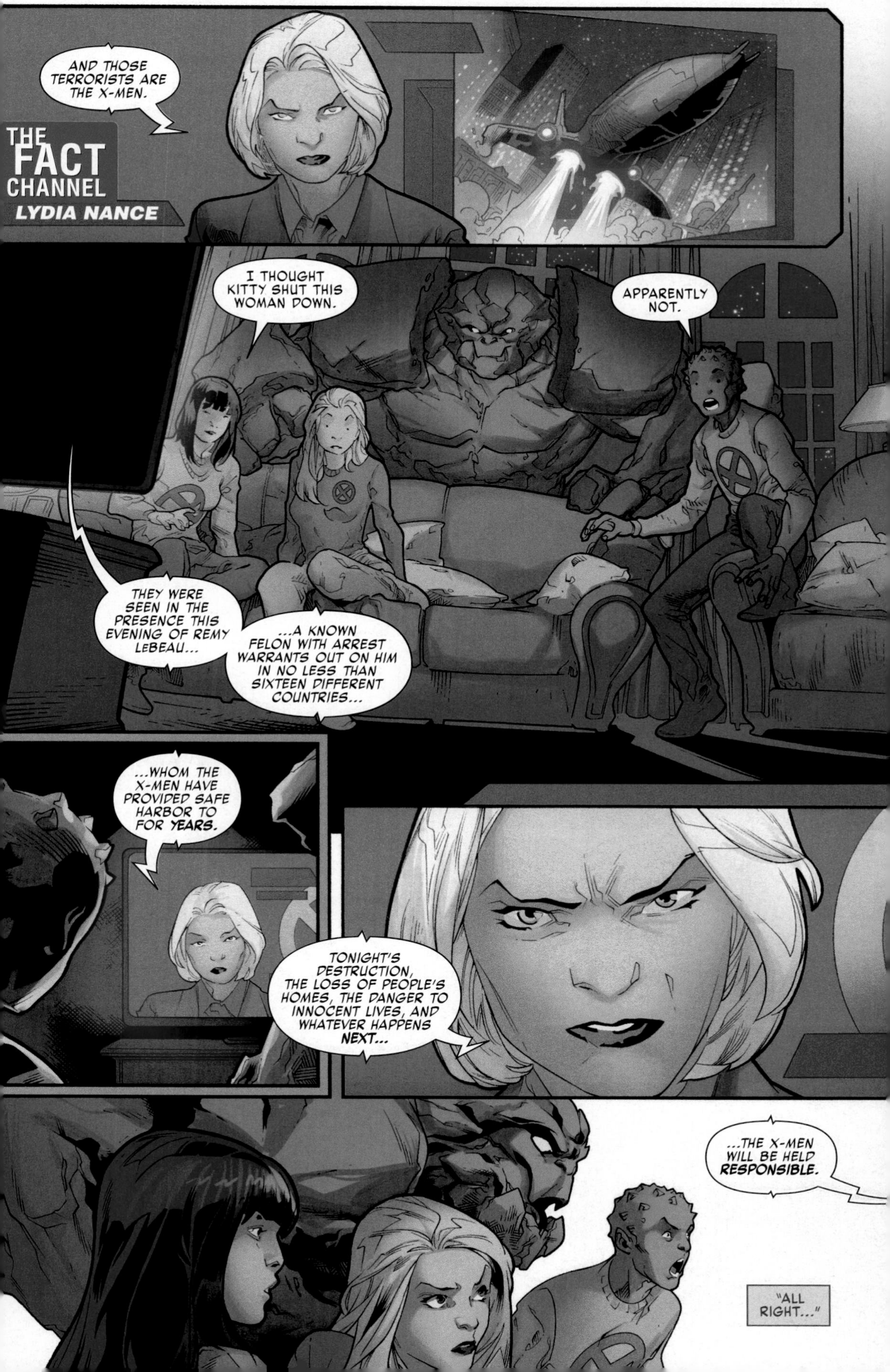
AND THOSE TERRORISTS ARE THE X-MEN.
THE FACT CHANNEL
LYDIA NANCE
I THOUGHT KITTY SHUT THIS WOMAN DOWN.
APPARENTLY NOT.
THEY WERE SEEN IN THE PRESENCE THIS EVENING OF REMY LeBEAU...
...A KNOWN FELON WITH ARREST WARRANTS OUT ON HIM IN NO LESS THAN SIXTEEN DIFFERENT COUNTRIES...
...WHOM THE X-MEN HAVE PROVIDED SAFE HARBOR TO FOR YEARS.
TONIGHT'S DESTRUCTION, THE LOSS OF PEOPLE'S HOMES, THE DANGER TO INNOCENT LIVES, AND WHATEVER HAPPENS NEXT...
...THE X-MEN WILL BE HELD RESPONSIBLE.
"ALL RIGHT..."

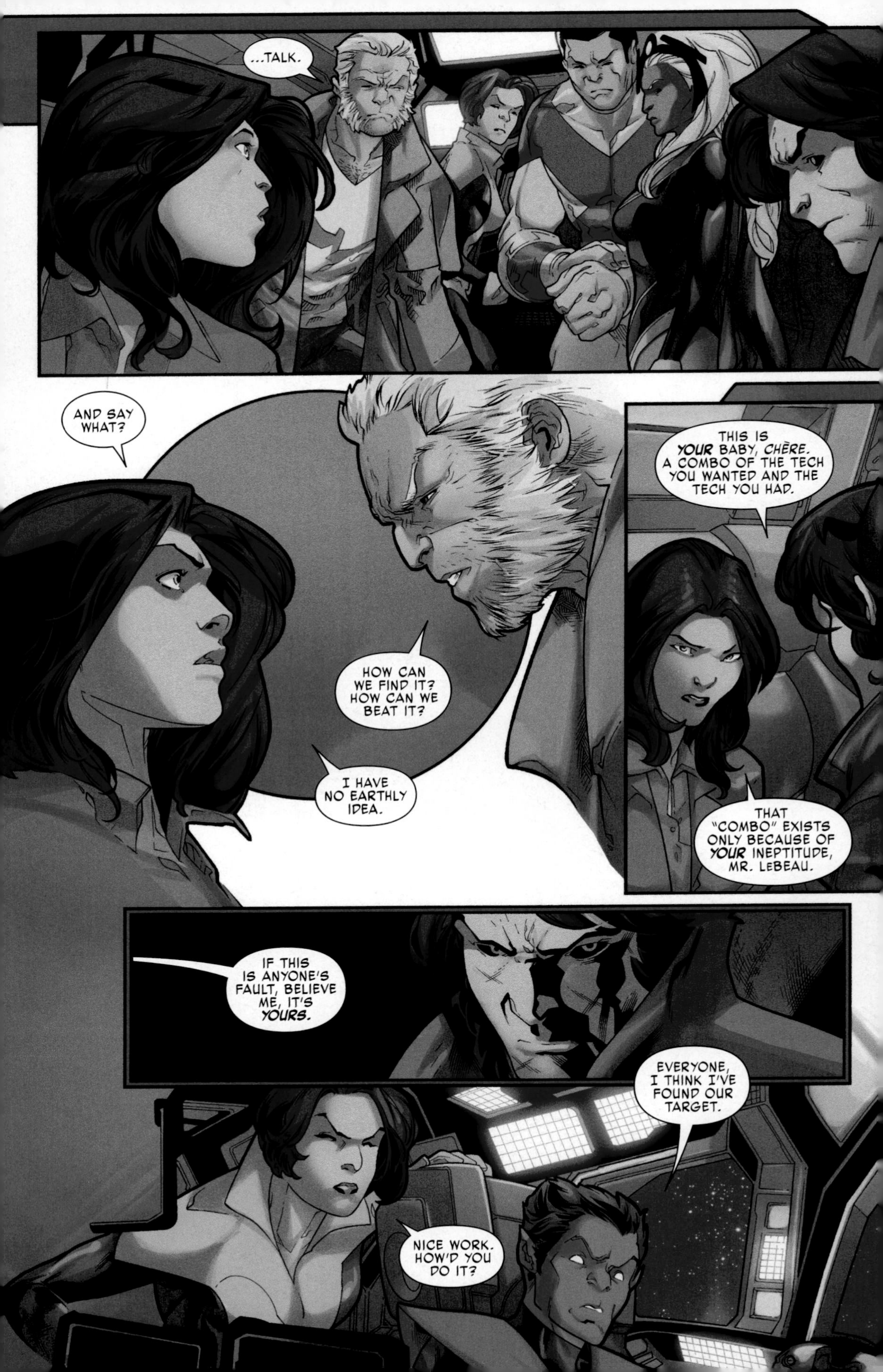
...TALK.
AND SAY WHAT?
HOW CAN WE FIND IT? HOW CAN WE BEAT IT?
I HAVE NO EARTHLY IDEA.
THIS IS *YOUR* BABY, *CHÈRE*. A COMBO OF THE TECH YOU WANTED AND THE TECH YOU HAD.
THAT "COMBO" EXISTS ONLY BECAUSE OF *YOUR* INEPTITUDE, MR. LEBEAU.
IF THIS IS ANYONE'S FAULT, BELIEVE ME, IT'S *YOURS.*
EVERYONE, I THINK I'VE FOUND OUR TARGET.
NICE WORK. HOW'D YOU DO IT?

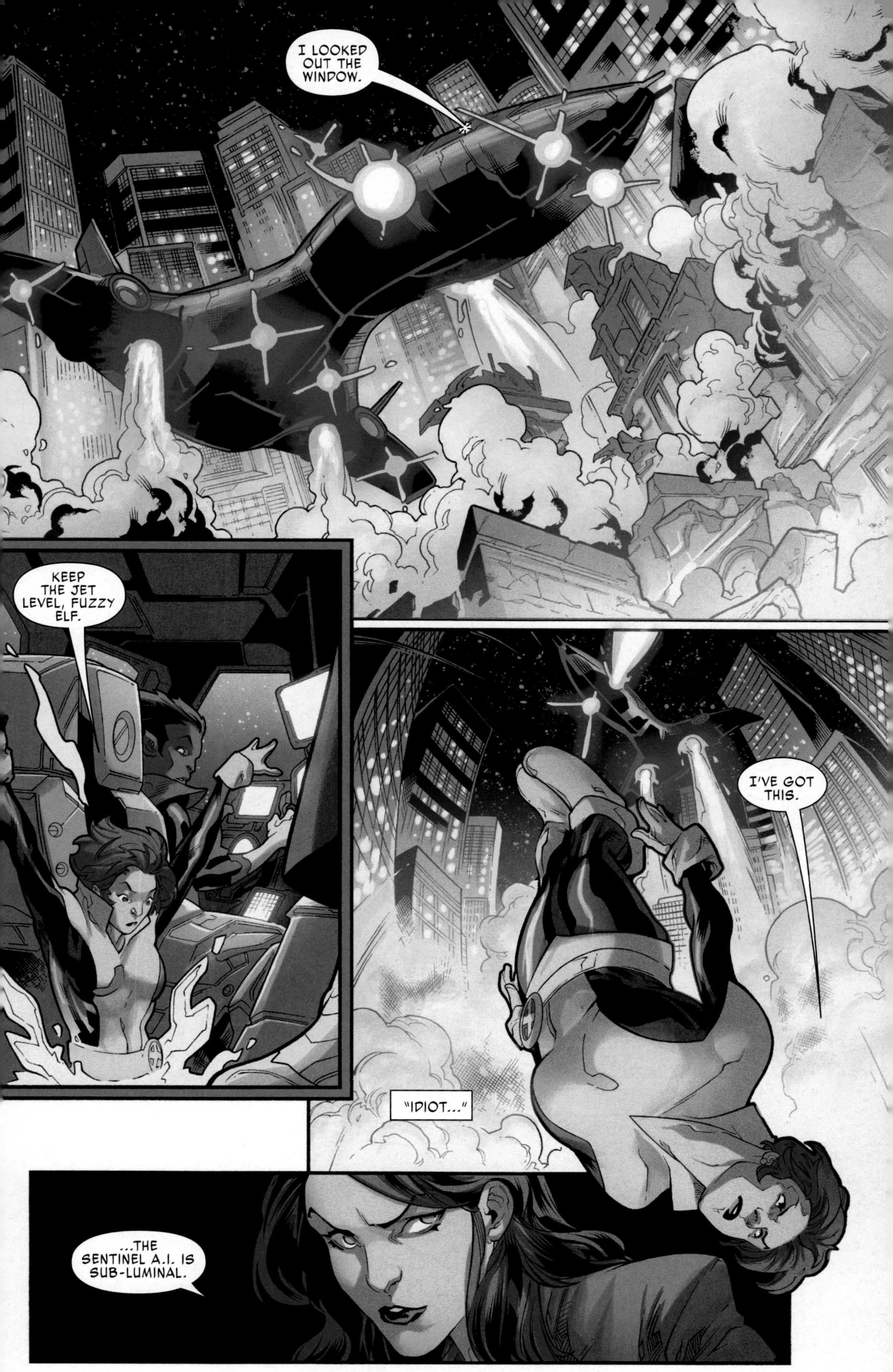
I LOOKED OUT THE WINDOW.
KEEP THE JET LEVEL, FUZZY ELF.
I'VE GOT THIS.
"IDIOT..."
...THE SENTINEL A.I. IS SUB-LUMINAL.

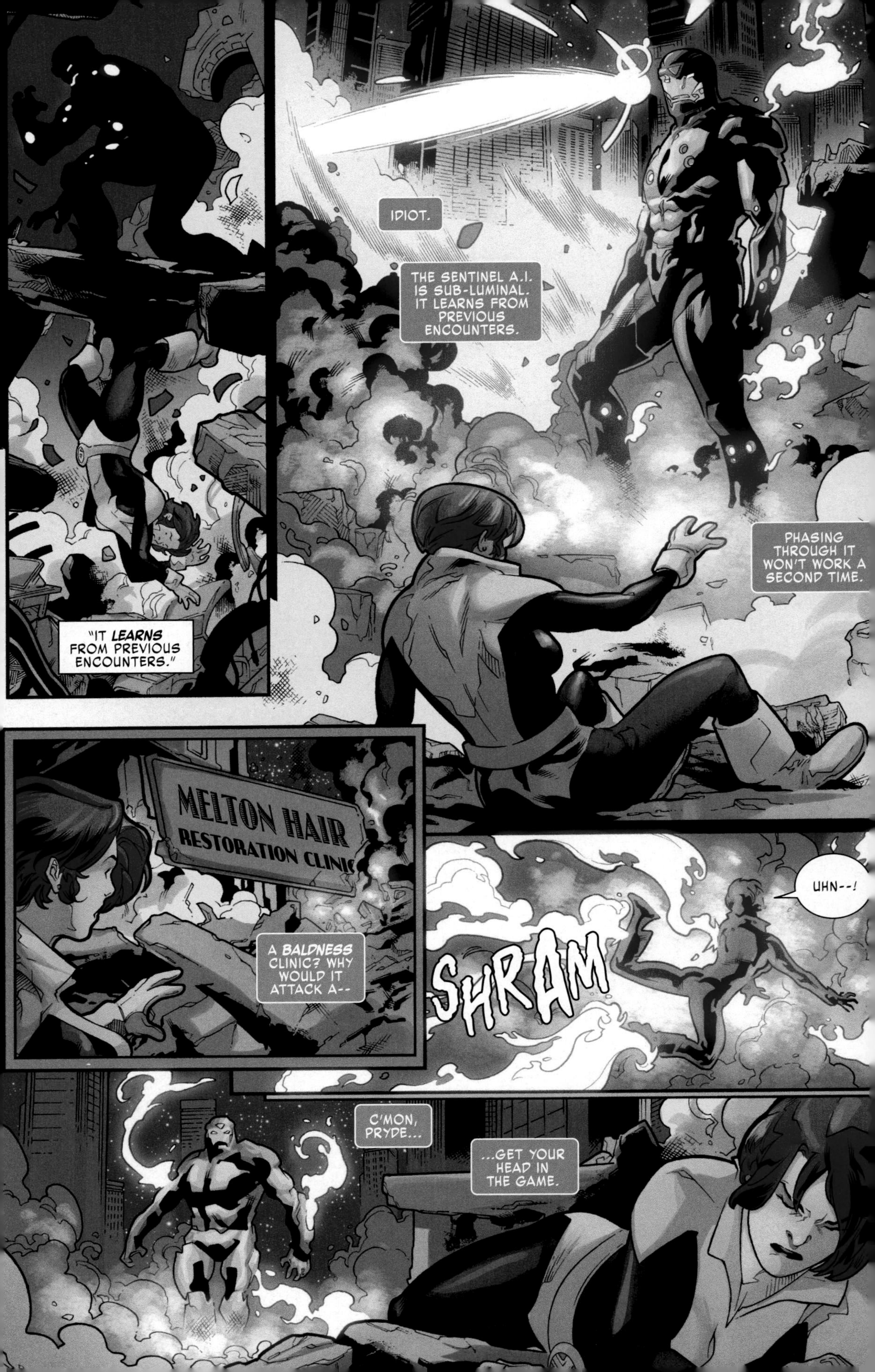
"IT LEARNS FROM PREVIOUS ENCOUNTERS."
IDIOT.
THE SENTINEL A.I. IS SUB-LUMINAL. IT LEARNS FROM PREVIOUS ENCOUNTERS.
PHASING THROUGH IT WON'T WORK A SECOND TIME.
MELTON HAIR RESTORATION CLINIC
A BALDNESS CLINIC? WHY WOULD IT ATTACK A--
SHRAM
UHN--!
C'MON, PRYDE...
...GET YOUR HEAD IN THE GAME.

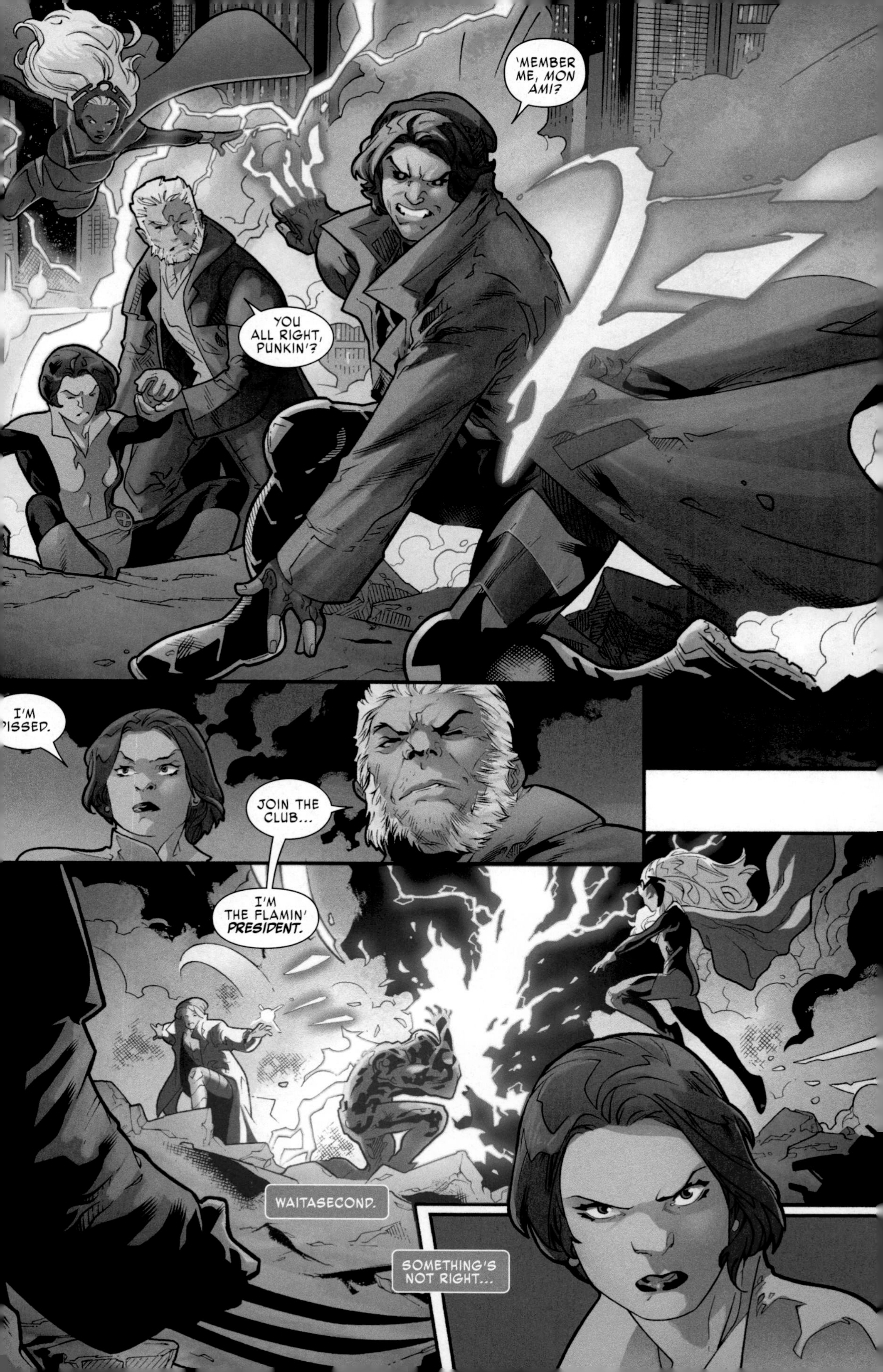
'MEMBER ME, MON AMI?
YOU ALL RIGHT, PUNKIN'?
I'M PISSED.
JOIN THE CLUB...
I'M THE FLAMIN' PRESIDENT.
WAITASECOND.
SOMETHING'S NOT RIGHT...

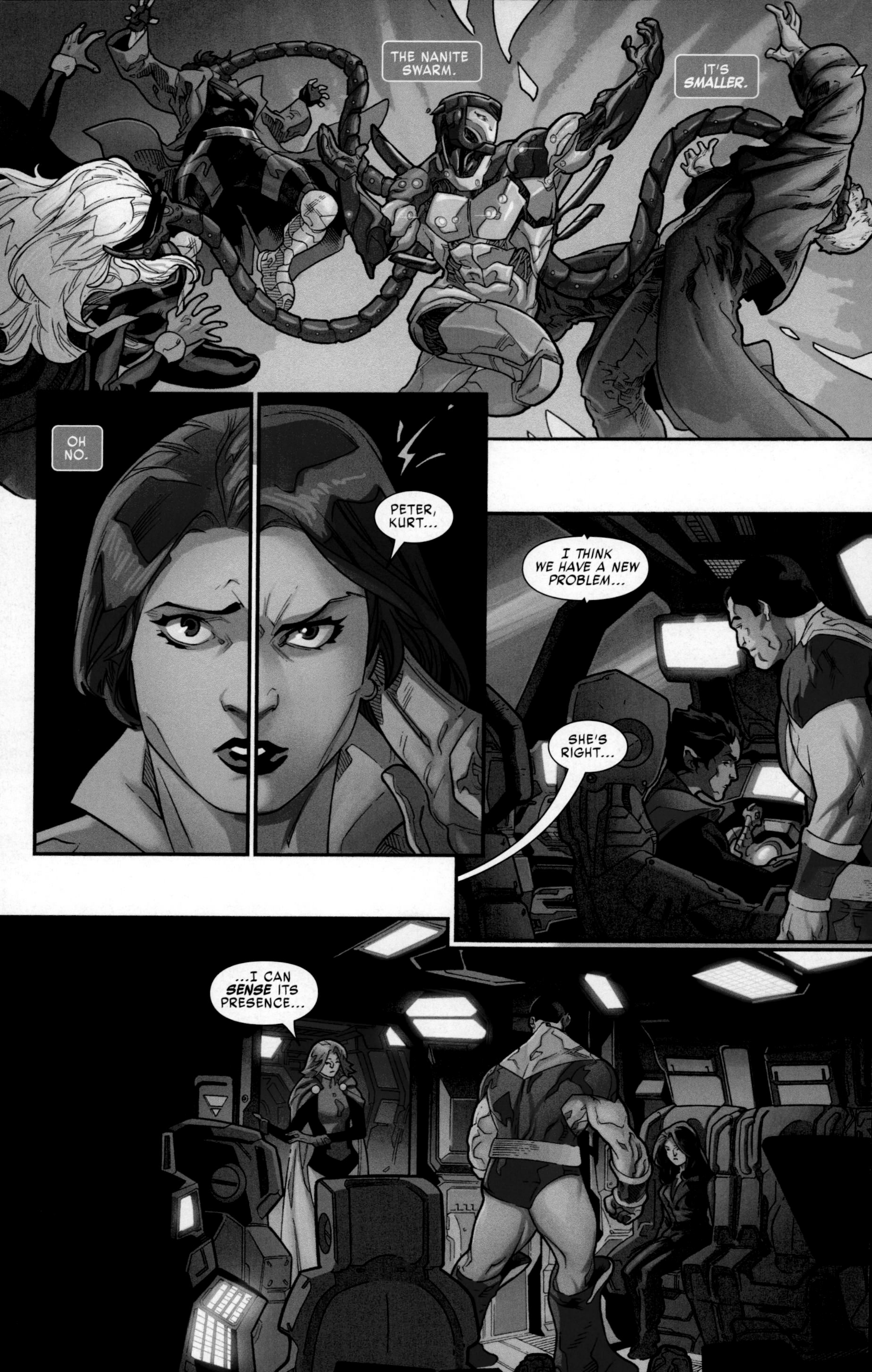
THE NANITE SWARM.
IT'S SMALLER.
OH NO.
PETER, KURT...
I THINK WE HAVE A NEW PROBLEM...
SHE'S RIGHT...
...I CAN SENSE ITS PRESENCE...

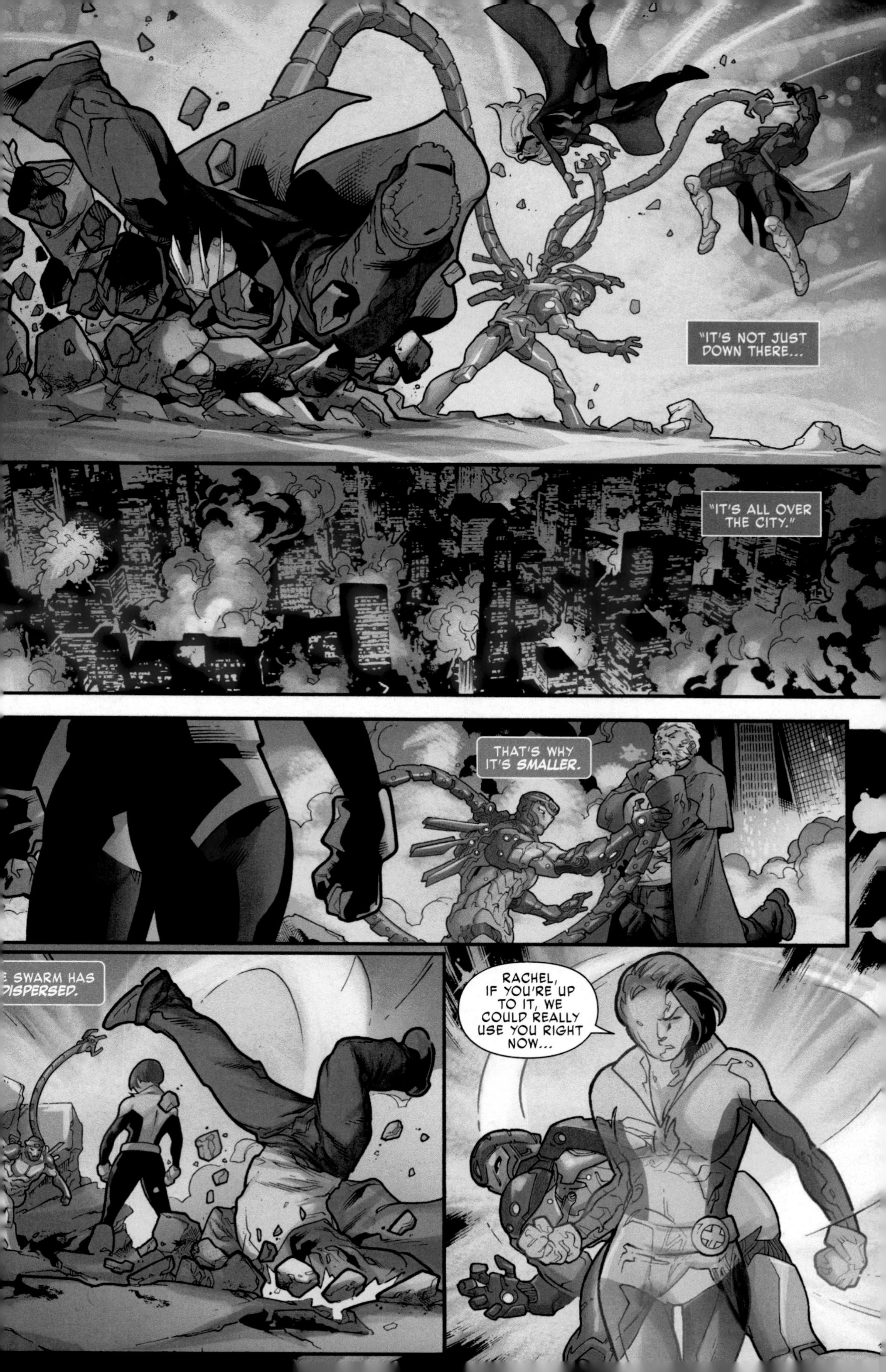
"IT'S NOT JUST DOWN THERE...
"IT'S ALL OVER THE CITY."
THAT'S WHY IT'S SMALLER.
SWARM HAS DISPERSED.
RACHEL, IF YOU'RE UP TO IT, WE COULD REALLY USE YOU RIGHT NOW...

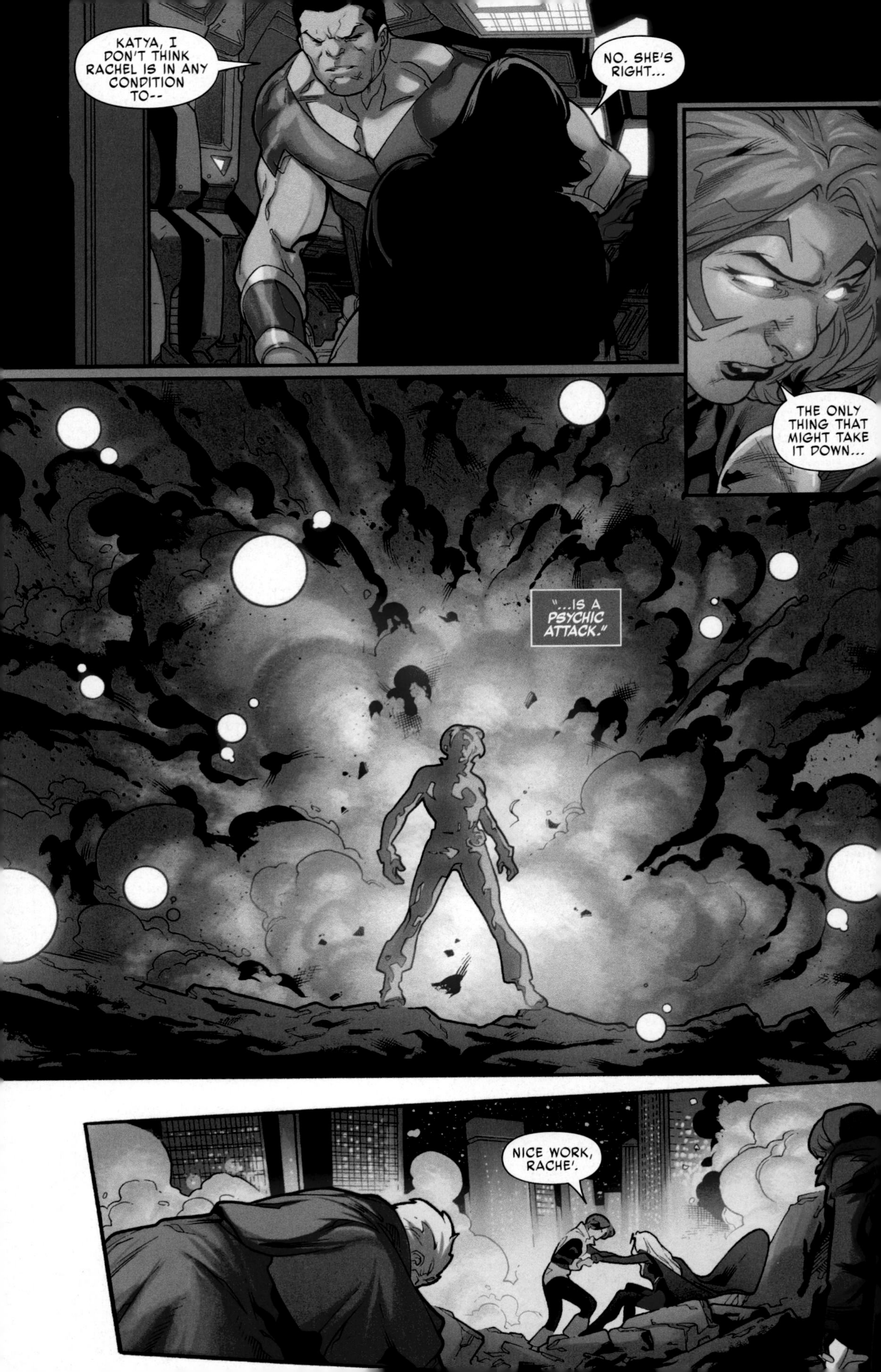
KATYA, I DON'T THINK RACHEL IS IN ANY CONDITION TO--
NO. SHE'S RIGHT...
THE ONLY THING THAT MIGHT TAKE IT DOWN...
"...IS A PSYCHIC ATTACK."
NICE WORK, RACHE'.

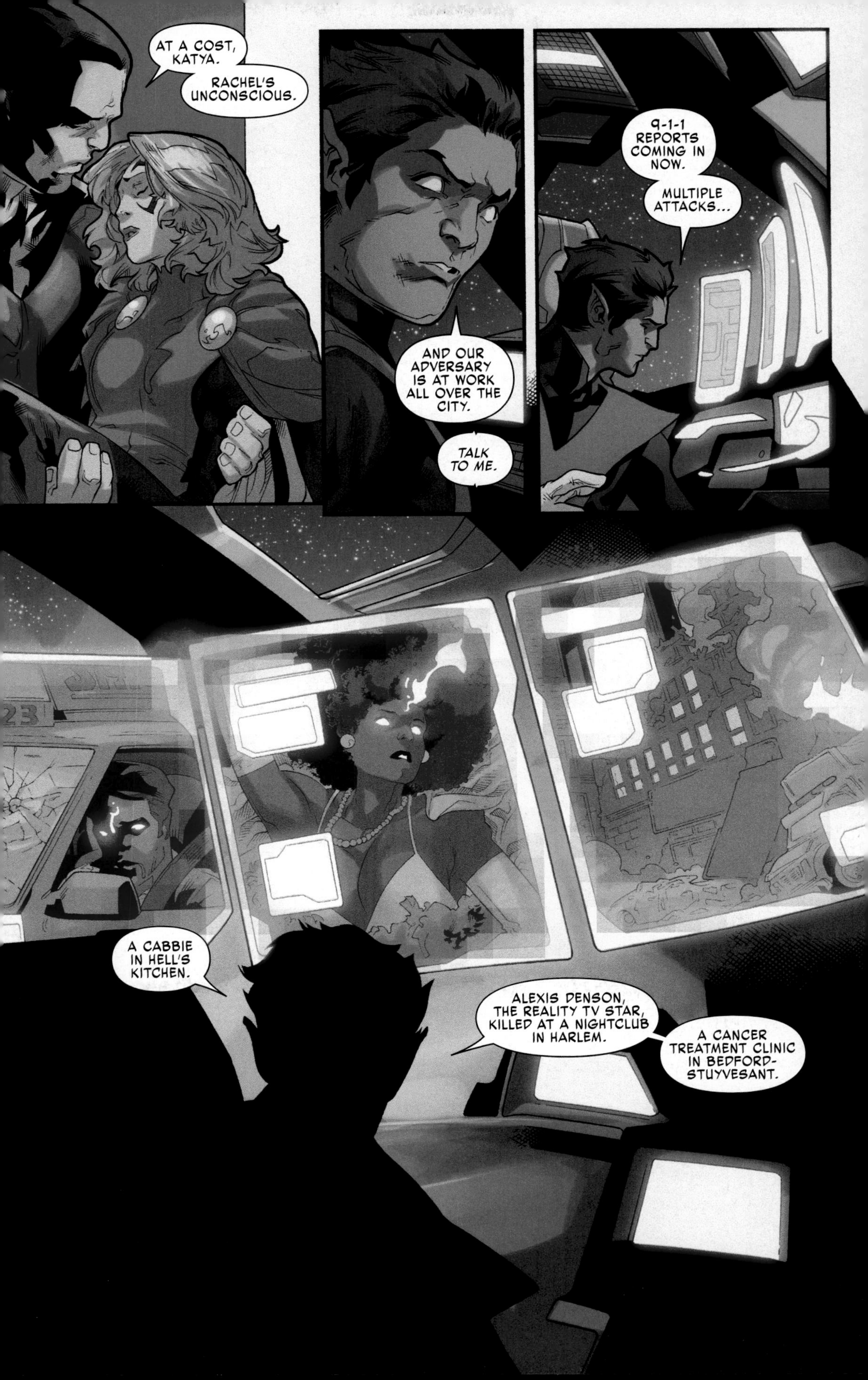
AT A COST, KATYA.
RACHEL'S UNCONSCIOUS.
AND OUR ADVERSARY IS AT WORK ALL OVER THE CITY.
TALK TO ME.
9-1-1 REPORTS COMING IN NOW.
MULTIPLE ATTACKS...
A CABBIE IN HELL'S KITCHEN.
ALEXIS DENSON, THE REALITY TV STAR, KILLED AT A NIGHTCLUB IN HARLEM.
A CANCER TREATMENT CLINIC IN BEDFORD-STUYVESANT.

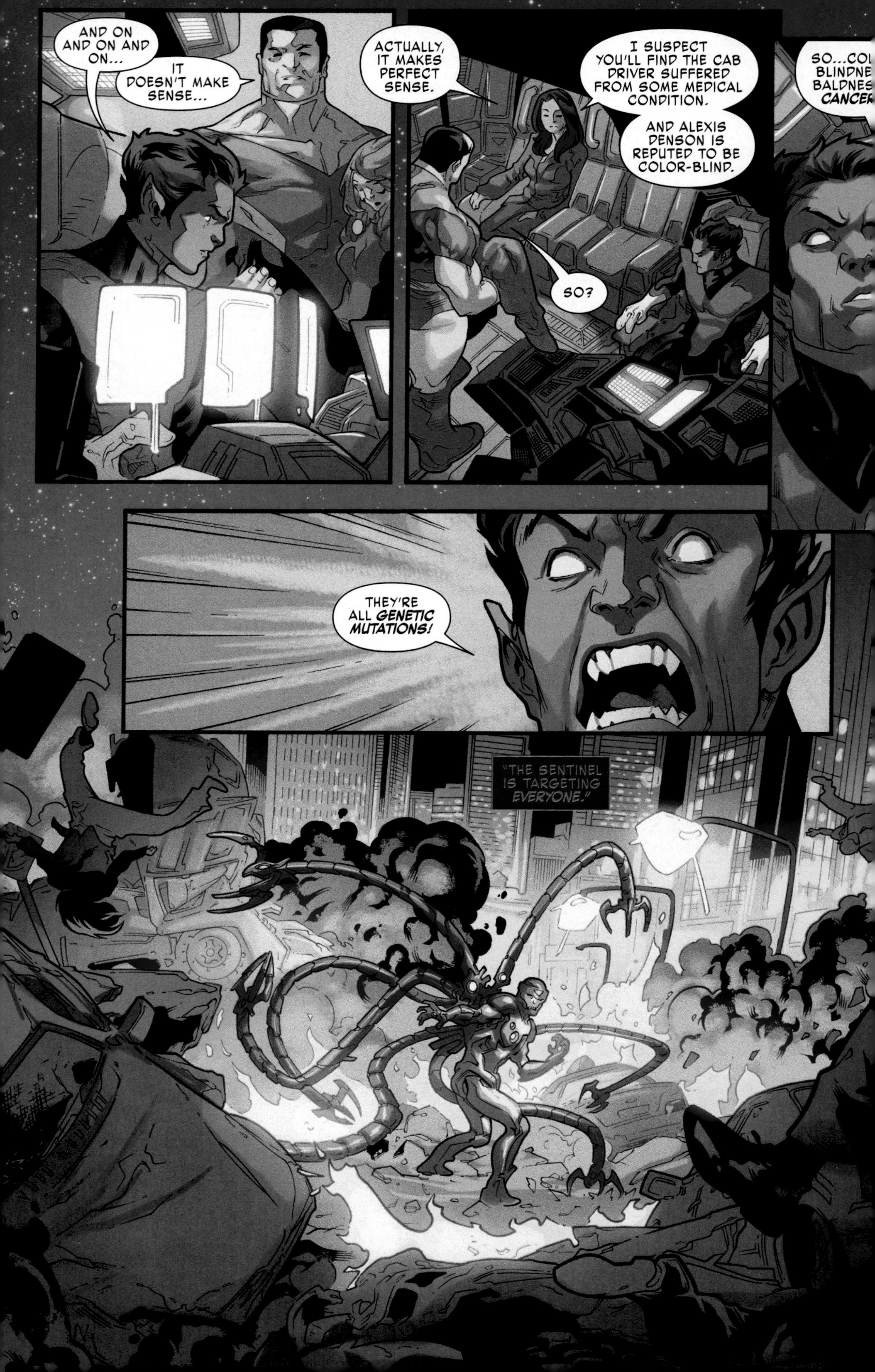
AND ON AND ON AND ON...
IT DOESN'T MAKE SENSE...
ACTUALLY, IT MAKES PERFECT SENSE.
I SUSPECT YOU'LL FIND THE CAB DRIVER SUFFERED FROM SOME MEDICAL CONDITION.
AND ALEXIS DENSON IS REPUTED TO BE COLOR-BLIND.
SO?
THEY'RE ALL GENETIC MUTATIONS!
"THE SENTINEL IS TARGETING EVERYONE."

6

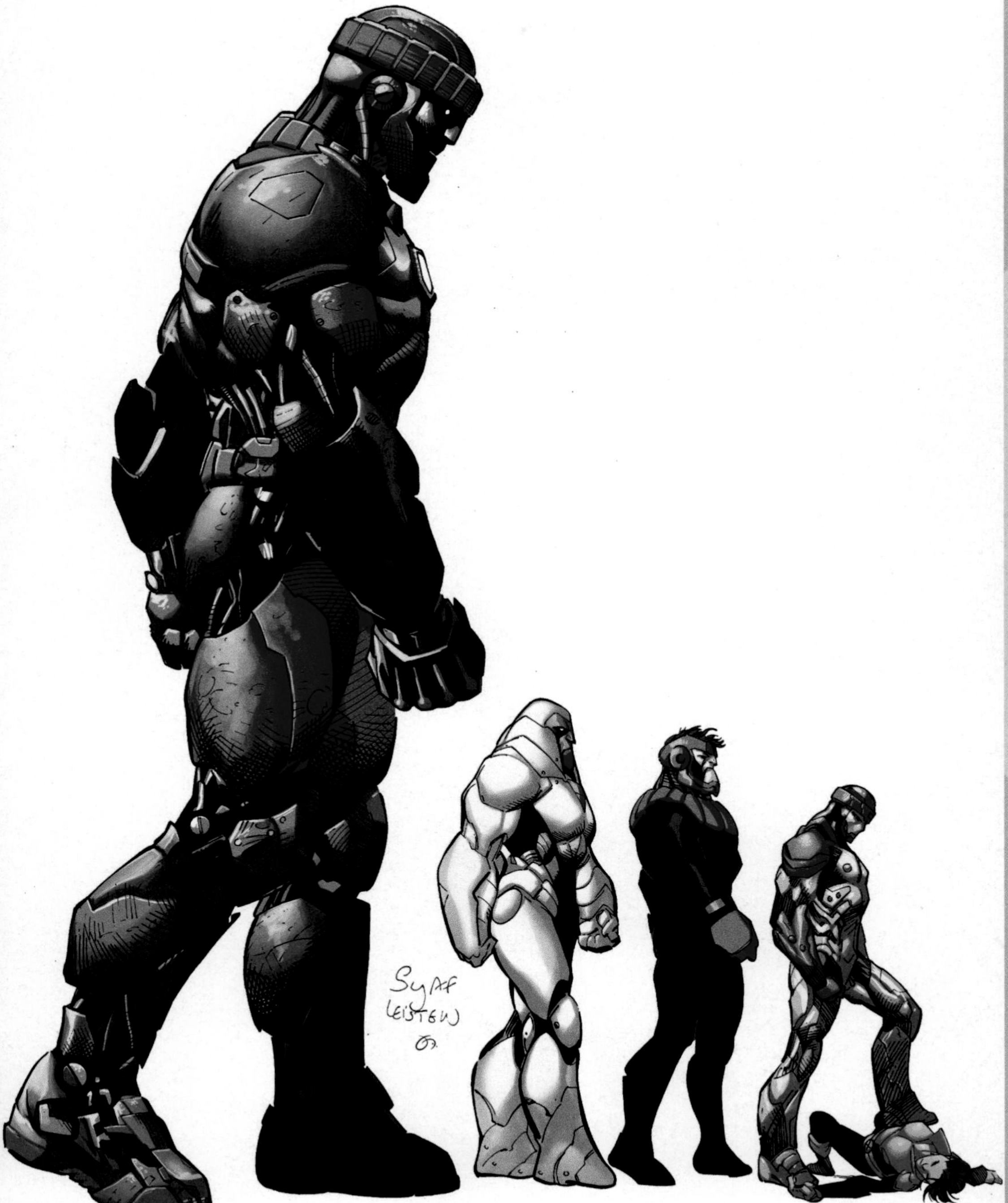

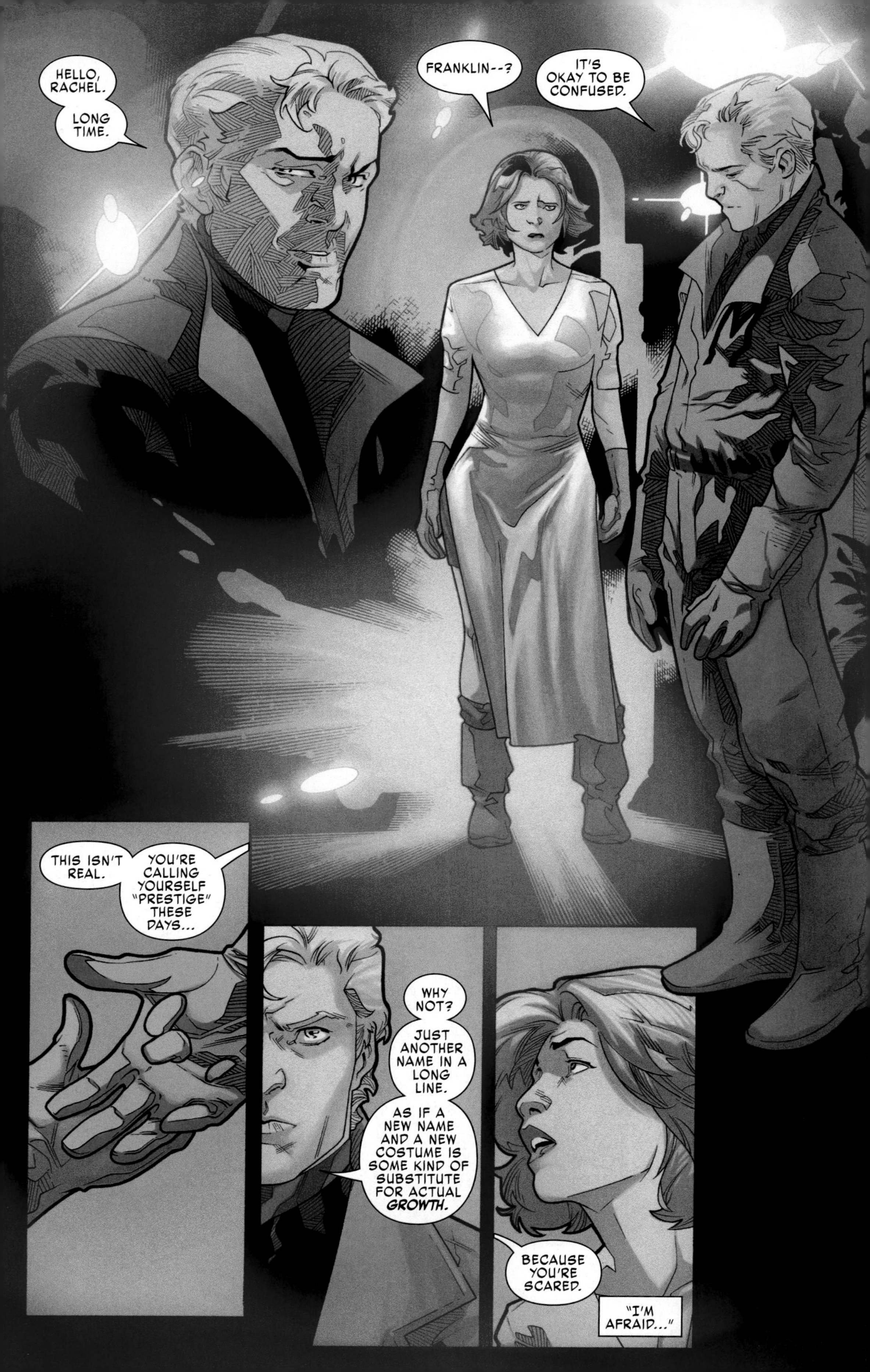
HELLO, RACHEL.
LONG TIME.
FRANKLIN--?
IT'S OKAY TO BE CONFUSED.
THIS ISN'T REAL.
YOU'RE CALLING YOURSELF "PRESTIGE" THESE DAYS...
WHY NOT?
JUST ANOTHER NAME IN A LONG LINE.
AS IF A NEW NAME AND A NEW COSTUME IS SOME KIND OF SUBSTITUTE FOR ACTUAL GROWTH.
BECAUSE YOU'RE SCARED.
"I'M AFRAID..."

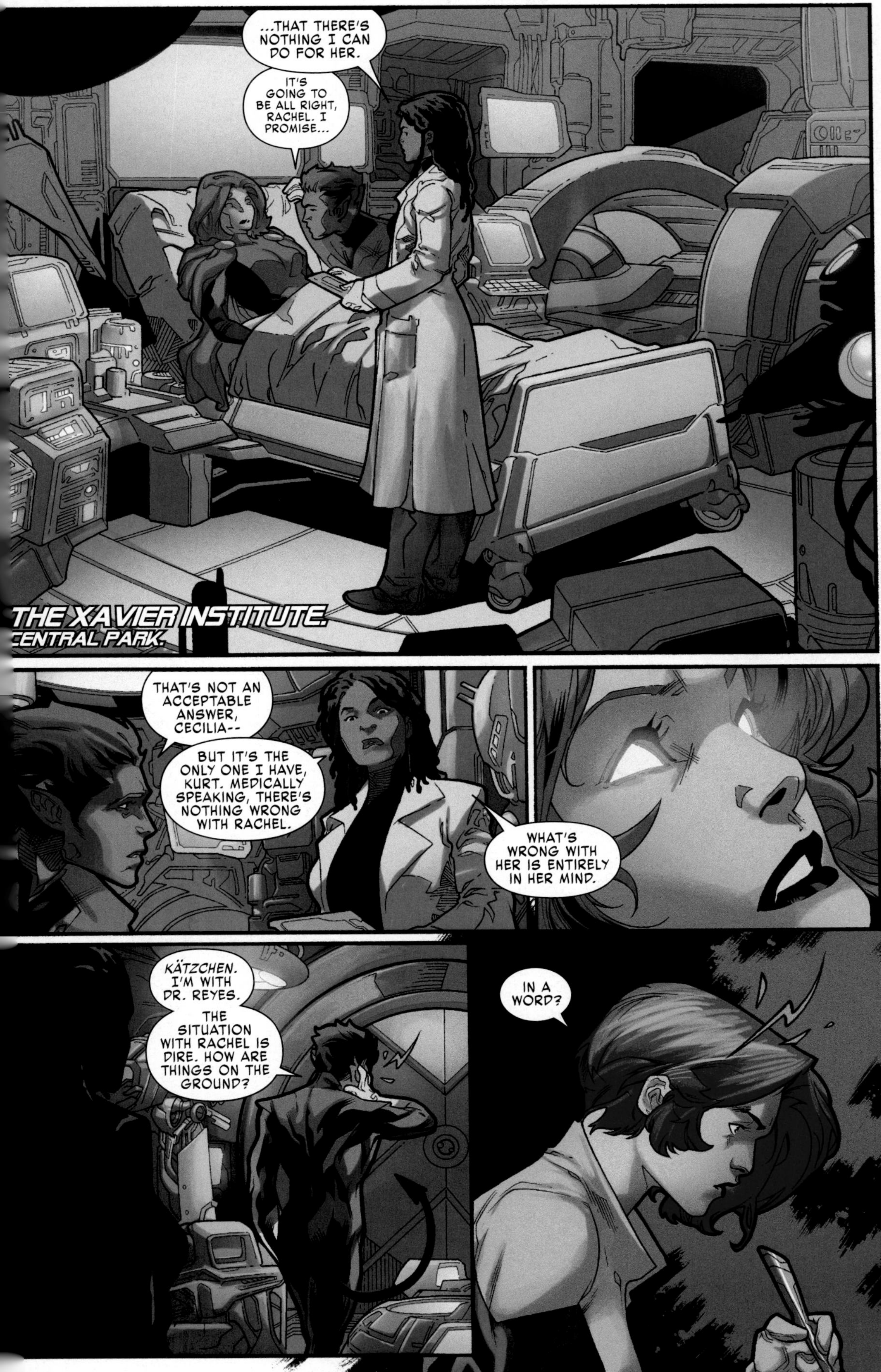
...THAT THERE'S NOTHING I CAN DO FOR HER.
IT'S GOING TO BE ALL RIGHT, RACHEL. I PROMISE...
THE XAVIER INSTITUTE. CENTRAL PARK.
THAT'S NOT AN ACCEPTABLE ANSWER, CECILIA--
BUT IT'S THE ONLY ONE I HAVE, KURT. MEDICALLY SPEAKING, THERE'S NOTHING WRONG WITH RACHEL.
WHAT'S WRONG WITH HER IS ENTIRELY IN HER MIND.
KÄTZCHEN. I'M WITH DR. REYES.
THE SITUATION WITH RACHEL IS DIRE. HOW ARE THINGS ON THE GROUND?
IN A WORD?

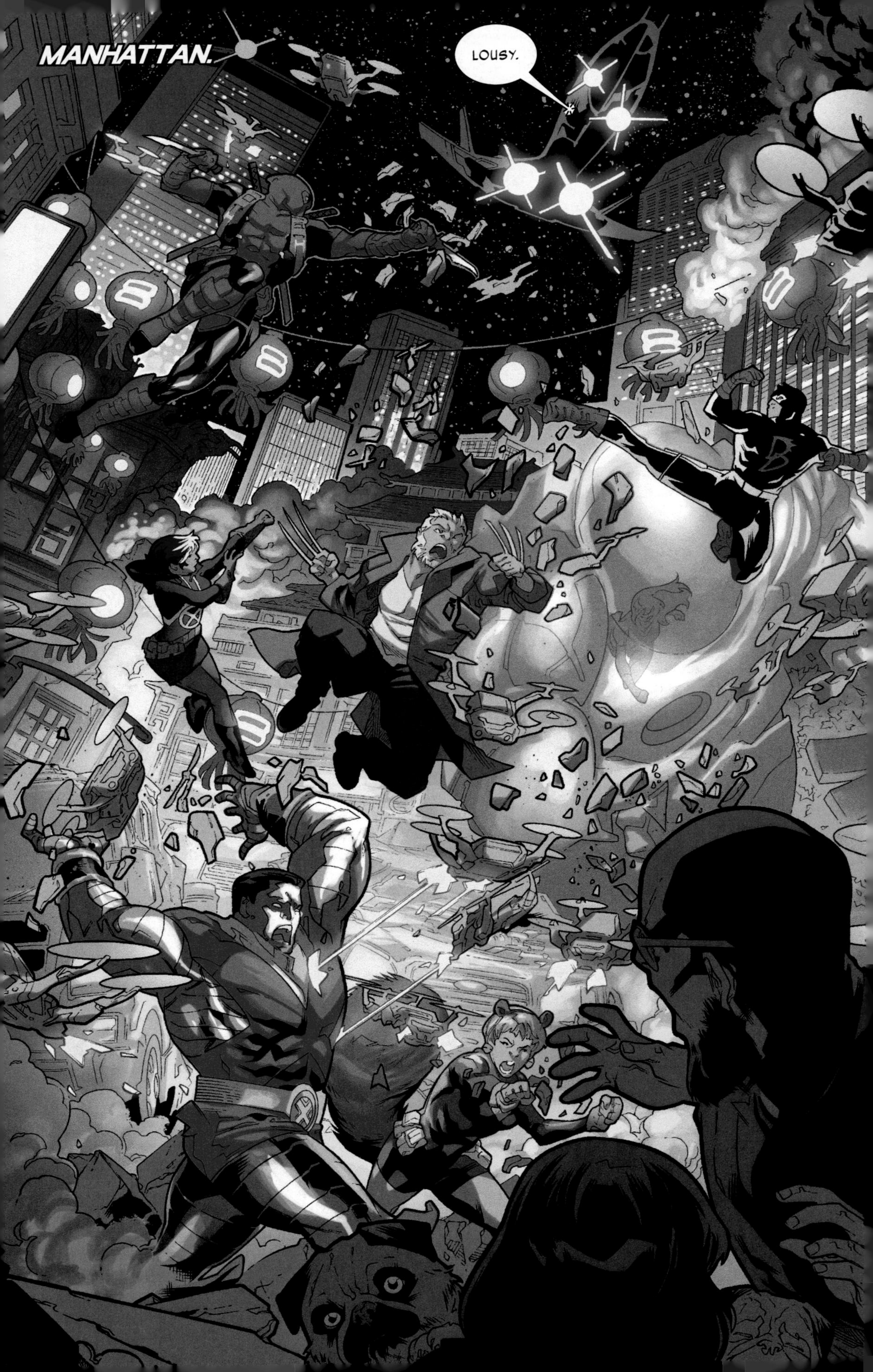
MANHATTAN.
LOUSY.

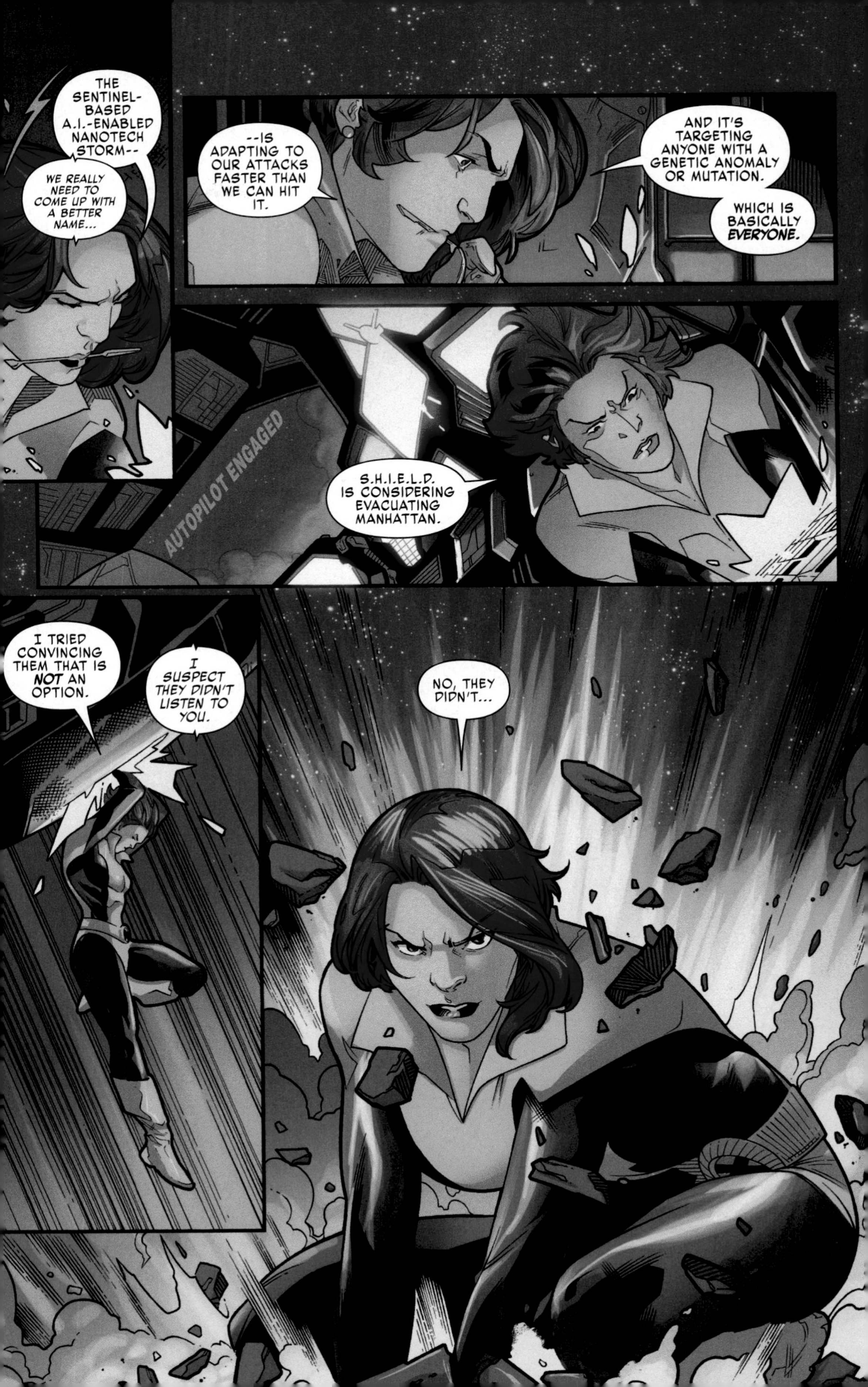
THE SENTINEL-BASED A.I.-ENABLED NANOTECH STORM--
WE REALLY NEED TO COME UP WITH A BETTER NAME...
--IS ADAPTING TO OUR ATTACKS FASTER THAN WE CAN HIT IT.
AND IT'S TARGETING ANYONE WITH A GENETIC ANOMALY OR MUTATION.
WHICH IS BASICALLY *EVERYONE.*
AUTOPILOT ENGAGED
S.H.I.E.L.D. IS CONSIDERING EVACUATING MANHATTAN.
I TRIED CONVINCING THEM THAT IS *NOT* AN OPTION.
I SUSPECT THEY DIDN'T LISTEN TO YOU.
NO, THEY DIDN'T...

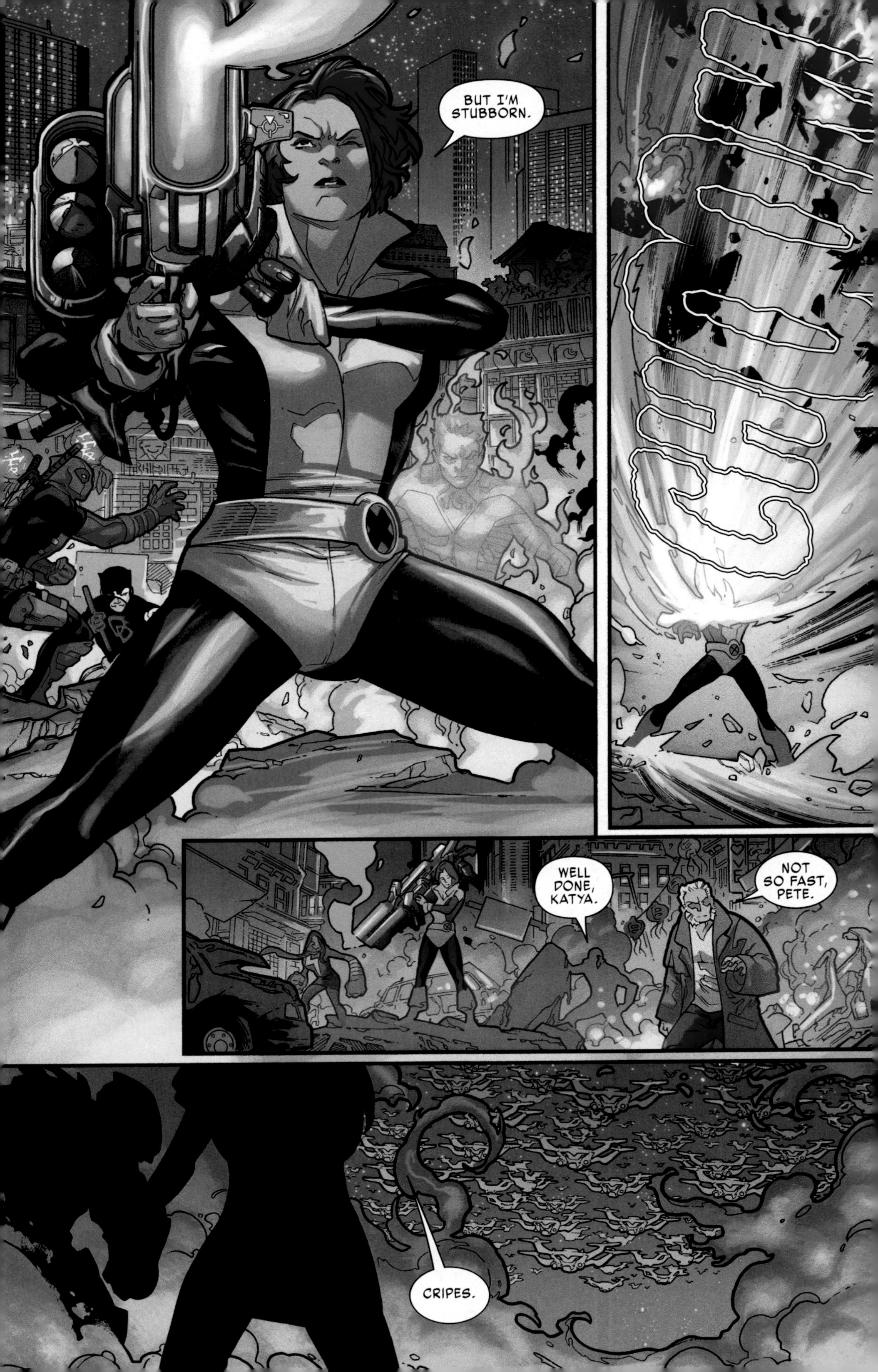
BUT I'M STUBBORN.
WELL DONE, KATYA.
NOT SO FAST, PETE.
CRIPES.

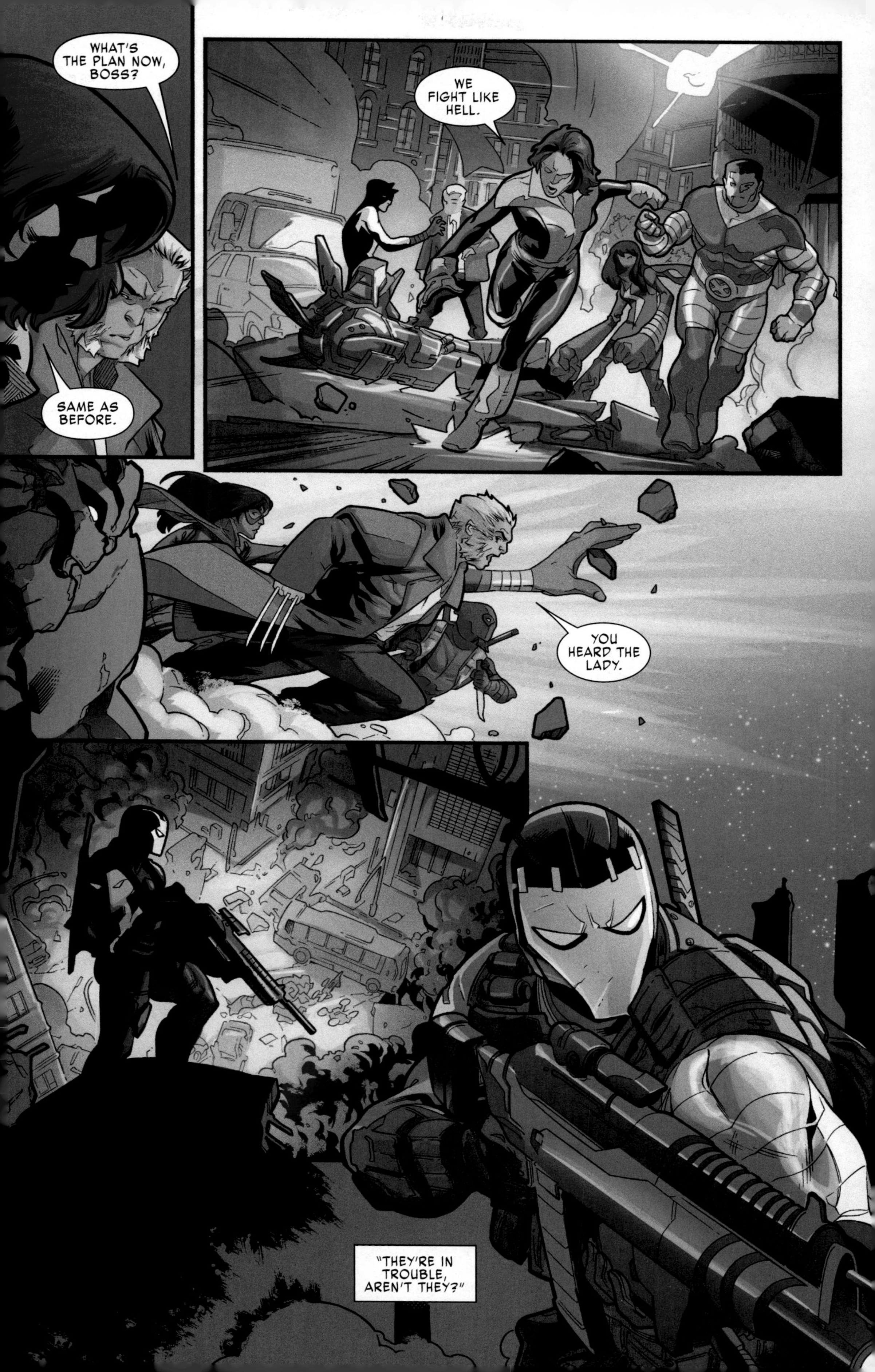
WHAT'S THE PLAN NOW, BOSS?
SAME AS BEFORE.
WE FIGHT LIKE HELL.
YOU HEARD THE LADY.
"THEY'RE IN TROUBLE, AREN'T THEY?"

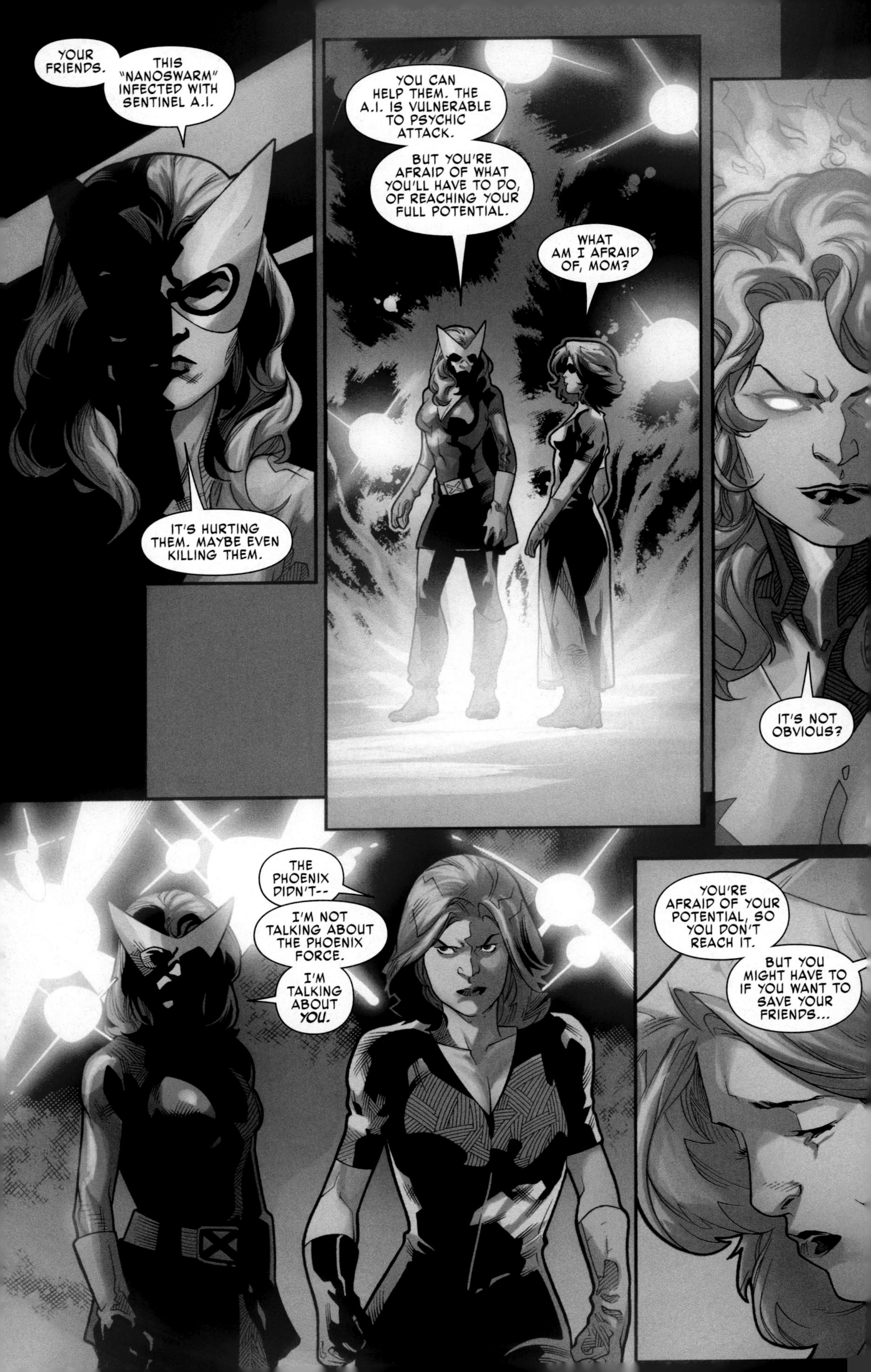
YOUR FRIENDS.
THIS "NANOSWARM" INFECTED WITH SENTINEL A.I.
IT'S HURTING THEM. MAYBE EVEN KILLING THEM.
YOU CAN HELP THEM. THE A.I. IS VULNERABLE TO PSYCHIC ATTACK.
BUT YOU'RE AFRAID OF WHAT YOU'LL HAVE TO DO, OF REACHING YOUR FULL POTENTIAL.
WHAT AM I AFRAID OF, MOM?
IT'S NOT OBVIOUS?
THE PHOENIX DIDN'T--
I'M NOT TALKING ABOUT THE PHOENIX FORCE.
I'M TALKING ABOUT *YOU.*
YOU'RE AFRAID OF YOUR POTENTIAL, SO YOU DON'T REACH IT.
BUT YOU MIGHT HAVE TO IF YOU WANT TO SAVE YOUR FRIENDS...

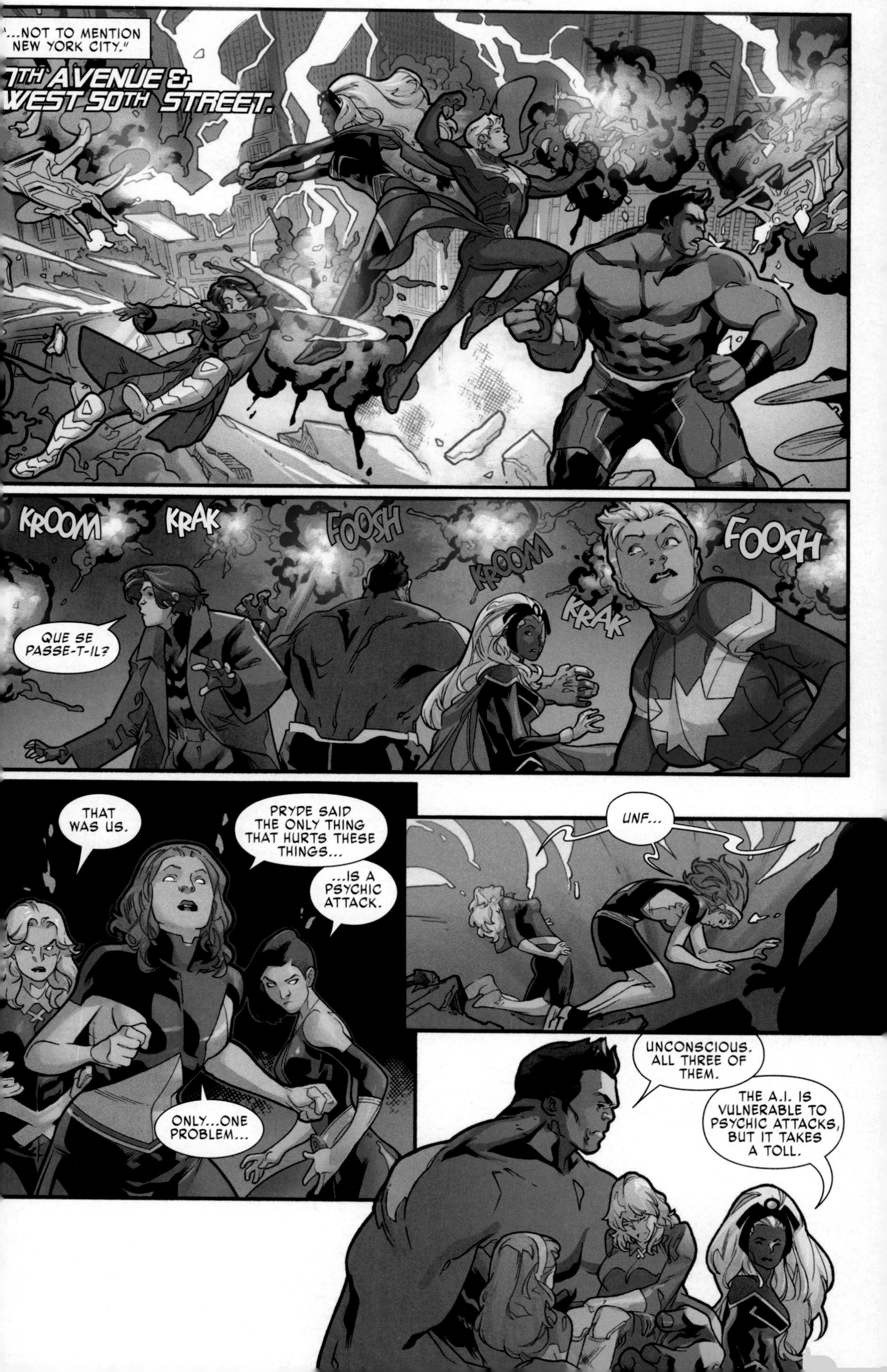
"...NOT TO MENTION NEW YORK CITY."
7TH AVENUE & WEST 50TH STREET.
KROOM
KRAK
FOOSH
KROOM
KRAK
FOOSH
QUE SE PASSE-T-IL?
THAT WAS US.
PRYDE SAID THE ONLY THING THAT HURTS THESE THINGS...
...IS A PSYCHIC ATTACK.
ONLY...ONE PROBLEM...
UNF...
UNCONSCIOUS. ALL THREE OF THEM.
THE A.I. IS VULNERABLE TO PSYCHIC ATTACKS, BUT IT TAKES A TOLL.

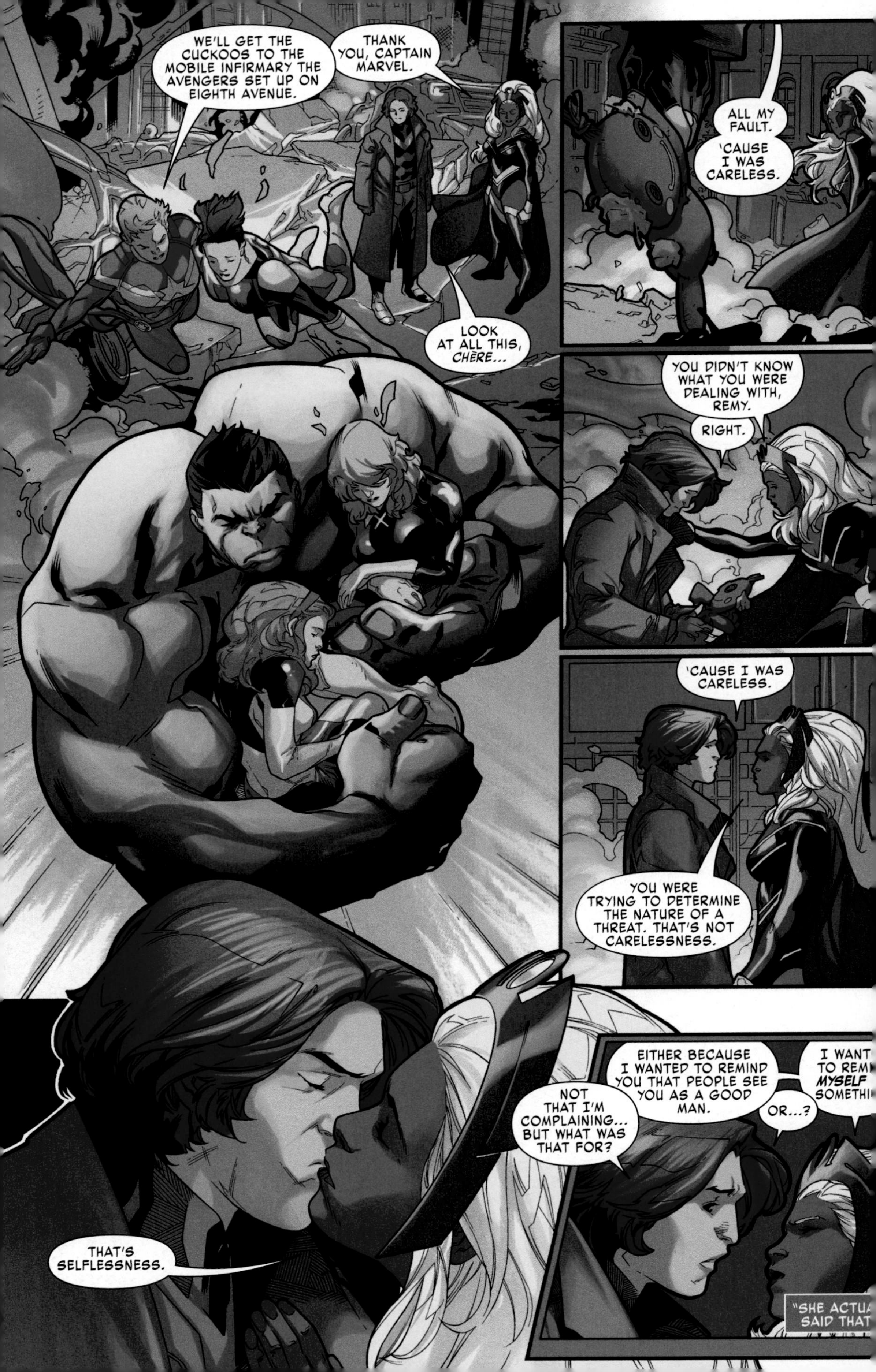
WE'LL GET THE CUCKOOS TO THE MOBILE INFIRMARY THE AVENGERS SET UP ON EIGHTH AVENUE.
THANK YOU, CAPTAIN MARVEL.
LOOK AT ALL THIS, *CHÈRE*...
ALL MY FAULT.
'CAUSE I WAS CARELESS.
YOU DIDN'T KNOW WHAT YOU WERE DEALING WITH, REMY.
RIGHT.
'CAUSE I WAS CARELESS.
YOU WERE TRYING TO DETERMINE THE NATURE OF A THREAT. THAT'S NOT CARELESSNESS.
THAT'S SELFLESSNESS.
NOT THAT I'M COMPLAINING... BUT WHAT WAS THAT FOR?
EITHER BECAUSE I WANTED TO REMIND YOU THAT PEOPLE SEE YOU AS A GOOD MAN.
OR...?
I WANT TO REM *MYSELF* SOMETHI
"SHE ACTUA SAID THAT

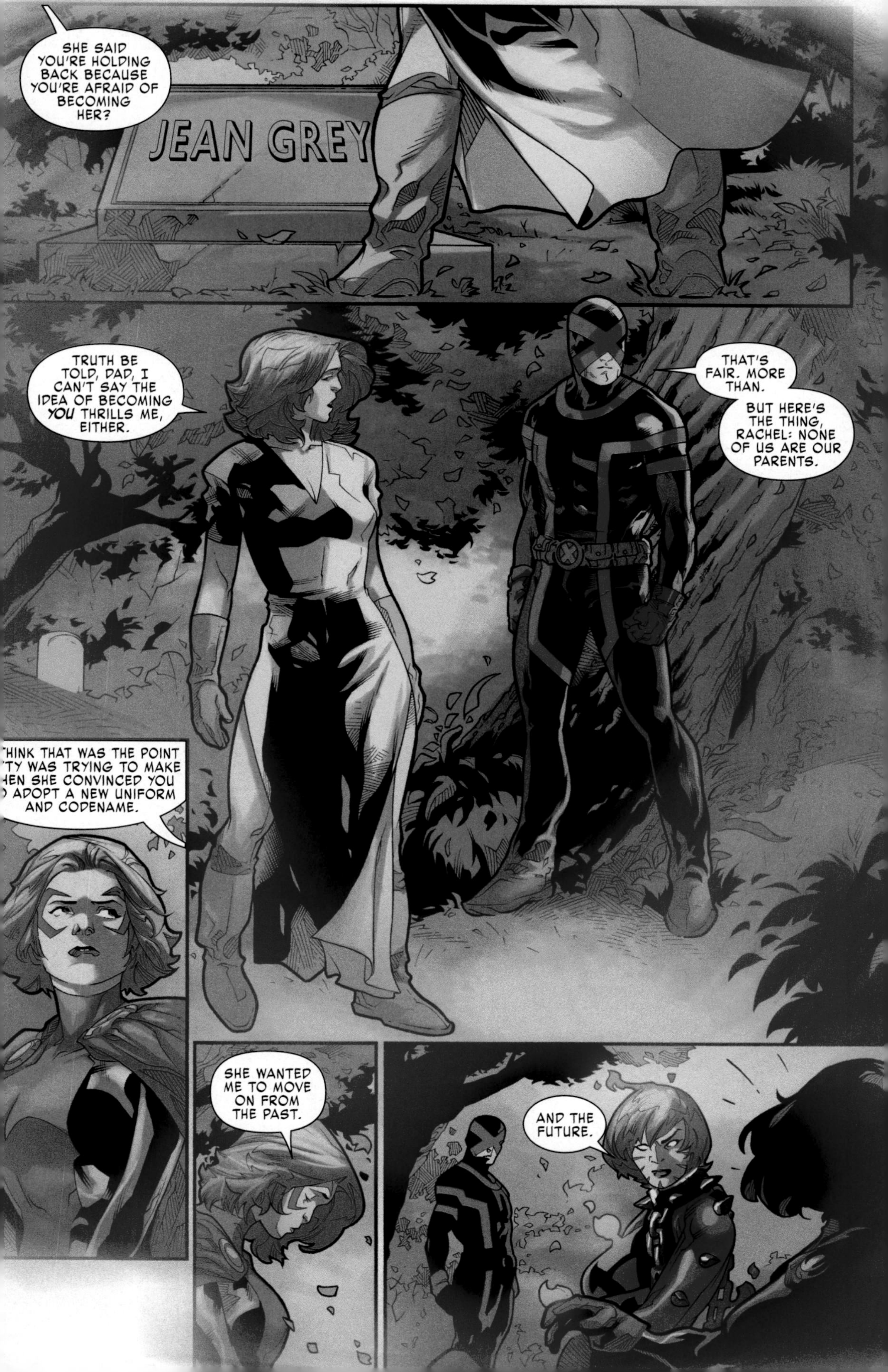
SHE SAID YOU'RE HOLDING BACK BECAUSE YOU'RE AFRAID OF BECOMING HER?
JEAN GREY
TRUTH BE TOLD, DAD, I CAN'T SAY THE IDEA OF BECOMING *YOU* THRILLS ME, EITHER.
THAT'S FAIR. MORE THAN.
BUT HERE'S THE THING, RACHEL: NONE OF US ARE OUR PARENTS.
THINK THAT WAS THE POINT TY WAS TRYING TO MAKE HEN SHE CONVINCED YOU ADOPT A NEW UNIFORM AND CODENAME.
SHE WANTED ME TO MOVE ON FROM THE PAST.
AND THE FUTURE.

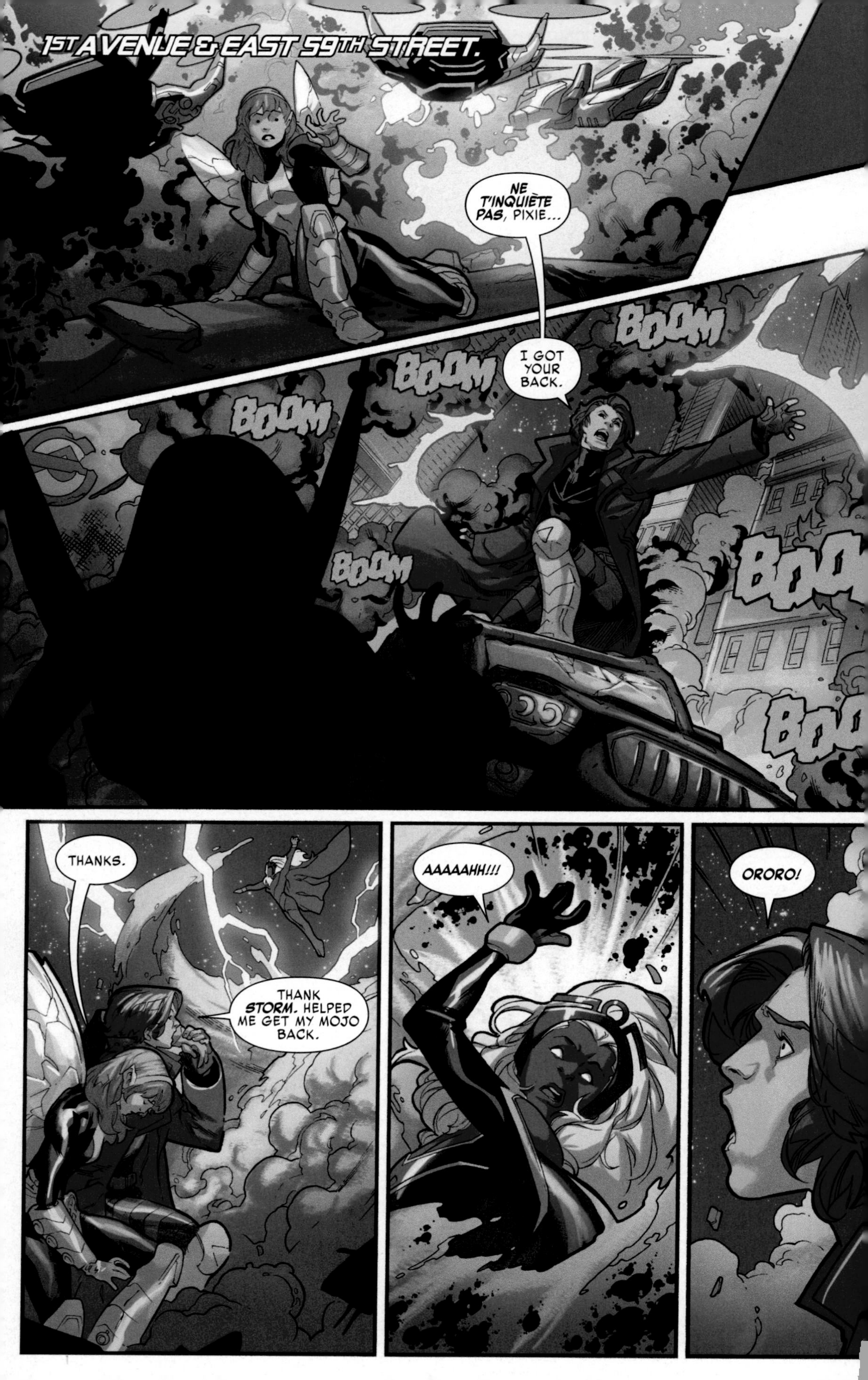
1ST AVENUE & EAST 59TH STREET.
NE T'INQUIÈTE PAS, PIXIE...
I GOT YOUR BACK.
BOOM
BOOM
BOOM
BOOM
THANKS.
THANK STORM. HELPED ME GET MY MOJO BACK.
AAAAAHH!!!
ORORO!

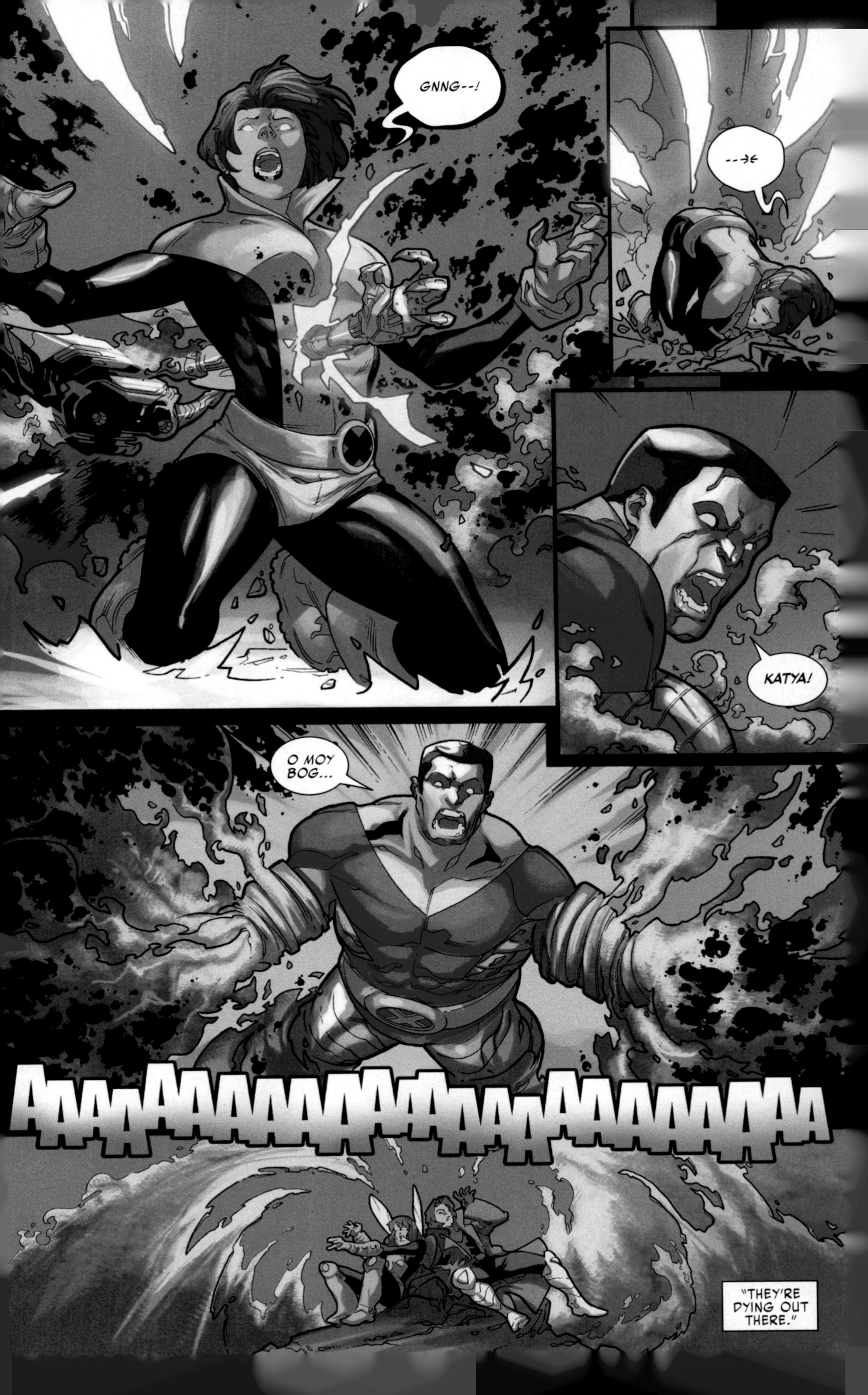
GNNG--!
--⚡
KATYA!
O MOY BOG...
AAAAAAAAAAAAAAAAAAAAAAA
"THEY'RE DYING OUT THERE."

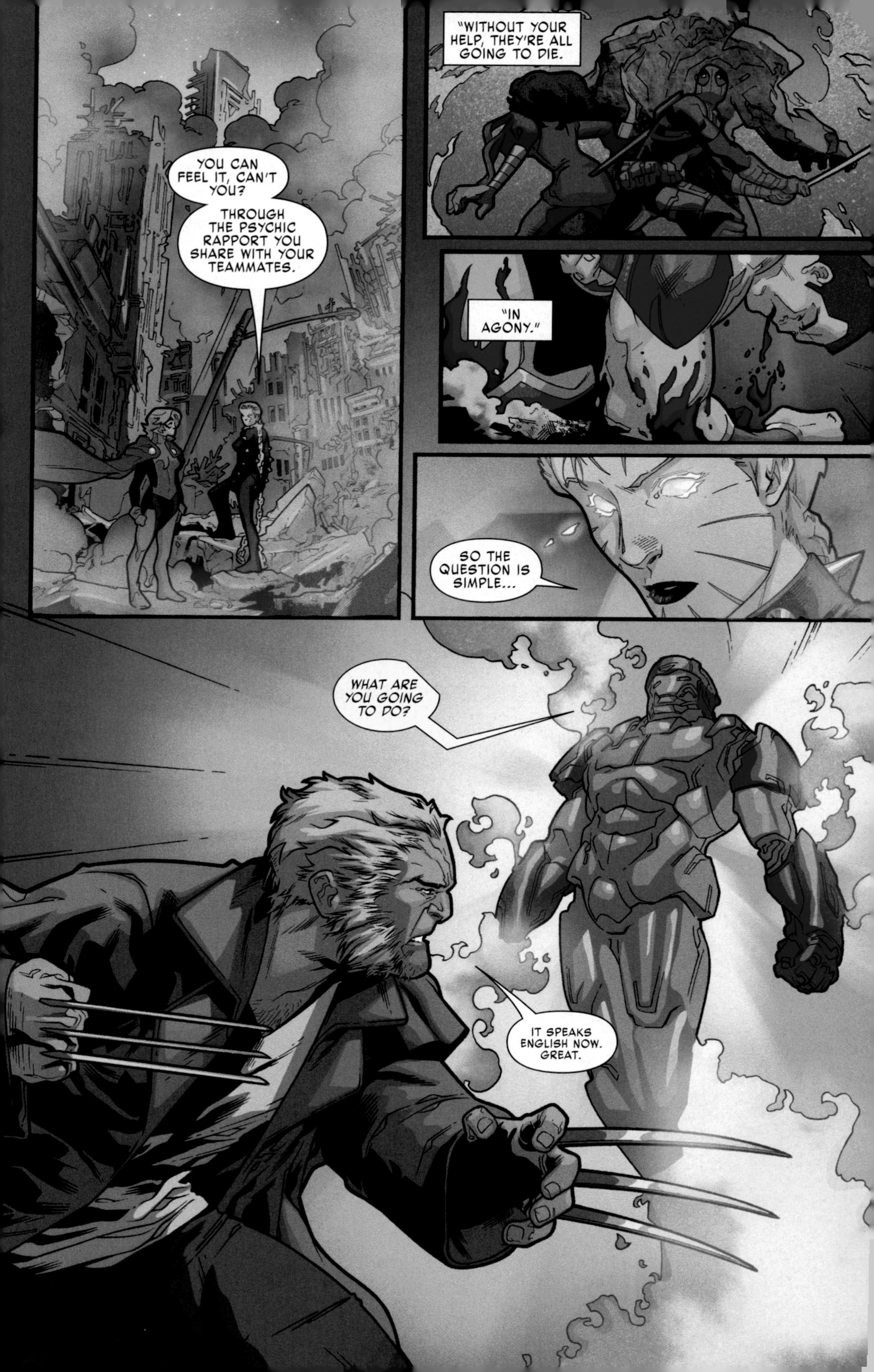
YOU CAN FEEL IT, CAN'T YOU?
THROUGH THE PSYCHIC RAPPORT YOU SHARE WITH YOUR TEAMMATES.
"WITHOUT YOUR HELP, THEY'RE ALL GOING TO DIE.
"IN AGONY."
SO THE QUESTION IS SIMPLE...
WHAT ARE YOU GOING TO DO?
IT SPEAKS ENGLISH NOW. GREAT.

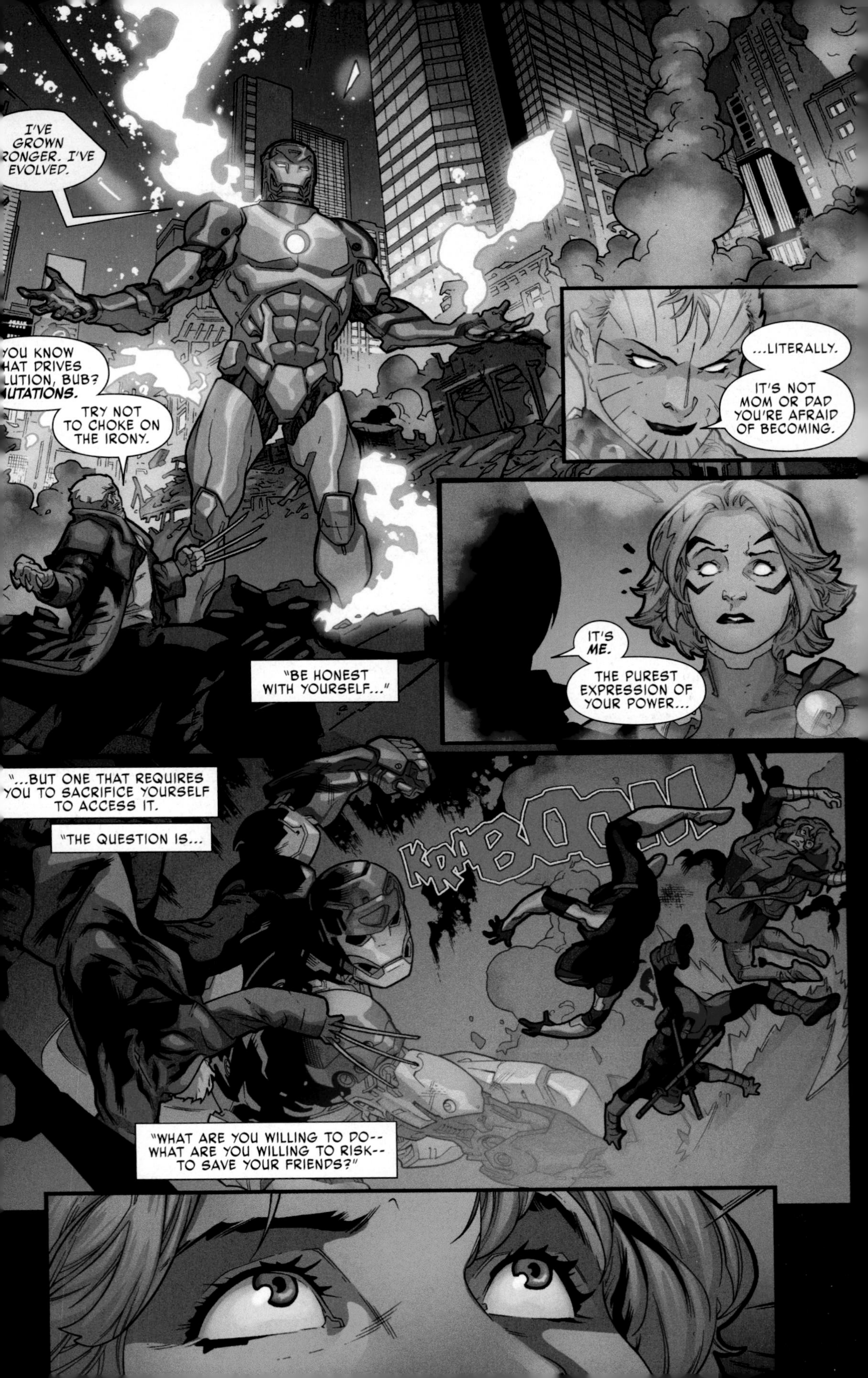

I'VE GROWN
RONGER. I'VE EVOLVED.
YOU KNOW
HAT DRIVES
LUTION, BUB?
UTATIONS.
TRY NOT TO CHOKE ON THE IRONY.
...LITERALLY.
IT'S NOT MOM OR DAD YOU'RE AFRAID OF BECOMING.
IT'S ME.
THE PUREST EXPRESSION OF YOUR POWER...
"BE HONEST WITH YOURSELF..."
"...BUT ONE THAT REQUIRES YOU TO SACRIFICE YOURSELF TO ACCESS IT.
"THE QUESTION IS...
KRABOOM
"WHAT ARE YOU WILLING TO DO-- WHAT ARE YOU WILLING TO RISK-- TO SAVE YOUR FRIENDS?"

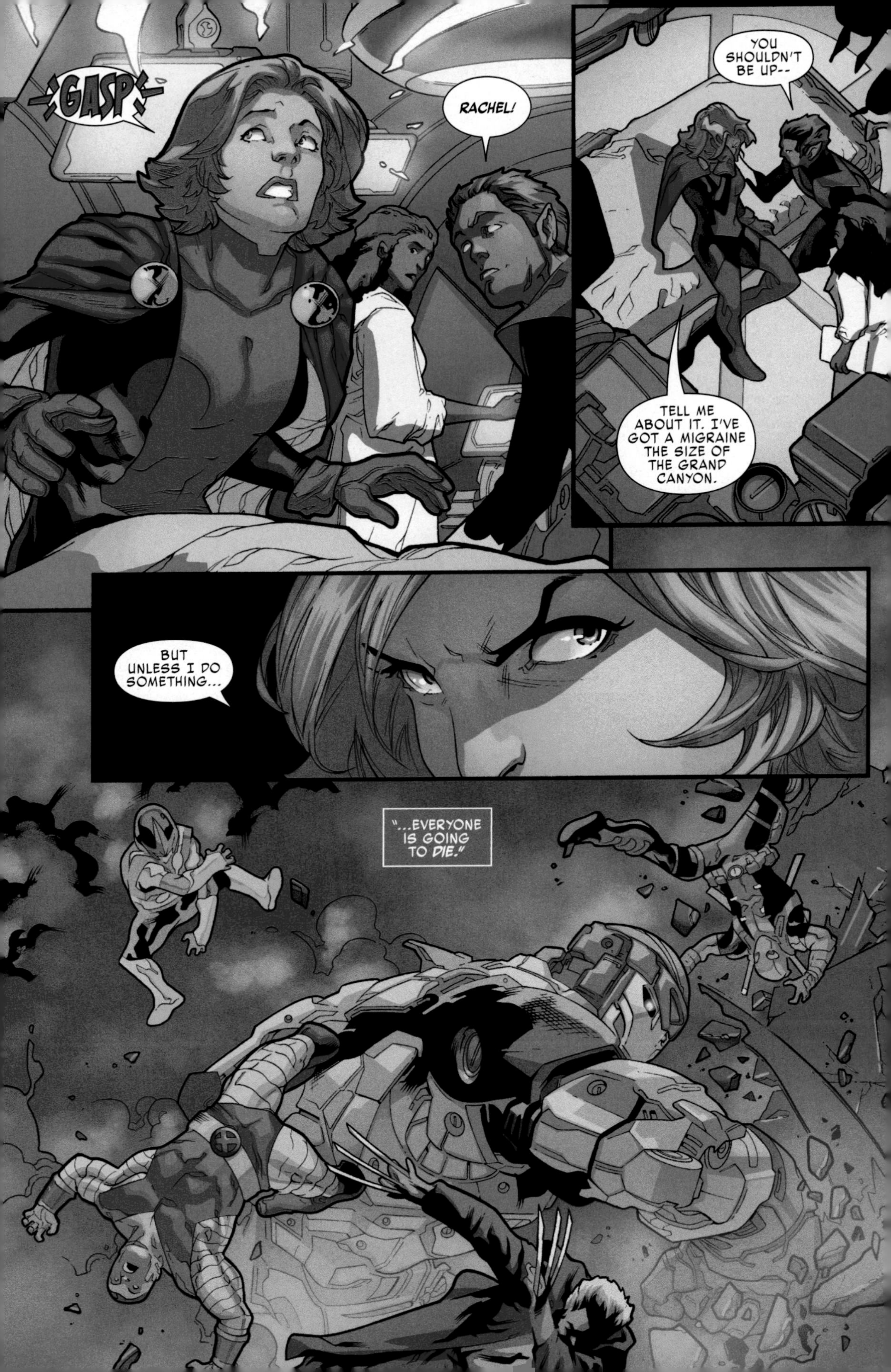
GASP
RACHEL!
YOU SHOULDN'T BE UP--
TELL ME ABOUT IT. I'VE GOT A MIGRAINE THE SIZE OF THE GRAND CANYON.
BUT UNLESS I DO SOMETHING...
"...EVERYONE IS GOING TO DIE."

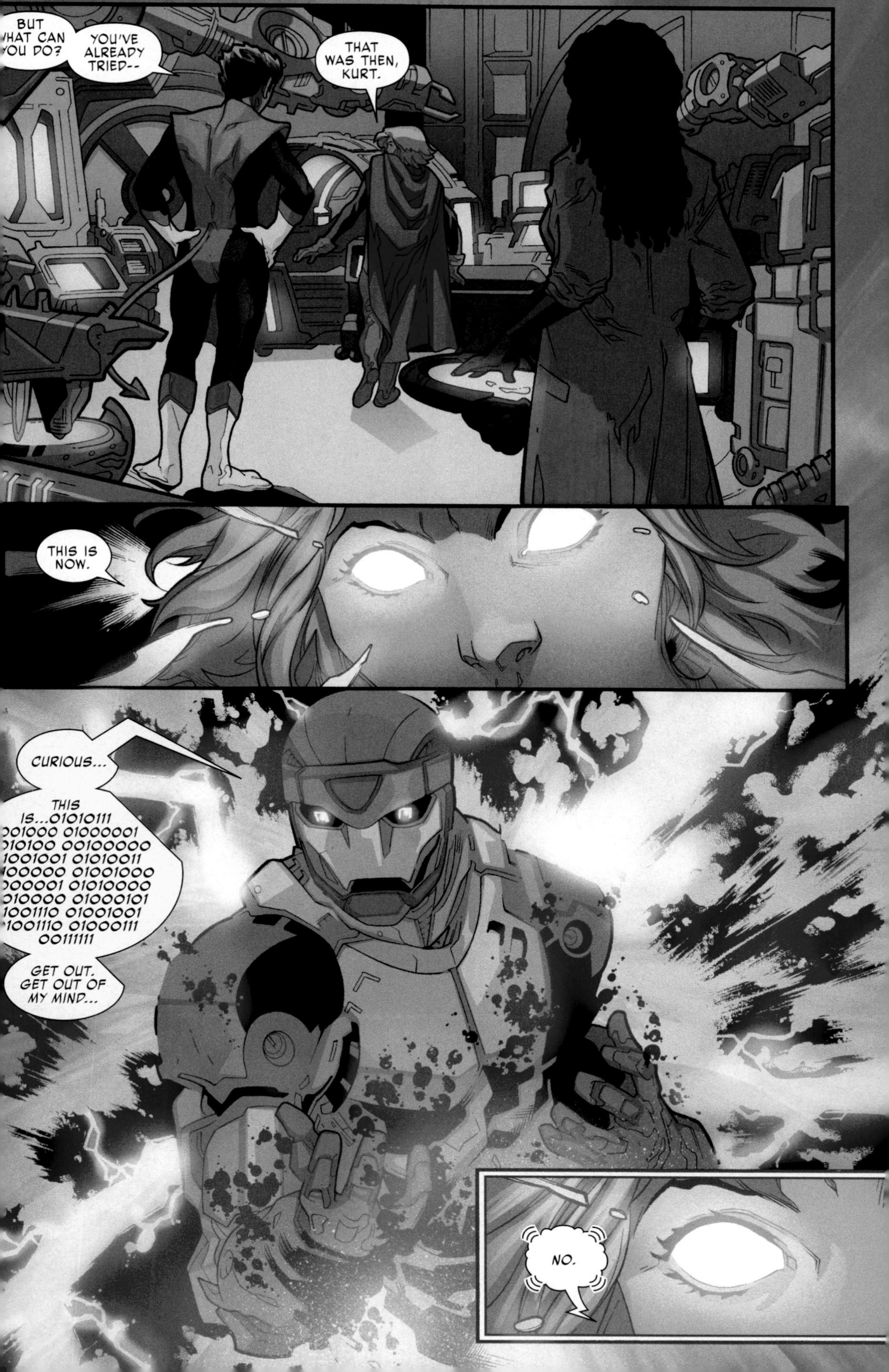
BUT WHAT CAN YOU DO?
YOU'VE ALREADY TRIED--
THAT WAS THEN, KURT.
THIS IS NOW.
CURIOUS...
THIS IS...01010111 001000 01000001 010100 00100000 1001001 01010011 100000 01001000 000001 01010000 010000 01000101 1001110 01001001 1001110 01000111 00111111
GET OUT. GET OUT OF MY MIND...
NO.

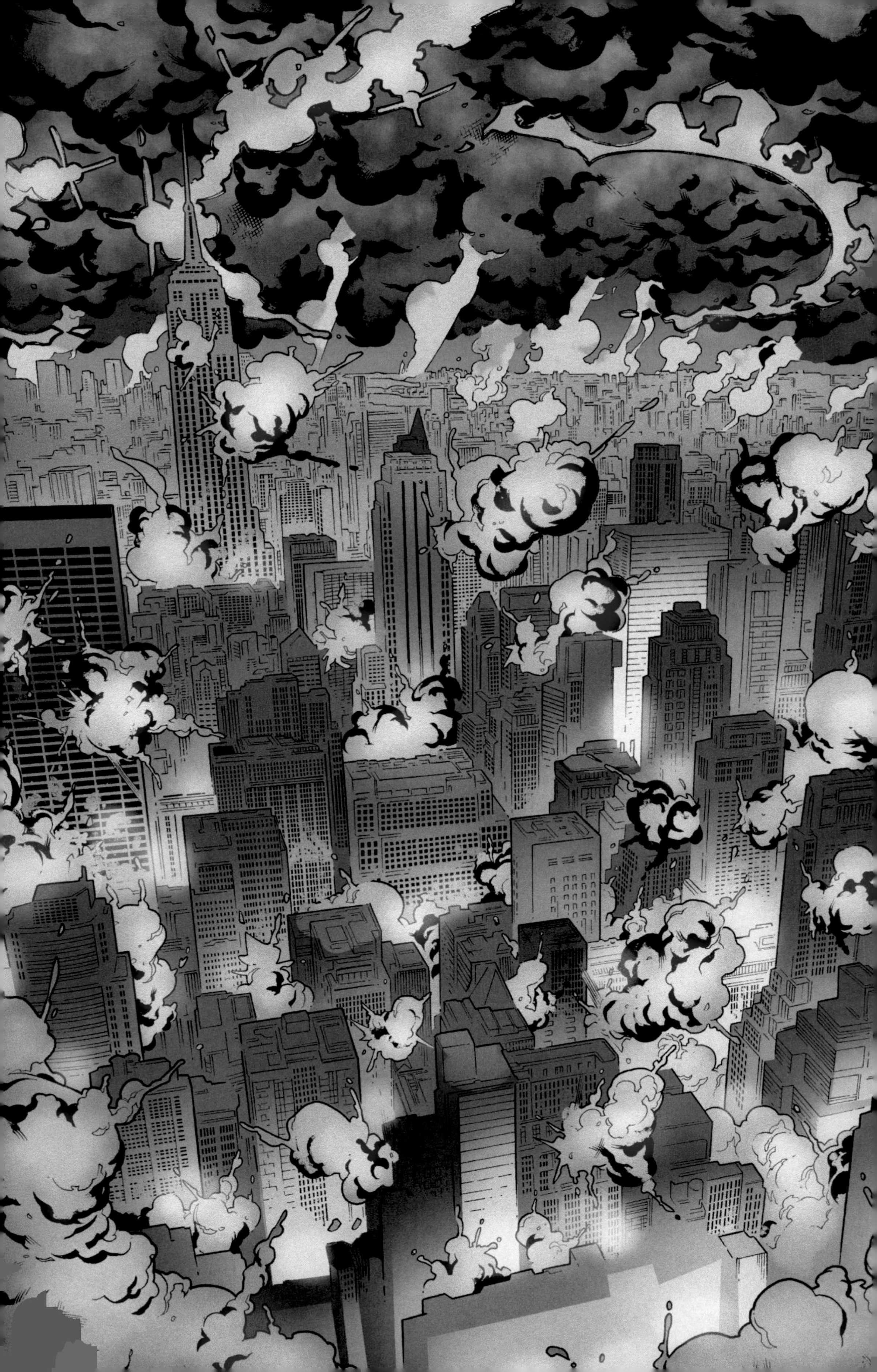

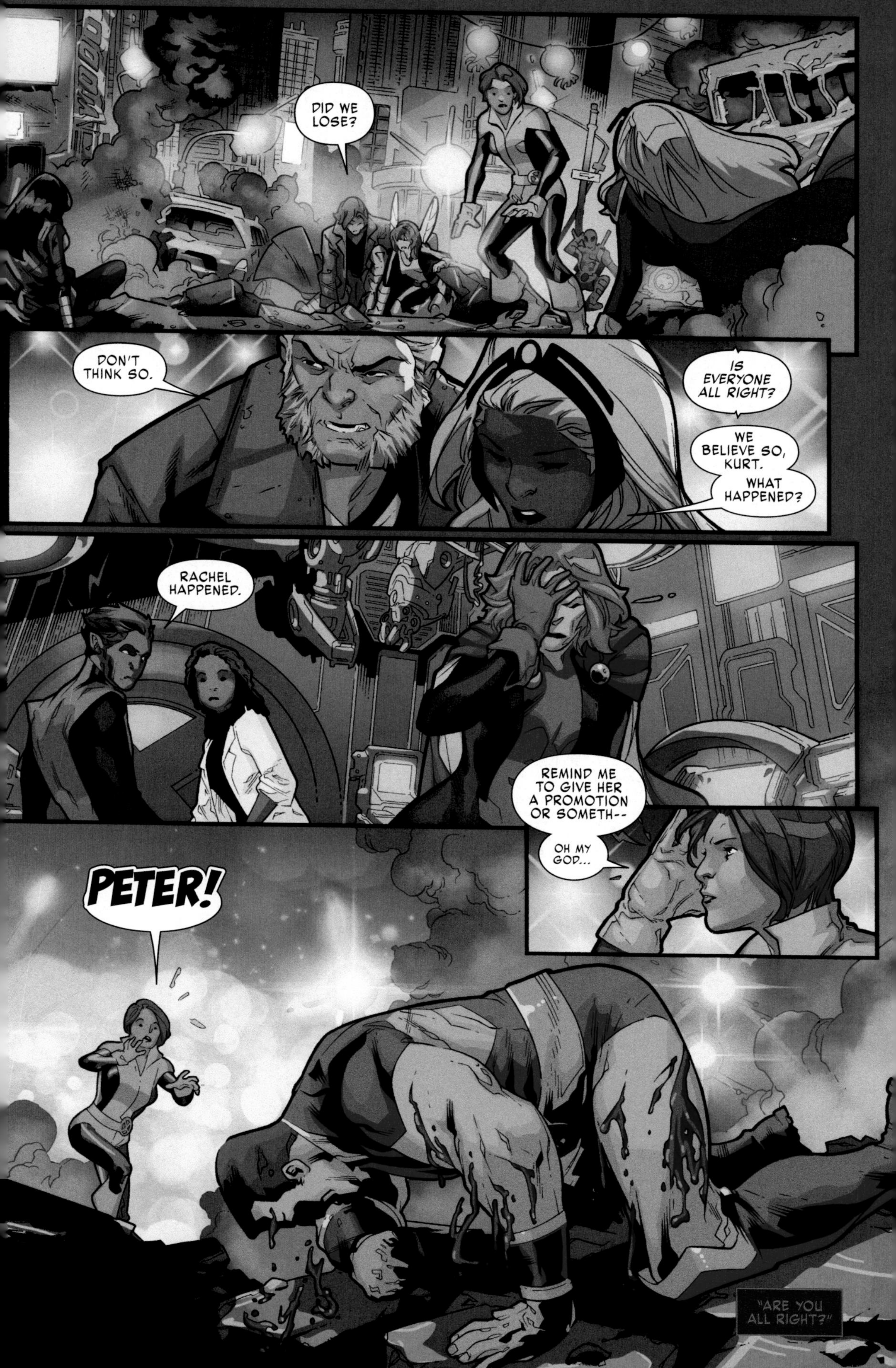
DID WE LOSE?
DON'T THINK SO.
IS EVERYONE ALL RIGHT?
WE BELIEVE SO, KURT.
WHAT HAPPENED?
RACHEL HAPPENED.
REMIND ME TO GIVE HER A PROMOTION OR SOMETH--
OH MY GOD...
PETER!
"ARE YOU ALL RIGHT?"

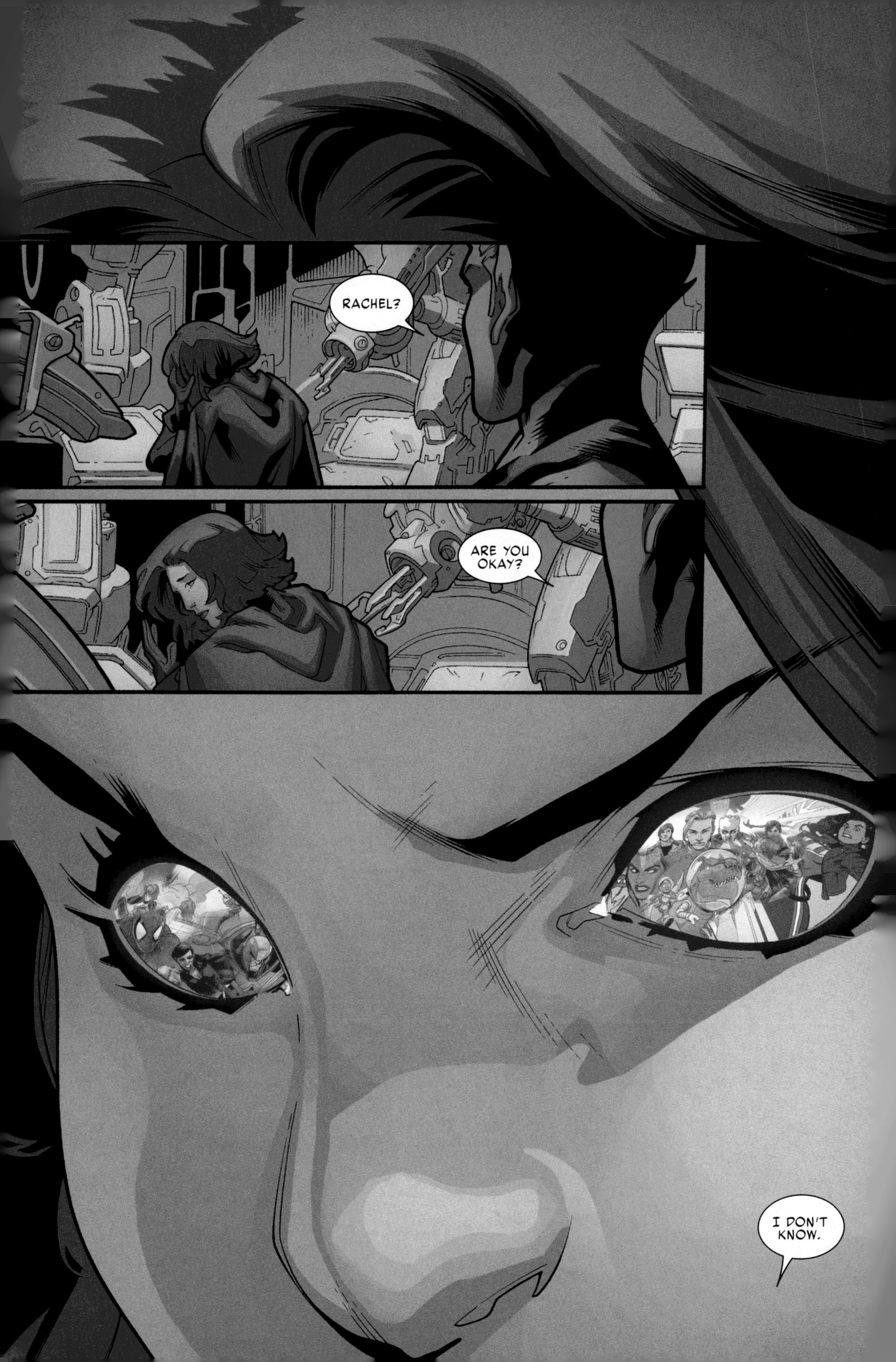
RACHEL?
ARE YOU OKAY?
I DON'T KNOW.

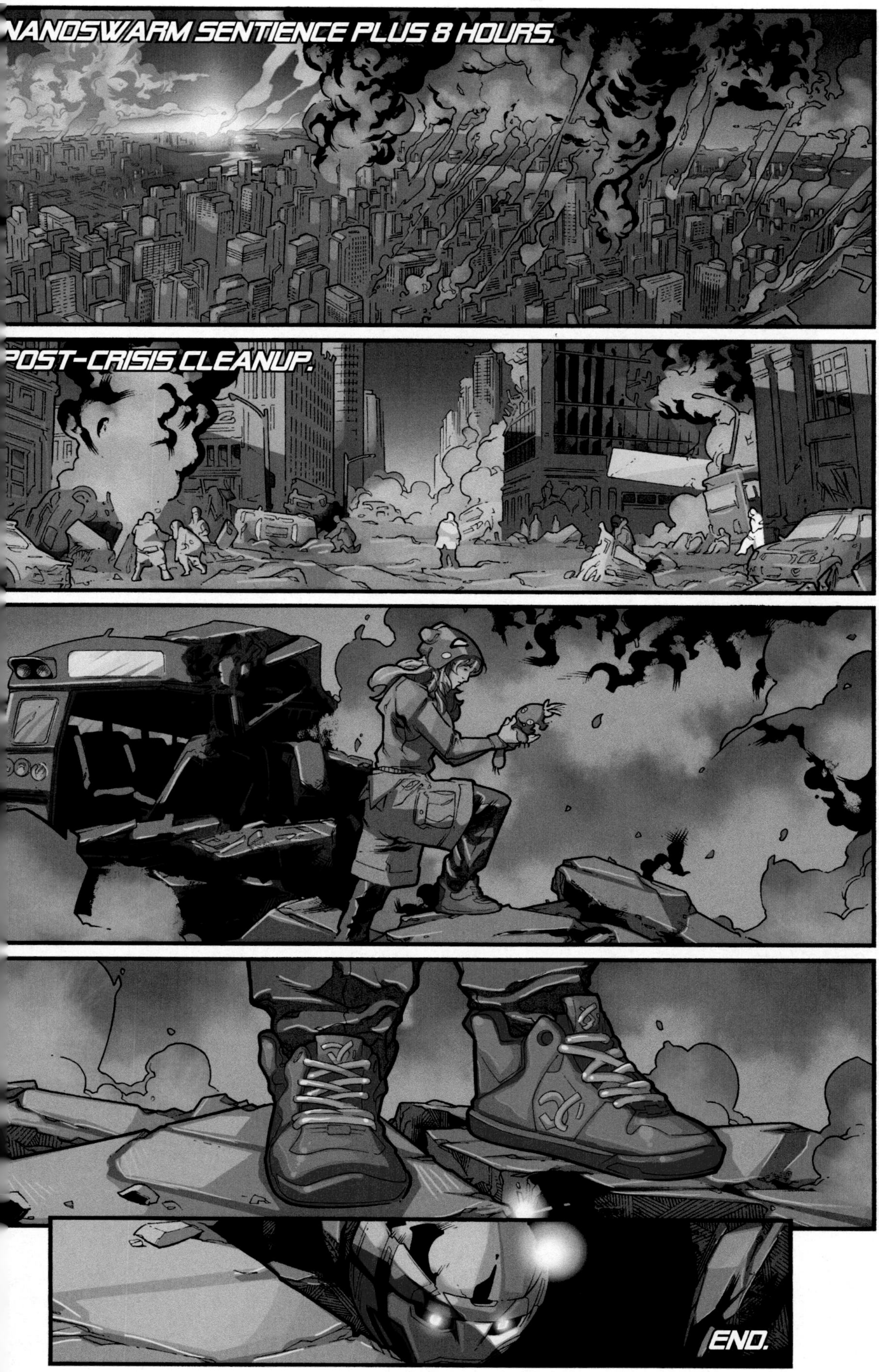
NANOSWARM SENTIENCE PLUS 8 HOURS.
POST-CRISIS CLEANUP.
END.

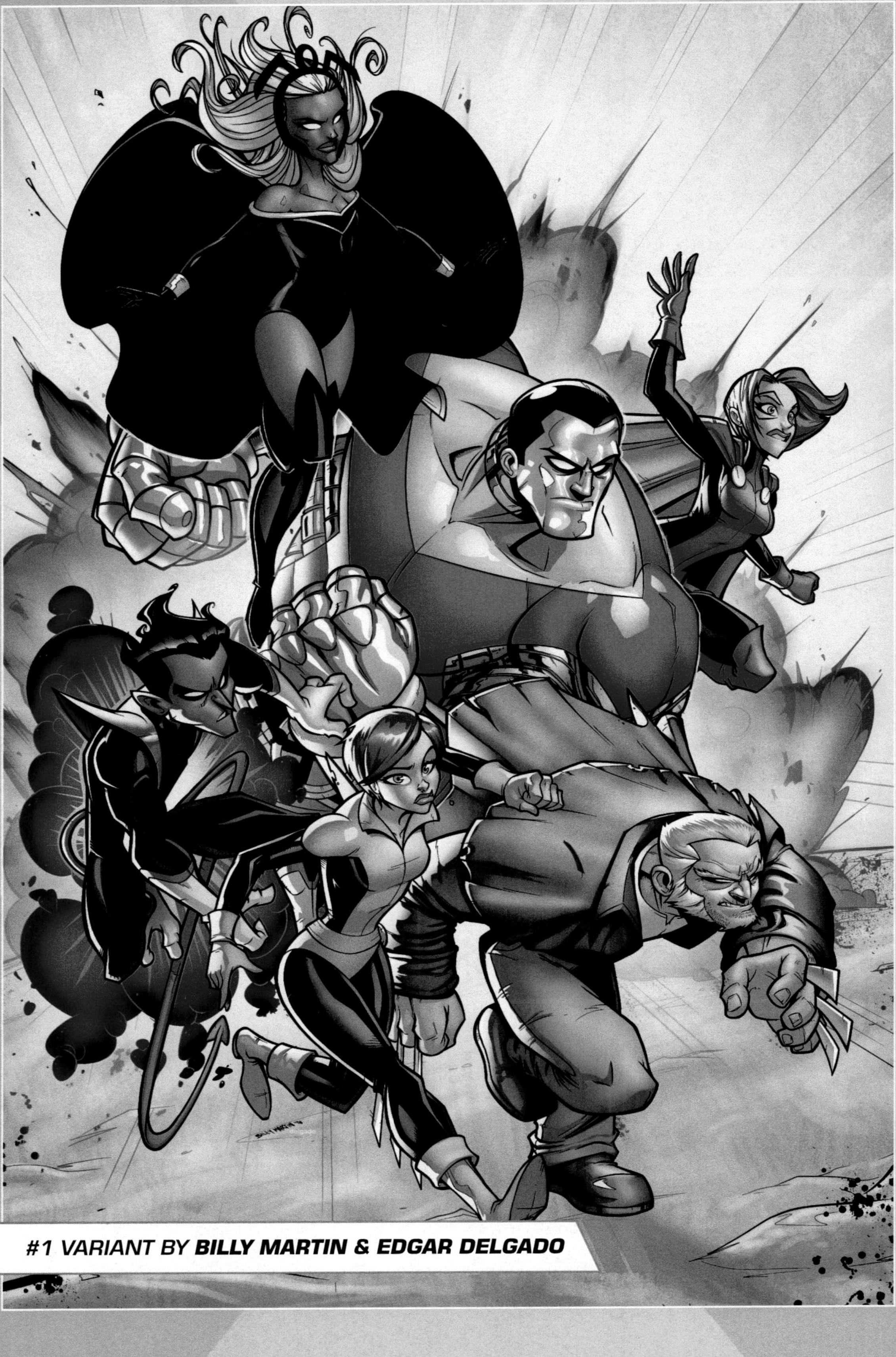

#1 VARIANT BY **BILLY MARTIN & EDGAR DELGADO**

#1 VARIANT BY **BOB McLEOD**

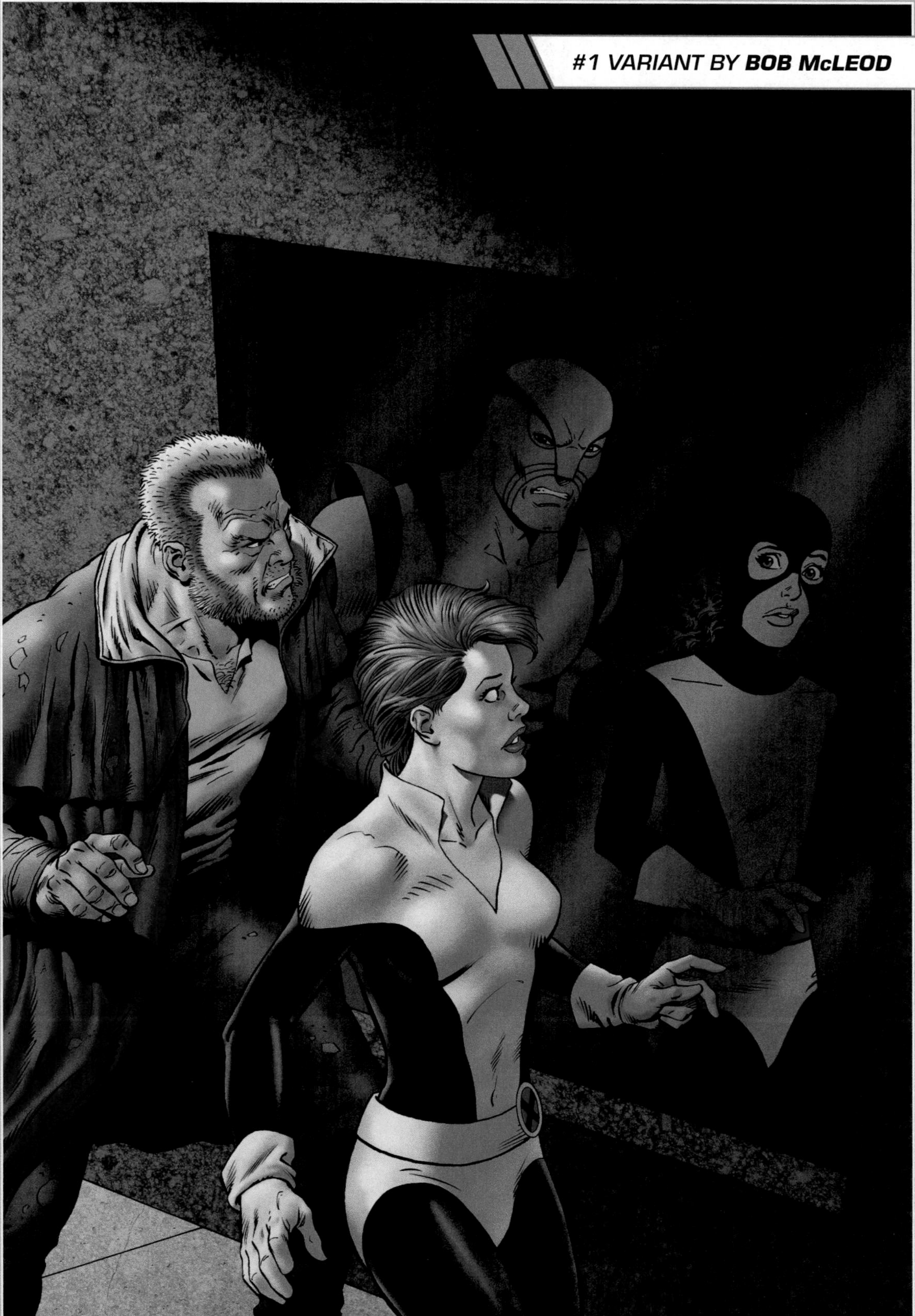

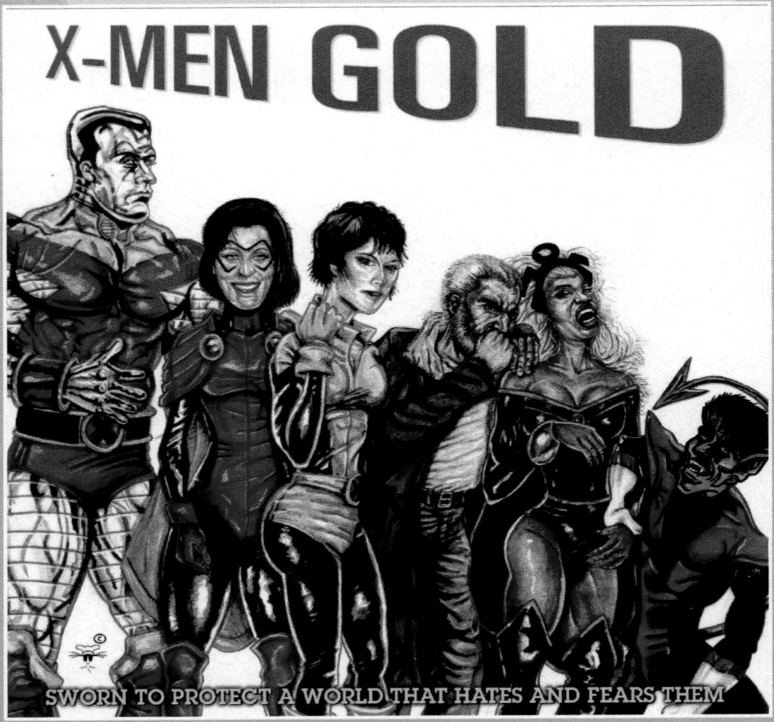
X-MEN GOLD
SWORN TO PROTECT A WORLD THAT HATES AND FEARS THEM

#1 HIP-HOP VARIANT
BY **ANDRÉ LeROY DAVIS**

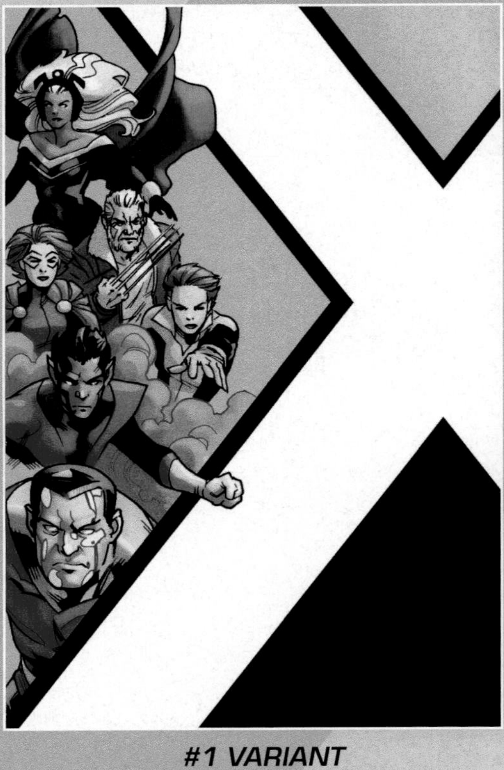

#1 VARIANT
BY **LEONARD KIRK**
& **MICHAEL GARLAND**

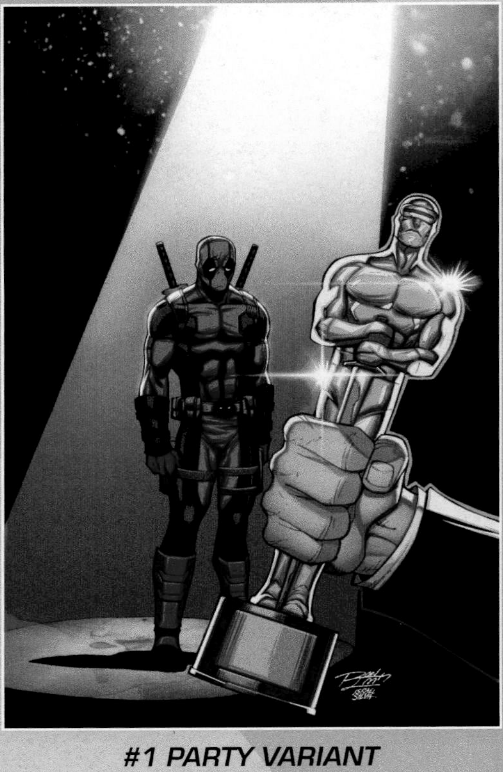

#1 PARTY VARIANT
BY **RON LIM**
& **ISRAEL SILVA**

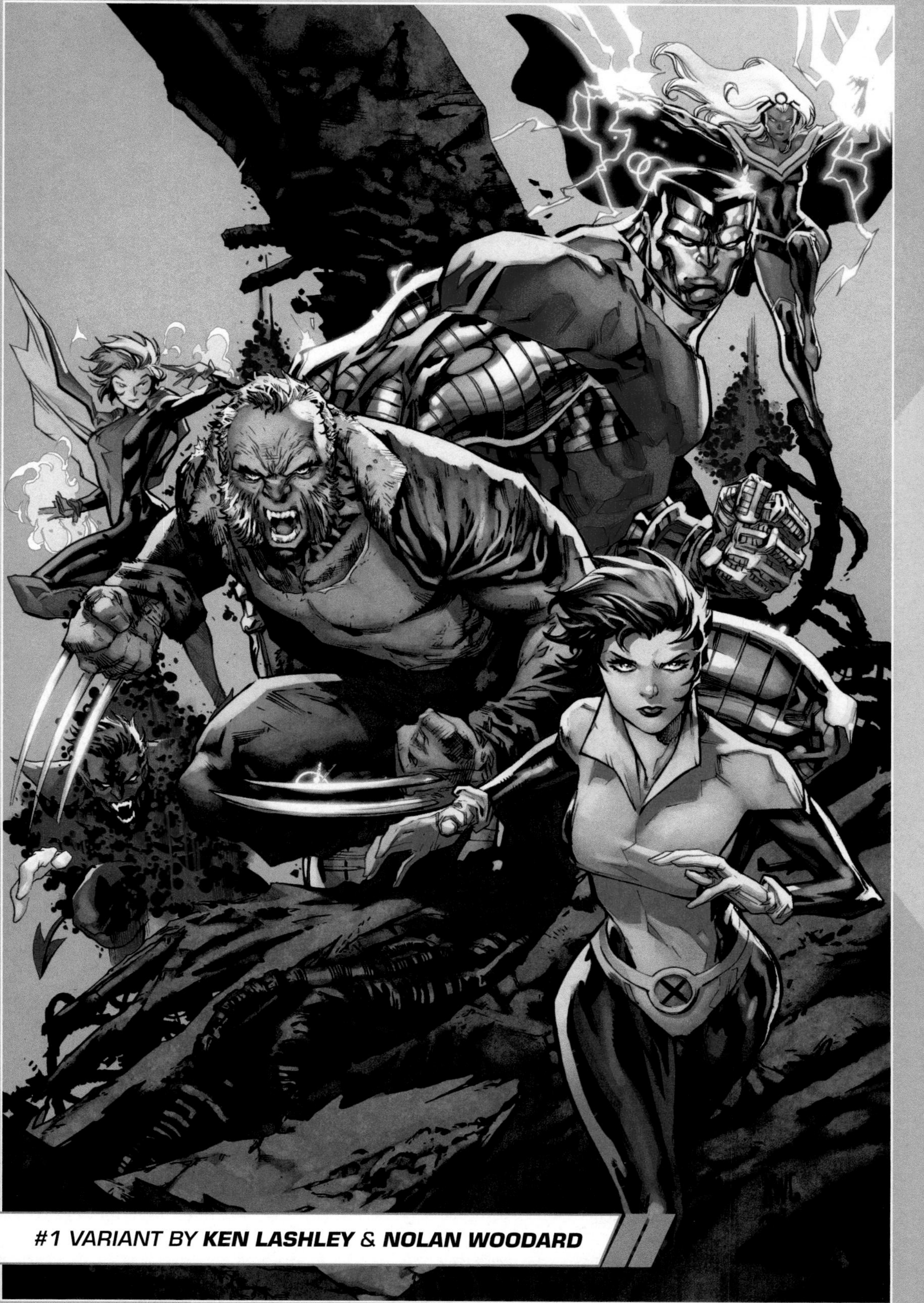

#1 VARIANT BY **KEN LASHLEY** & **NOLAN WOODARD**

#1 VARIANT BY **SKOTTIE YOUNG**

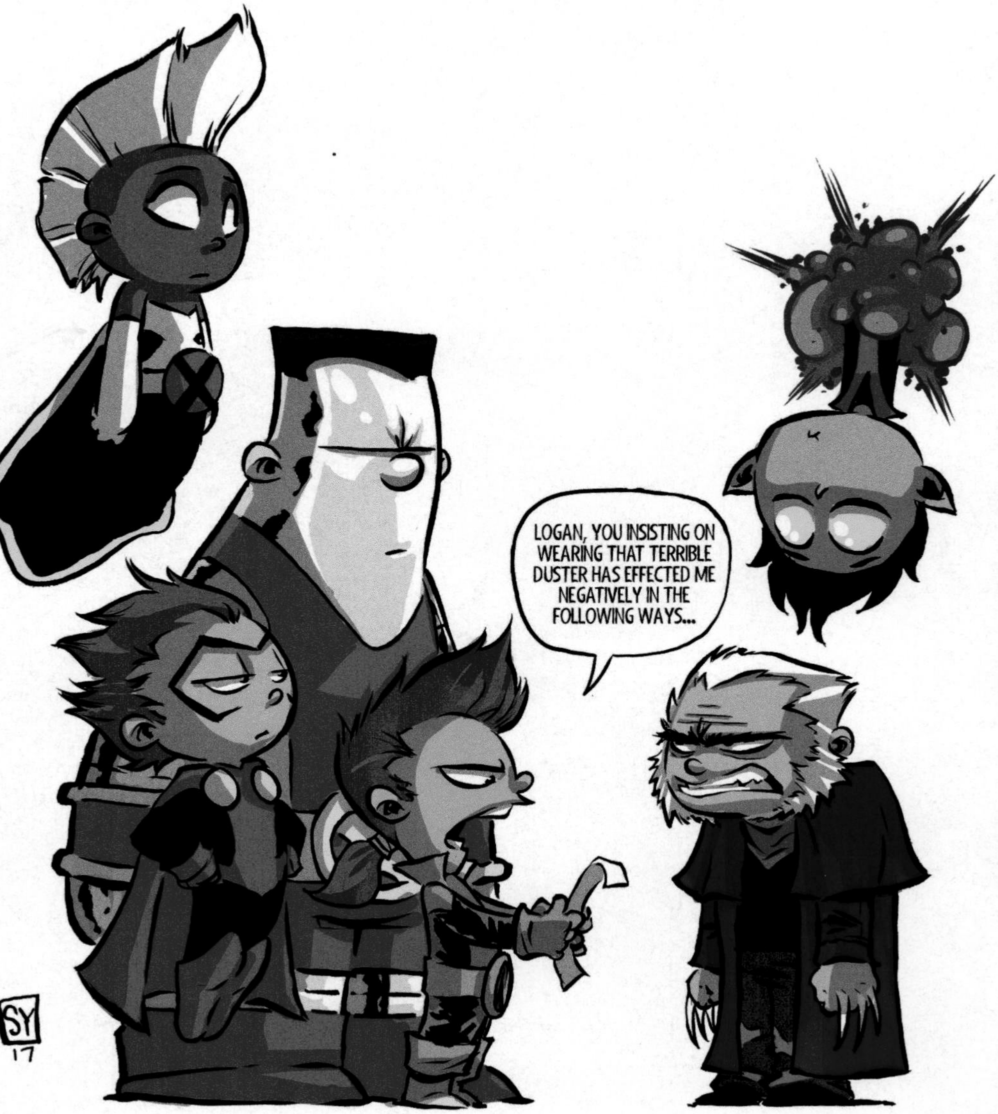
LOGAN, YOU INSISTING ON WEARING THAT TERRIBLE DUSTER HAS EFFECTED ME NEGATIVELY IN THE FOLLOWING WAYS...
SY 17

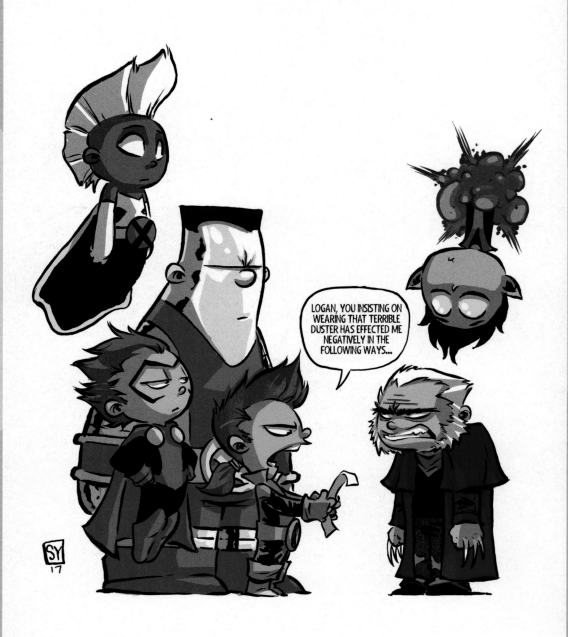

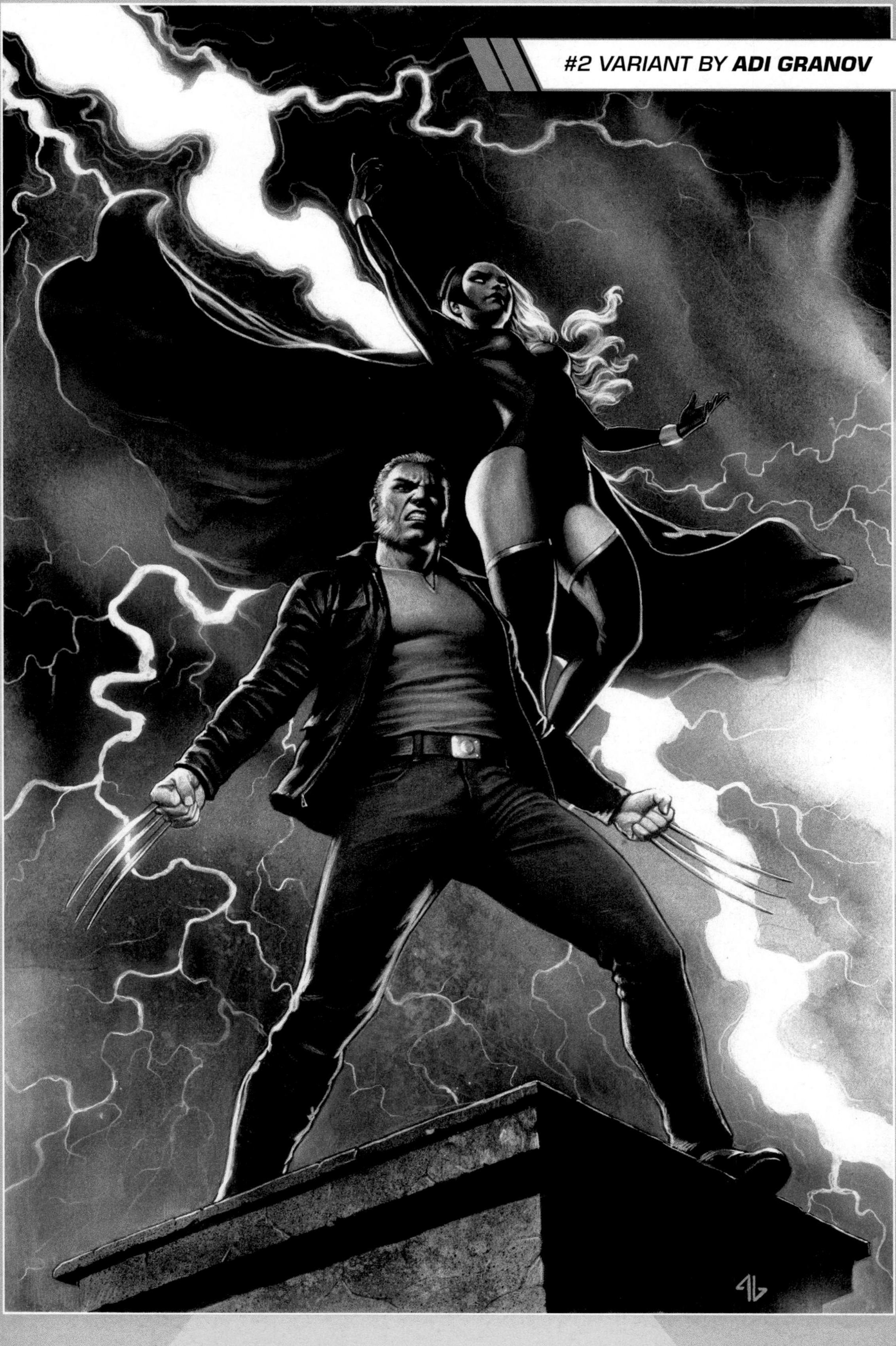

#2 VARIANT BY **ADI GRANOV**

#3 VARIANT BY ***J. SCOTT CAMPBELL*** *&* ***MARTE GRACIA***

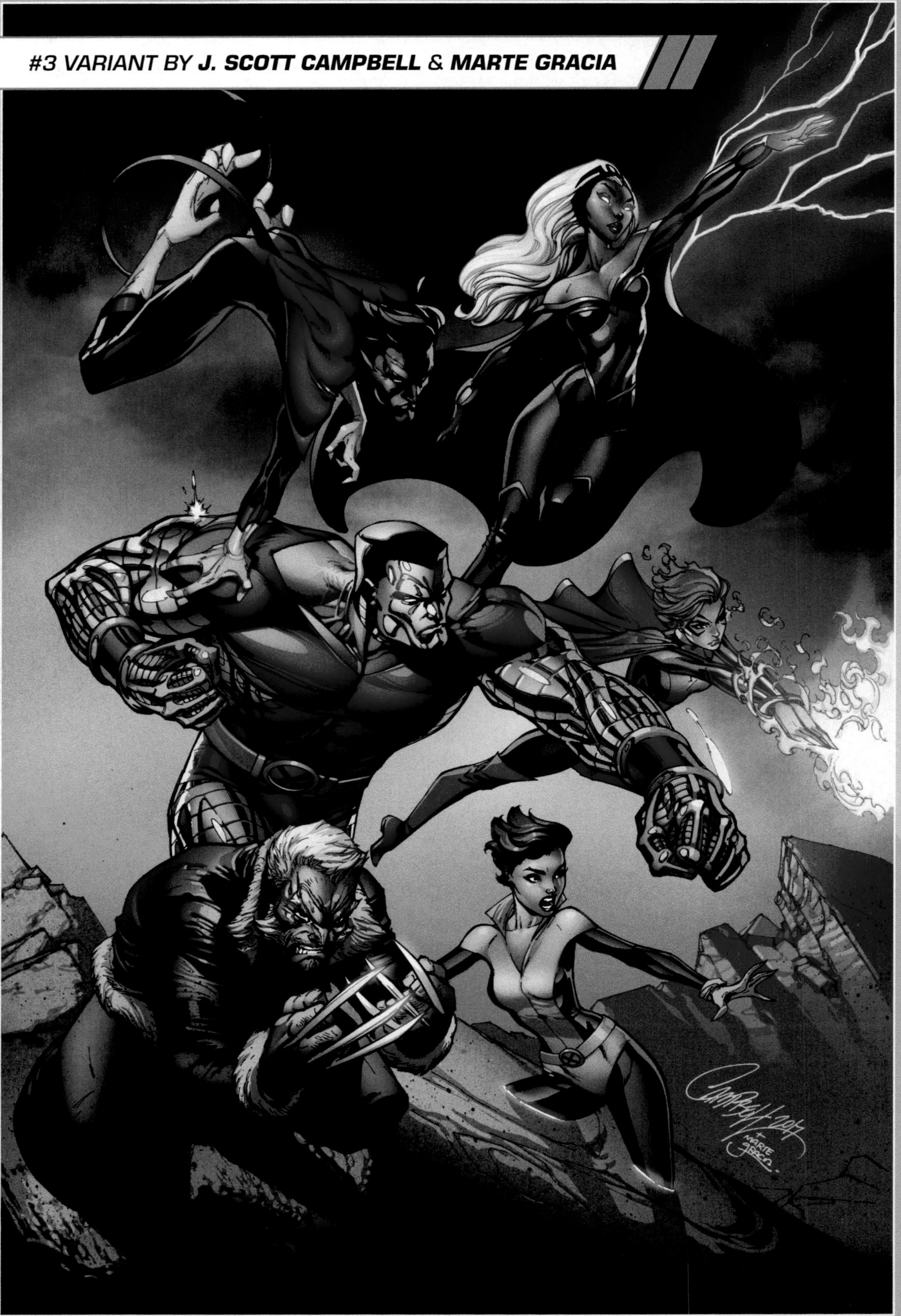

#4 VARIANT BY **DAVID MARQUEZ** & **MARTE GRACIA**

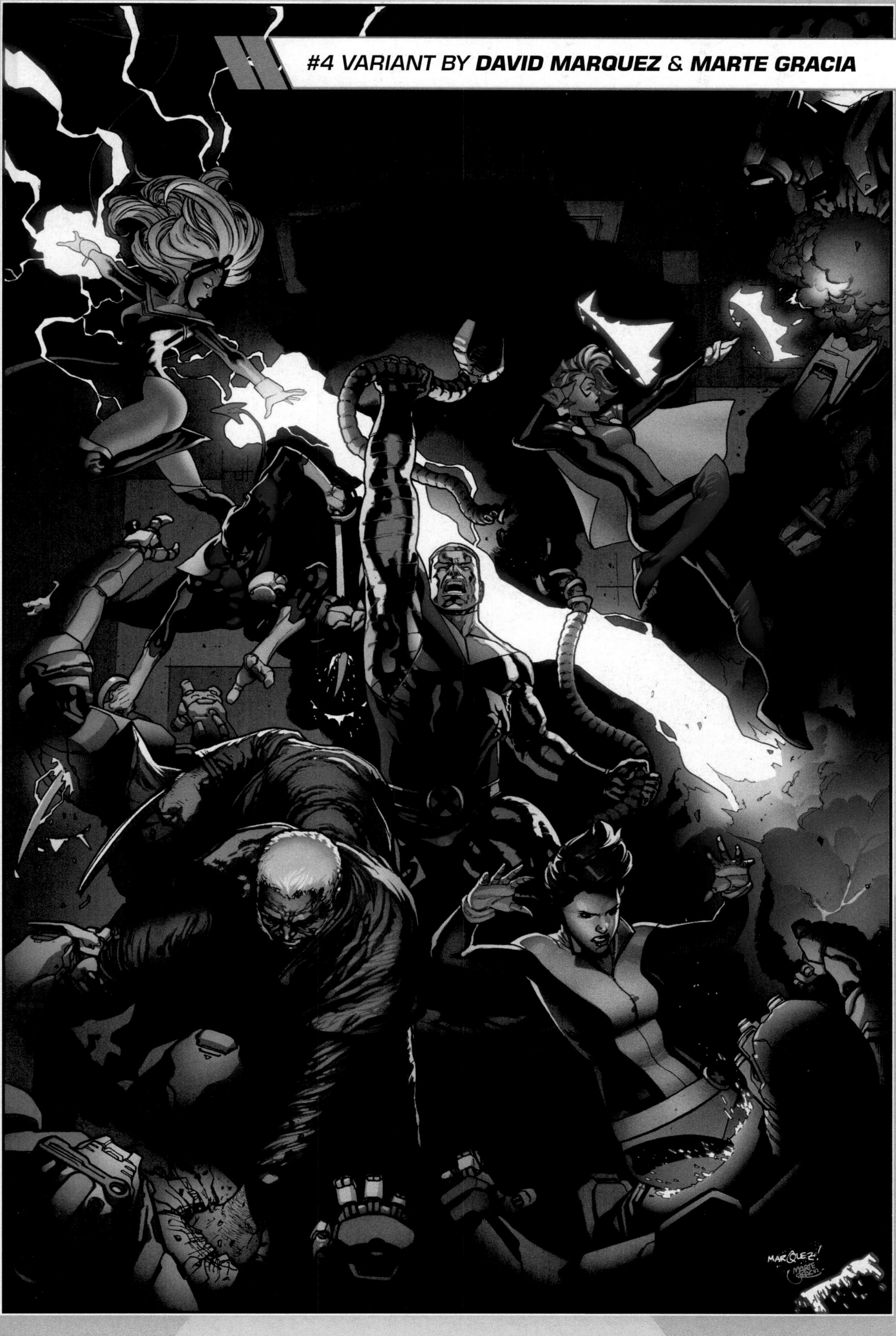
MARQUEZ!
MARTE GRACIA

#5 MARY JANE VARIANT BY **ANTHONY PIPER**

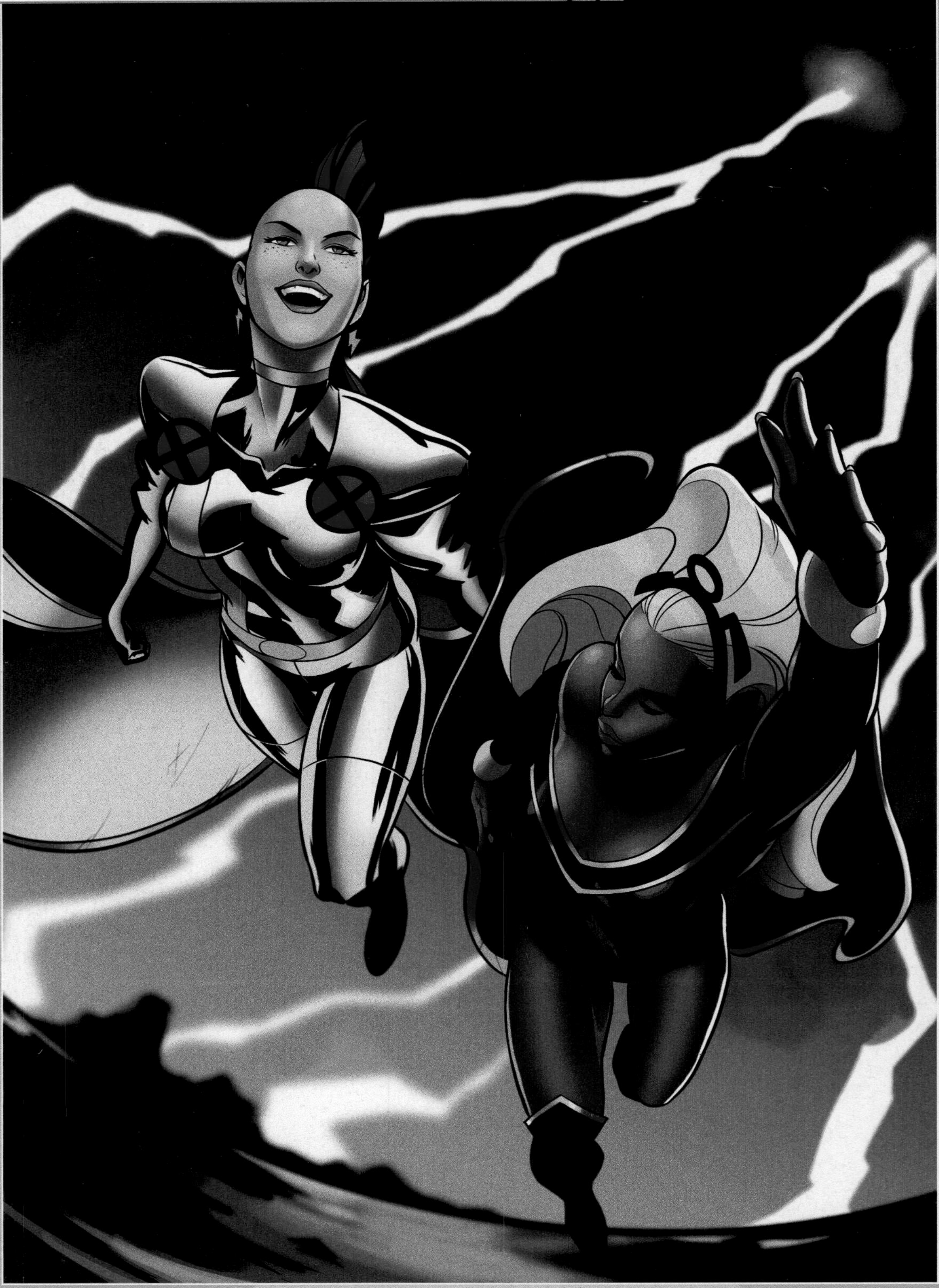